Harcourt Religion Publishers

Call to Faith

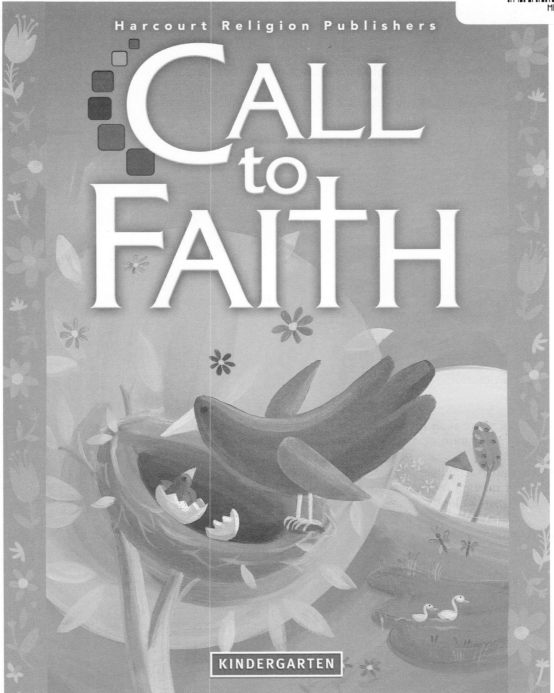

KINDERGARTEN

KINDERGARTEN

Harcourt Religion Publishers

www.harcourtreligion.com

3 4 5 6 7 8 9 10 015016 13 12 11 10

CONTENTS

Opening Prayer

Sign of the Cross

In the name of the Father,
    and of the Son,
    and of the Holy Spirit.
                    Amen.

We Are Called

O God, Teacher and Giver of Life,
    we begin today a new journey,
    a journey of faith.
We are ready to learn from each other in this
ministry,
    to support one another in love,
    and to work together as the Church.
Grant us your wisdom
    to deepen our understanding of you.
Grant us your love
    to grow in our love for each other.

Walk with us on this journey
    as we answer the call to faith
    and help others do so as well.
Lead us to make loving choices in everything
we do.
Guide us with the witness of the saints,
    the words of Sacred Scripture,
    and the teachings of the Church.

We pray for these gifts,
    confident in your goodness,
    through Jesus Christ, our Lord. Amen.

CALL to FAITH

Philosophy

Call to Faith is shaped around the following catechetical principles:

- **Conversion is central to catechesis.** The aim of *Call to Faith* is to form participants into disciples who act with the mind and heart of Christ.

- **Catechesis is a lifelong process.** Catechesis is gradual, systematic, and lifelong. We are touched and transformed by the living God and by the lived Tradition of the community throughout our lives.

- **Catechesis is the responsibility of all baptized members of the Church.** The whole parish community (including parents, family members, catechists, and pastors) is called to hand on the faith through faith sharing and the witness of daily life.

Sources of Catholic Wisdom

Call to Faith is deeply rooted in Church Tradition. In its dependence on and faithfulness to both the *Catechism of the Catholic Church* and the *General Directory for Catechesis*, it remains true to the *magisterium*, or teaching office of the Church, and draws from the following sources of Catholic wisdom:

Scripture In *Call to Faith*, the treasure of God's word is highlighted and integrated into the program's instruction, reflection, sharing, and prayer. Throughout the program students, catechists, and families are provided with both the content and the tools necessary to explore the Scriptures and to enrich their faith.

Doctrine   Each lesson of *Call to Faith* draws on and instructs in Church doctrine in ways that help students, catechists, and families understand and appreciate the Church's teachings as they apply to life today.

Lives of Saints and People of Faith   *Call to Faith* takes seriously the importance of models and witnesses of faith as a factor in the faith development of both children and adults. The story of one person of faith whose life witnesses to the lesson theme is presented at the end of each lesson, and stories of other saints and people of faith are interwoven into the lessons when appropriate.

Cultural Customs and Celebrations   Many communities have customs and devotions that address or celebrate the faith. These customs and devotions involve the lived experience and wisdom of the Christian community, and they respect the context and the culture of the local community. The inclusion of many of these rituals and customs is a unique component of *Call to Faith* and assists parishes in making the curriculum their own.

Catechetical approaches in CALL to FAITH

Because of the many ways children learn, and because of the communal nature of the Church itself, *Call to Faith* uses a variety of catechetical approaches, which are designed to help you succeed and be faithful to the task of catechesis.

Content-centered catechesis

The presentation of the core elements of the faith is essential in religious formation and instruction. *Call to Faith* provides you with accurate and comprehensive content based on Scripture and the *Catechism of the Catholic Church*, as well as a teaching method that will help you effectively communicate the content to your students.

Catechesis in the whole community

Call to Faith is the first textbook series designed for use in a catechetical program that encompasses the whole parish community. Although these textbooks are designed for children of various ages, they are also specifically designed to be the basis for catechesis in the rest of the community. The *Pastoral Leader's Source Book*, which accompanies *Call to Faith*, provides resources that will extend catechesis to the entire faith community.

Liturgical catechesis

Call to Faith includes a generous amount of liturgical catechesis to help students and families become, as the Second Vatican Council's document on the liturgy expressed, "full, conscious, and active" participants of the assembly at Mass. *Call to Faith* students who learn by celebrating the rites and feasts, rather than by merely reading about them, are formed for life in the rich liturgical tradition of the Catholic Church.

Lectionary-connected catechesis

For Catholics, the Scriptures are proclaimed week after week in the Liturgy of the Word at Sunday Mass. The "Break Open the Word" feature in *Call to Faith* provides an ongoing opportunity to reflect on these Scriptures. Care is also taken to provide opportunities to reflect on the readings for the seasons and feasts of the Church year. Harcourt Religion Publishers' Web site, **www.harcourtreligion.com**, serves the entire catechetical community in this effort.

 Visit **www.harcourtreligion.com** for weekly scripture readings and seasonal resources.

Generations of Faith &

Households of Faith

The first catechists in any young adolescent's life are the family members with whom he or she lives. What happens at home—both positive and negative—provides lessons for life. In the family, faith is shared as part of the unfolding of daily life. The home, known as the "domestic Church," provides a real place in which adolescents can grow in their faith.

Call to Faith is committed to partnering with parents and guardians to develop households of faith.

► Family connections are made throughout the program in the presentation of the content and in the issues raised in the stories that open the chapters.

► Complete Home Lessons for each chapter available at **www.harcourtreligion.com.**

► Additional family and community connections at **www.harcourtreligion.com.**

► *Faith at Home: Nurturing Households of Faith* is a yearly magazine for families who wish to enrich what their children are learning in the classroom. It empowers parents and guardians to be the primary religious educators of their young adolescents.

Today, parish and school leaders are seeking ways to meet the catechetical needs of several generations. They want an approach to catechesis that provides a systematic and comprehensive presentation of the faith while using a pedagogy that itself is drawn from the teaching style of Christ. They want to serve the entire community, giving parents, grandparents, guardians, and other adults the tools they need to develop households of faith. And they want to encourage everyone to participate fully in parish life, especially in the Sunday Liturgy.

To help leaders meet these goals, Harcourt Religion Publishers has partnered with the Generations of Faith Project of the Center for Ministry Development. This partnership resulted in the all-new, systematic catechetical program *People of Faith: Generations Learning Together*. This program enables the parish community to create a program of lifelong faith formation that is centered in the events of Church life. It embraces all ages and generations, promotes faith growth at home, and, most importantly, promotes participation in Church life.

People of Faith: Generations Learning Together and *Call to Faith*, working together, will provide you with an innovative approach to lifelong faith formation that engages all generations. All members of the community are invited to learn and grow in faith together.

Lifelong Catechesis and *Call to Faith*

Call to Faith incorporates lifelong catechesis in its curriculum. Through regular moments of faith sharing, connections to the Sunday lectionary, and options for family-centered catechesis and adult formation, *Call to Faith* engages not only the specific learner but the larger community of faith.

Call to Faith

Catechetical Process

Call to Faith uses a proven three-step catechetical process: Invite, Explore, Celebrate.

Invite   This step invites the learner into the catechetical process through simple and engaging reflections that draw out the life experience of the learner.

Explore   This step explores, in an age-appropriate way, the living Tradition of our Catholic faith as it is expressed in Scripture and doctrine. Through the use of a variety of stories, literary forms, and questions students enter more deeply into the chapter content and are helped to connect faith with their lives.

In order to show reverence for the word of God, Scripture is clearly labeled and set apart in each lesson. The "Words of Faith" feature included in this step helps build a common language of faith.

Celebrate   In this step, students celebrate what they believe through prayer celebrations that model the diverse ways in which Catholics pray. Prayers of praise, meditations, litanies, and celebrations of the word are included.

Music and song are included in each celebration. The *Call to Faith* music CD tracks are listed by chapter for ease of use.

Call to Faith Activity Process

Each chapter includes an integrated activity strand designed to lead the student from personal faith reflection to communal participation.

Let's Begin helps children reflect on their own varied experiences.

Share Your Faith helps children dialog with others and act on their faith.

Connect Your Faith helps children connect with the faith life of the Church.

Live Your Faith helps children put their faith into action.

The Family Faith page also includes a "Live Your Faith" activity, emphasizing that it is in the family setting—the "domestic Church"—that students primarily live out their faith.

Call to Faith SCOPE AND SEQUENCE

	Grade K		Grade 1	
Revelation	• God made the world. • God made people to be like him. • God made people to love him and others.		• God created everything. All that God made is good. • God knows and loves everyone. • God's world is a gift to you. • You can learn about God and his love from the world he made. • All creation is a gift from God. • Everyone must help care for God's world.	
	Psalm 148:7–10, Genesis 1:27–28, 6–8, 1 Corinthians 13:4–7	CCC: 337; 356; 288	Genesis 2:7–22, 1:5–25, 1:26–30	CCC: 282, 286–287, 290, 299, 355–361, 364; 32, 297, 301, 293–295, 2402
Trinity	• God shows his love through others. • When we pray, we are talking to God. • All people care for God's world.		• The Holy Trinity is God the Father, God the Son, and God the Holy Spirit. • Jesus is the Son of God • Jesus is both God and man. • Jesus, Mary, and Joseph are the Holy Family. • Jesus told stories, or parables, to teach about God's love. • The Bible is God's word written in human words.	
	1 John 3:1, 1 Thessalonians 5:16–18, Genesis 1:28–30, 6–8	CCC: 238; 278; 373	John 14:7-9, Luke 2:51–52, 15:3–6	CCC: 232–234, 240, 423, 458–459, 516; 464, 531–533; 105–110, 136
Jesus Christ	• Jesus is the Son of God and the Son of Mary. • Jesus taught us to live through his life. • All Christians are called to follow Christ.		• Jesus' healing actions show God's power and love. • Faith is the gift of believing in God. • The Great Commandment is about love of God and others. • You are to love God above all else and love others as you love yourself. • Prayer is listening and talking to God. • Jesus taught his friends how to pray the Lord's Prayer.	
	Luke 2:1–7, 6:27–36, 10:25–37, Mark 1:16–19	CCC: 422, 723; 561; 940–942	Luke 8:40–56, 10:25–28, Ephesians 5:18–20	CCC: 547–550, 153, 1814; 2052–2056, 2196; 2560, 2564, 2601, 2607, 2759, 2761
The Church	• The Church is a large family that belongs to God. • The Holy Spirit helps the Church family to love. • Each person has special talents to serve others.		• God invites everyone into his kingdom. • The Church is people who follow Jesus and say "yes" to God's call. • God the Holy Spirit is the third Person of the Holy Trinity. • The Holy Spirit fills people's hearts with love and guides the Church. • Saints are friends of God who can show you how to live. • People in the Church are called to live holy lives, as the saints did.	
	Colossians 3:12–17, Acts 2:1–4, Matthew 25:42–46, Luke 2:1–20	CCC: 751, 752; 253, 791; 910, 2447	Genesis 6:14–22, 7:1–23, Luke 14:16–23, John 14:25–26	CCC: 541–545, 551, 781–782, 768; 243, 685; 684, 688, 731–733, 828, 829, 1023, 825, 956
Morality	• Love one another as Jesus loves you. • God's rules help people make good choices. • Tell others when you are sorry.		• Jesus' words and actions teach us how to love and serve God. • When you serve others, you are serving God. • The Ten Commandments are God's laws to help people love God and others. • God gives people the freedom to choose. • God always forgives those who are truly sorry and want to do better. • God asks that we forgive others and ourselves.	
	John 15:9, 11, Matthew 18:21–35, 19:18–19	CCC: 1825; 2472; 270; 1421, 2227, 1435	John 13:4–17, Deuteronomy 10:12–13, Luke 18:9–13	CCC: 565, 459, 2825; 2053, 2058, 2067, 1730–1734; 982, 1431, 2840, 1446–1450
Sacraments	• The words and actions of the sacraments show the wonders of God. • Water is a source of life and also brings new life. • The bread becomes Jesus at Mass.		• God loves you so much that he sent his Son to save you. • Jesus died and rose to new life. • The Church has seven sacraments. They are signs of God's love. • Jesus gave the sacraments to remind people that he is with them always. • Your sharing in God's love and life is called grace. • Baptism is your welcome into the Church family.	
	Mark 8:22–26, 14:22–31, Acts 8:35–40	CCC: 459, 1749, 1131; 1, 1218, 1228; 1333, 1337, 1341	Luke 23–24, John 14:18–19, Acts 1:5, 8	CCC: 416–418, 422, 601, 654–655, 683; 1113, 1130, 1123; 1279, 1263–1270
The Kingdom of God	• God is great and we must serve him first. • The saints pray for us to God the Father every day. • To praise God for the wonderful things he does is adoration.		• At Mass the Church family celebrates God's love. • Jesus gives himself to us in the Eucharist. • Heaven is being happy with God forever. • God invites all people to heaven. All who show love will go to heaven. • The signs of God's kingdom are justice, peace, and love. • Christians work here and now to help God bring his kingdom to its fullness.	
	1 Corinthians 2:9, Matthew 25:35–39, Luke 24:1–12	CCC: 30, 1844, 223; 833, 958, 955; 54, 2639, 2097	I Corinthians 11:23–25, John 14:1–3, 16:22, Romans 14:17–19	CCC: 1359–1361, 1374, 1325; 1024, 1023; 2819, 2818, 543–54

Call to Faith SCOPE AND SEQUENCE

	Grade 2		Grade 3	
Revelation	• God is the creator of all that is good. • Jesus is God's greatest gift. Jesus is the Son of God. • God sent his Son, Jesus, to bring all people back to his friendship. • Jesus is the Savior and the Good Shepherd. • God tells us about himself through the Bible. • The Bible is God's word written by humans.		• God created everything. All creation shows God's goodness. • God created humans in his image and likeness. • The Bible is the word of God written in human words. • The Church is the People of God gathered in the name of Jesus. • Children first learn about God's love through their families. • The family home is called the "domestic Church."	
	Psalm 8:2, 7–9, Genesis 2–3, 6–9, John 10:11–14, Matthew 4:23–25	CCC: 290, 355, 422–464, 2415–2418; 430, 220, 389–390, 1441, 1846; 51–55, 80–82	**Genesis 1:1–2:3, Acts 2:42–47, Luke 1:39–56**	CCC: 315, 355, 293–301; 831, 836, 771; 1657, 1666, 2204–2207
Trinity	• You can call God "Father" because he created you and cares for you like a good parent. • You can trust in God because he loves you. • Jesus is the beloved Son of God. • Jesus is the Savior of the world. • The Holy Trinity is the three Persons in one God. • The Holy Spirit guides the Church and helps you to be a disciple.		• The Holy Trinity is three Persons in one God. • Jesus, God the Son, taught about God the Father and God the Spirit. • The Mass is the Church's most important form of worship. • In the Mass the Church remembers what Jesus did at the Last Supper. • Prayer is the raising of one's mind and heart to God. • Prayer is an important part of a Christian's daily life.	
	Matthew 6:26–32, Luke 1–2, 2:41-52, 3:13–17, John 14:15–26, Acts 1–2	CCC: 355–356, 238–242; 461, 495, 437, 464–469; 685, 253, 1831, 1845, 731, 249–253	**John 14:6–7, 16–17, Luke 18:9–14, 22:14-20, Matthew 6:5–8**	CCC: 253, 240, 243, 234; 61, 69, 1083; 2559, 2659, 2688
Jesus Christ	• The Ten Commandments are God's laws to his people. • Jesus teaches you to love God above all things and to love others as you love yourself. • Conscience is God's gift that helps you know right from wrong. • Sin is a free choice to do what is wrong. • God is merciful and forgiving. • God will always forgive you if you are truly sorry.		• Jesus shared the good news about God's kingdom of justice, love, and peace. • Jesus is the Messiah, the chosen one, and Savior. • Jesus died and rose to new life to save all people from the power of sin. • The Church celebrates the Paschal mystery in all the sacraments. • The Church is the Body of Christ to which all members belong. • Church members continue Jesus' work when they help others.	
	John 15:12, 18:17–18, 25–27, Luke 10:25–37, 15:11–32	CCC: 2060–2068, 2055, 1730–1731, 1847, 1996–2005, 1786–1789; 1428, 2839, 1846, 1870	**Luke 4:16–22, John 20:11–18, Matthew 25:34–40**	CCC: 546, 1154, 2688; 613, 2099–2100; 521, 1267, 2427–2428
The Church	• Grace is sharing in God's life. • Sacraments are holy signs that come from Jesus and give grace. • In the Sacrament of Reconciliation, you receive God's forgiveness. • This sacrament also celebrates your friendship with God and the Church. • The Church year celebrates the life, death, and Resurrection of Jesus. • The Resurrection is the mystery of Jesus being raised from death.		• The bishops are the successors of the Apostles. • The pope, bishops, and pastors lead and guide the Church. • The Holy Spirit unites the Church and makes its members holy. • Many cultures together make up the unity of the Church. • The Church's mission is to share Jesus' good news with the people of all nations. • The Church is catholic because it is everywhere and welcomes everyone.	
	Genesis 6:14–22, 7:1–23, Acts 8:4–12, Luke 14:16–23, 7:36–50, John 14:25	CCC: 1131, 1996–1997, 1212, 1113–1130; 1849, 1440–1448; 1168, 1169, 1194	**Matthew 16:15–19, 26:69-75, John 21:15–17, Luke 1:46–50, 1 Corinthians 3:5–9**	CCC: 880, 884, 890; 813, 791, 957; 831, 830, 864
Morality	• The kingdom of God is love, peace, and justice for all. • Everyone is welcome in God's kingdom and the Catholic Church. • Jesus' disciples share in his life and in his work. • Followers of Jesus are to proclaim his good news to the world. • Prayer is being with God in your heart and mind. • Jesus taught his followers the Lord's Prayer.		• Jesus' law of love is to love one another as Jesus loves each of us. • Jesus teaches that we should love and forgive our enemies. • God's gifts of faith, hope, and love help you live a good and moral life. • Christians are called by Jesus to be the light of the world. • The Holy Spirit and the teachings of the Church help you make good choices. • Your conscience and grace also help you follow God.	
	Luke 19:1–8, Matthew 6:5–9, 19:13–15, 28:20, John 15:4–5	CCC: 541, 543–544, 1826–1827, 2816; 1716–1717, 747, 902; 2762–2763, 2620, 2564	**Matthew 5:14–16, 43–48, Acts 9:1–30**	CCC: 1822, 1825, 1970; 1813, 2105, 1697; 2041, 1496, 1444
Sacraments	• Mass is another name for the celebration of the Eucharist. • The assembly uses songs, prayer, and actions to worship. • In the Liturgy of the Word, God's word is read from the Bible. • We say what we believe about God and pray for the needs of the Church and the world. • The Eucharist is a memorial of the sacrifice of Jesus. • The Liturgy of the Eucharist is the second main part of the Mass.		• Sacraments are signs that come from Jesus and give grace. • The Sacraments of Initiation are Baptism, Confirmation, and Eucharist. • The Sacraments of Healing are Reconciliation and Anointing of the Sick. • In these sacraments the Church prays for spiritual and physical healing. • The Sacraments of Service are Holy Orders and Matrimony. • These sacraments celebrate people's commitment to God and the community.	
	Acts 2:42–47, Matthew 13:31–32, 19:21–22	CCC: 1071, 1167, 1083, 1140–1144; 546, 1349, 1354, 101–104; 1357, 1374, 1356–1381	**Acts 2:38–41, Luke 8:40–42, 49–56, 1 Corinthians 4:1–2**	CCC: 1229, 1271, 1272; 1421, 1514, 1531; 1534, 1535
The Kingdom of God	• Through the Eucharist, Jesus' followers are united with him and one another. • The gift of Holy Communion is received with reverence. • The Church's mission is to share Jesus' message of love and to spread the news of the kingdom of God. • All members of the Church share in its mission. • Heaven is life and happiness forever with God. • The Eucharist is a sign of joy and of what heaven will be like.		• God kept his promise to be forever faithful when he sent his Son, Jesus. • The Church continues to be a sign of God's covenant. • All members of the Church share in its mission to work for peace and justice. • The Church is a sign of the kingdom of God. • People who die in God's friendship live forever in God's presence. • At the end of the world, Christ will judge all people on the way they lived their lives.	
	Luke 9:10–17, 14:15–23, Acts 10:42–48, Matthew 22:2–10	CCC: 1358, 1390; 846, 791, 850, 849–856; 542–543, 545, 546	**Matthew 10:5–14, Revelation 21:1–4, 22:13**	CCC: 781, 1612, 813–822; 2046, 2443, 2448; 673, 681, 1041

Grade 4	Grade 5
• God loves and cares for all creation and has a plan for the world. • All God wants you to know about him is in Scripture and Tradition. • God's covenant with Abraham reveals that God is always faithful to his people. • Sin is present in the world because of human choice. • The Ten Commandments help you be faithful to him and his covenant. • The commandments tell you ways to love God and others.	• True happiness can come only through communion with God. • Religion expresses a relationship with God through beliefs, prayer, and practices. • Humans share in the Creator's loving plan by caring for creation. • God's providence is his care and plan for all creation. • God communicates through signs. • Through the signs and symbolic actions of the sacraments, God's life becomes truly present in your life.
Jonah, Genesis 3, 12, 15, 17, 21, 37, 42, 44, 45, Exodus 2, 5, 14, 17–20 CCC: 302–308, 80–83, 50; 59–61, 385–389; 2055, 2060–2061, 577–580	John 4:7–29, Psalm 98:4–9, Exodus 3:1–15 CCC: 27, 28, 142–143, 153–155, 160, 162; 307, 302, 2404; 1147, 774, 1152
• Every person is worthy of respect because he or she is created in God's image. • Each person has a soul that will live forever. • God created people for one another, and all must work for the common good. Such love of neighbor reflects the love of the Holy Trinity. • No one can believe alone, just as no one can live alone. • God has given you free will so that you can make good choices. • Your conscience is the "inner voice" that helps you choose what is good.	• The Trinity is the central mystery of Christian faith and life. • Virtue is the habit of doing good. The theological virtues are faith, hope, and love. • Prayer and worship are ways to show love for God. • When we pray and worship, God fills us with joy, strength, and hope. • The Great Commandment states that you will love the Lord, your God, with all your heart, soul, and mind and your neighbor as yourself. • The cardinal virtues play a central role in helping people lead morally good lives.
Genesis 1:27, Acts 2:42–45, Luke 10:30–37 CCC: 355–357, 362–366, 1928–1933; 1905–1906, 1878, 1757; 1706–1786, 1704-106	John 1:32–34, 2 Samuel 6:1–15, Mark 12:28–34 CCC: 234, 1813, 253–255; 1083, 2638, 1082; 1071, 2565; 1804–1809, 1811
• The Beatitudes describe the reign of God that Jesus announced. • The Beatitudes show you how to live and act as a follower of Jesus. • The Great Commandment is to love God with all your heart, strength, and mind and to love your neighbor as yourself. • The Great Commandment sums up all the teachings of the Ten Commandments. • The first three commandments are to honor, respect, and worship God. • These commandments tell you to believe in, trust, and love God.	• The Incarnation is the belief that the Son of God became a human being. • Jesus is both human and divine, truly God and truly human. • God's kingdom is present and grows until God's reign comes in fullness. • Jesus proclaimed the kingdom of God through his actions and parables. • Through the sacraments, Christ unites his followers to his Passion, death, Resurrection, and Ascension. • Jesus Christ is the Redeemer of the human race.
Matthew 5:1–10, 19:16–22, Exodus 32:1–20 CCC: 1716, 1720, 1723, 1078–1079; 2055, 2083, 2196, 2447; 2062, 2077, 2113	Luke 8:5–8, 24:5–9 CCC: 461, 464, 1701–1702; 763–769, 546–547, 567; 1076, 618, 654
• Every person is called by God to a vocation. • Through your vocation, you can help God increase his reign. • The Church's holiness shines in the saints. All who live their love of God are saints. • Mary is the perfect model of holiness, and she is called the Mother of the Church. • Jesus gave the leaders of the Church the authority to interpret Scripture and Tradition for the faithful. • The Holy Spirit directs the Church in teaching and guiding the People of God.	• As members of the Church, we are all united in living out the mission of Christ. • The Church is expressed in the images of the Body of Christ and the People of God. • The Apostles proclaimed God's good news and cooperated with God's reign. • Under the guidance of the Holy Spirit, the pope and the bishops continue the Apostles' mission to teach. • Mary and the saints provide the Church with models of holiness. • Canonization declares that a model Christian is enjoying eternity with God.
Jeremiah 1:5–8, Luke 1:46–50, Mark 8:27–30 CCC: 941, 2046, 2030; 828, 829; 85, 87, 940–943	I Peter 2:4–5, Matthew 16:15–19, 28:19–20, Luke 1:30–31, 38 CCC: 811, 776, 775; 551, 85–86, 863; 1173, 828, 2013
• God created humans to live in strong, loving families. • The fourth, sixth, and ninth commandments provide basic laws of family love and respect. • All human life is sacred because it comes from God. • The fifth commandment forbids anything that takes a human life. • Because God is truth, his people are called to live in the truth. • The eighth commandment forbids lying.	• Evil is the result of humans' turning away from God's goodness. • God sent his Son to redeem people from the power of sin and evil. • The process of becoming Catholic is called the Rite of Christian Initiation of Adults. • The Sacraments of Initiation are Baptism, Confirmation, and Eucharist. • The Church receives God's forgiveness through the Sacraments of Healing. • The Sacrament of Reconciliation includes contrition, confession, penance, and absolution.
Luke 2:41–52, Matthew 5:43–45, John 8:31–32, 14:6 CCC: 2203, 2197, 2204, 2380, 2233; 2258, 2268, 2303–2304; 2465, 1741, 2467	Romans 5:19, 6:10–11, Luke 15:11–32 CCC: 311, 614, 1854–1863; 1232, 1233, 1212, 1231; 1421, 1491, 1527
• The Church year celebrates the Paschal mystery. • The seasons of the liturgical year include Advent, Christmas, Lent, Easter, and Ordinary Time. • The seven sacraments are signs, instituted by Christ, that give grace. • The Sacrament of the Eucharist is at the heart of Christian life. • God's forgiveness is offered to all who seek it. • Reconciliation and the Anointing of the Sick celebrate God's healing love.	• The wheat bread and grape wine become the Body and Blood of Jesus in the Sacrament of the Eucharist. • In the liturgical assembly, the Holy Spirit strengthens the community. • The word of God is conveyed through Scripture and Tradition. • Jesus is truly present in the word as it is proclaimed and preached in the liturgy. • The Eucharist is the source and the summit of the Catholic Church. • The Eucharist closely unites Christ's followers to him and to one another.
Ecclesiastes 3:1–8, Luke 22:17–20, 19:1–10, John 9:1–38 CCC: 1067, 1171, 1140; 1210, 1407, 1370; 1489, 1421;	Colossians 3:16, Matthew 26:26–28 CCC: 1374, 1141, 1378; 80–82, 1088, 108; 1324, 1372, 1398
• The commandments call you to be generous and to have the right attitude toward possessions. • The goods of the earth are meant for the benefit of the whole human family. • The Church's mission is to proclaim the Gospel and to work for the good of all. • The Church is made up of people from many cultures united by belief in Christ. • The Church teaches that at the end of time, all will be raised from the dead. • All will come into the presence of Christ to be judged.	• The vocations of ordained and married people build the reign of God and serve others. • The Sacraments of Service are Holy Orders and Matrimony. • Faith in the Resurrection is the source of hope in eternal life and happiness. • Last rites of the Church include the Sacraments of Healing and the Eucharist. • The Church's mission is to bring the good news to all people everywhere. • Every baptized person has the responsibility of sharing the good news.
Mark 12:41–44, Matthew 25:34–40, 28:18–20 CCC: 299, 2402, 2407; 849, 1807, 942; 681, 682, 671	Matthew 9:35–38, 25:31–40, Luke 4:16–21 CCC: 1534, 1535, 1635; 989, 1525, 1024; 849, 863, 2820

Call to Faith

Grade 6

Revelation

- God reveals himself and his plan of salvation through Scripture.
- The most important truth of both Sacred Scripture and Tradition is that God is faithful and wants you to live with him forever.
- The stories of creation in Genesis reveal that God alone created the universe.
- God created humans in his own image to live in harmony with him forever.
- God fully revealed his faithfulness to humans by sending his only Son, Jesus.
- Humans have the ability to live in friendship with God.

Ruth 1:1–17, Genesis 1:1–30, 2:4-25   CCC: 51–55, 214, 108; 279–289, 355–361, 373; 396–411, 1730, 1468, 396

Trinity

- God calls you on a journey of faith toward salvation.
- The path toward salvation is paved with prayer.
- God rescued the Hebrews from slavery and sent his Son to save all people.
- The Passover and the Eucharist celebrate God's saving actions.
- The Ten Commandments are the laws of God's covenant with the Israelites.
- The Ten Commandments help you stay close to God and in right relationship with others.

The Book of Genesis, The Book of Exodus   CCC: 176–184, 2570–2572, 183; 62–64, 1150–1151, 430–431; 1961–1966, 1949–1953

Jesus Christ

- In Old Testament times, God chose leaders like Saul and David, who were anointed kings.
- God the Father anointed his Son Jesus to be prophet, priest, and king.
- The Bible teaches that true wisdom comes from trusting God and obeying his law.
- Jesus is the wisdom of God, sought in every age by those who are wise.
- Prophets of the Old Testament spoke for God, telling people to repent and obey God.
- Jesus is the Messiah described by the Old Testament prophets.

1 Samuel and 2 Samuel, 1 Kings, Job, Isaiah and Zechariah   CCC: 59–64, 695, 218–221; 156–158, 215–217, 1950; 2581–2584, 711–714, 702

The Church

- The Gospels are the good news of Jesus; they proclaim his life and teachings.
- The Gospels are interpreted by the Church through Tradition.
- Jesus laid the foundation for the Church through his life and teachings. He sent the Holy Spirit to help the Church fulfill its mission.
- The Holy Spirit continues to animate the Church today.
- The Church is one, holy, catholic, and apostolic.
- The Church is a community, united in faith, working together to share the Gospel.

Luke, Acts of the Apostles, 1 Corinthians 3:16, 12:12, Ephesians 1:22–23, 2:19–20   CCC: 124, 109–119, 772; 763–768, 849–854, 737–747; 811–813, 830–831, 823

Morality

- The Great Commandment allows you to achieve happiness and holiness.
- The Beatitudes and precepts of the Church help the faithful live holy lives.
- Working toward justice means respecting the dignity of persons and peoples.
- Justice is giving what is due to God and others.
- Your conscience helps you know when you have sinned.
- Through the sacrament of Reconciliation, God forgives sins and restores us to his friendship.

Matthew 17:1–8, 18:23–35, 22:37–40, Micah 6:8   CCC: 1716–1729, 2041–2043; 1939–1942, 2304–2306, 1807; 1777–1782, 1440–1445

Sacraments

- The mission of the Church is to proclaim the gospel in word and deed.
- Through the Sacraments of Initiation, Christians are given new life.
- All of the baptized are called to follow Christ by serving others.
- Ordained ministers serve God through preaching the word and through celebrating the sacraments.
- The Church celebrates marriage through the Sacrament of Matrimony.
- This sacrament helps a man and woman grow in love and holiness.

Acts 8:26–39, John 13:1–15   CCC: 849–856, 1212, 1285; 897–900, 1548–1553, 900; 1612–1617, 1646–1651, 2204

The Kingdom of God

- Members of the communion of saints can intercede, or pray to God for others.
- The communion of saints includes all holy persons, both living and dead, who are united in the Eucharist.
- Christ desires the unity of all his disciples.
- Ecumenism is the work of Christians toward unity.
- God will triumph over evil when Christ comes again in glory.
- In the new creation, God will reward good and punish evil.

Acts of the Apostles, The Gospel of John   CCC: 2634–2638, 946–948; 820–822, 813–819; 992–996, 1038–1041, 1042–1047, 991

SCOPE AND SEQUENCE

Grade 7	Grade 8

- God created the heavens and the earth, making humans in his image and likeness.
- God promised to restore the human race to his intended harmony and perfection.
- God is the author and inspiration of the sacred words of Scripture, recorded by humans.
- God continues to speak to us today through the Scriptures.
- We know God through Jesus Christ who is the sign of God the Father's love through the Holy Spirit.
- The natural and revealed laws help us choose what is good and to live as God's people.

Genesis 1:1—2:4a; 1 John 1:5; John 1:1–14, 3:16; Matthew 26:26–30; Exodus 20:1–17   CCC: 69, 315–319, 353, 410; 136–139, 521, 1802; 73, 1979–1983

- Humans can live in friendship with God because we have a soul, reason, and free will.
- God established a covenant with his people, promising to be faithful to them and to be their God.
- The Ten Commandments guide us in what it means to be and live in God's image.
- Scripture and the lived Tradition of the Church make up one source of revelation, or deposit of faith.
- Faith is both a gift from God and a free human choice and action.
- The Church is holy because her founder is holy and because the Holy Spirit lives within her.

1 Samuel 3:1–10; Mark 9:14–29; 1 Corinthians 13:1–13; Psalm 8:6–7   CCC: 44, 70–72, 228, 2080, 2081; 96–98, 176–182; 319, 353, 867, 2720

- The Trinity is a mystery, never totally understood by the mind, yet approached through faith.
- The love that the Father, the Son, and the Holy Spirit have for each other is a model for us.
- The Son of God has existed for all time, and through the Incarnation, became human.
- Jesus revealed his divinity through the working of miracles, which also reveal his human nature.
- The Holy Spirit gives the Church life and energy and unites us as the Body of Christ.
- The Holy Spirit guides the Church in her living Tradition and prayer.

Matthew 1:18–23, 28:16–20; John 1:1–21, 10:31–38, 14:15–17; Philippians 2:1   CCC: 261, 743, 1890, 2680; 479, 480, 483, 561; 747, 809, 2590, 2661, 2644

- Jesus' Transfiguration revealed his divine glory as the Son of God.
- The gift of grace helps us to know and love God.
- The Christian family (the domestic Church) has a special role in the establishment of God's kingdom.
- Through our Baptism we share in Jesus' mission as priest, prophet, and king.
- The gifts of the Holy Spirit help us live our Christian witness.
- The Holy Spirit lives in the Church, uniting, guiding, and giving her life.

Luke 9:28–36; 1 Peter 2:9–10, 15; 1 Cor 6:19–20; 2 Cor 6:16–18   CCC: 455, 2021; 804, 808, 942; 382, 747, 809, 1280, 1316, 1317, 1845

- Jesus is the second Person of the Blessed Trinity, at once fully human and fully divine.
- Jesus became human to show us how to live and reach our full potential as God's children.
- The Beatitudes reveal values of the kingdom and how to live in harmony with God and one another.
- By disobeying God the first humans introduced sin and suffering into the world.
- God promised a Messiah who would bring salvation and free his people from sin.
- Jesus conquered death and makes it possible for those who have faith to experience new life.

Luke 11:9–13; 1 Timothy 2:5–6; Matthew 5:3–12; 7:24–29; 1 John 4:10–11   CCC: 460, 479, 561; 1725, 1726, 1983; 70, 384, 415–419, 621, 985

- The first disciples worshiped together, followed Jesus' teachings, and cared for one another.
- Jesus offers eternal life to those who believe.
- Through Jesus we are forgiven and made whole again.
- Conversion is an ongoing process, nurtured by the Holy Spirit.
- The Catholic Church is made up of Eastern Catholics and Roman Catholics, united by a common creed, the sacraments, and the leadership of the pope.
- Christ desires that we work and pray toward the unity of all baptized Christians.

Mark 10:46–52; Luke 7:36–50, 19:1–10; John 15:1–10, 17:20–26; Romans 8:10   CCC: 1948; 1490, 2018–2020, 2025, 2027; 810, 816–819, 838, 1208, 1318, 1320

- Jesus sent his disciples into the world and asks us to work together to spread his message.
- The Holy Spirit uses many different ways to teach us how to pray.
- Jesus is the head of the Church, the Mystical Body of Christ.
- We are all united with one another as part of Christ's Body to help build God's kingdom.
- The Church is both a sign and instrument of the communion between God and his people.
- A personal relationship with God, nourished by prayer, helps us bring his love and truth to others.

Acts 9:1–5; Matthew 6:9–13, 18:12–20; John 1:43–51, 8:12   CCC: 935, 940, 2644, 2693; 779, 805–807; 45, 183, 620, 780, 2591, 2744

- The bishops are direct successors of the Apostles, and the pope is the direct successor of Peter.
- Guided by the Holy Spirit, the Church continues to teach the truth of Christ.
- The Church is universal, reaching out to the whole world and welcoming all people.
- Missionaries bring the Good News to people who have not yet come to know and believe.
- The pope and bishops belong to the Church's hierarchy, and guide the priests, deacons, religious communities, and the lay faithful.
- The laity bring the truth of God's kingdom to the world in which they live and work.

Matthew 13:31–33, 16:13–19; John 4:13–42; Acts 1:8–9, 2:1–4, 6:1–7   CCC: 869, 935, 936, 1593–1596, 2050, 2051; 849, 851, 854, 868; 937–945, 1591

- God made us with a free will, an intellect, and a soul, all of which help us choose to do good.
- Morally good actions require that their object, intention, and circumstance be good.
- A well-formed conscience will guide us to do what is right and good.
- All people possess the human dignity that comes from being made in God's image.
- We are to honor and protect the human dignity of all people from conception to death.
- Theological and cardinal virtues guide us in our choices and actions.

Matthew 5:38–48, 6:2–4, 7:12; Psalm 139:14–16; Philippians 4:8,13   CCC: 1711, 1713, 1757–1761, 1796, 1798, 1871–1876; 2319–2326; 1833–1841, 2393–2395

- We are called to put God first in our lives, to trust and hope in him.
- God's name is holy, and his name deserves respect and reverence.
- The Holy Family stands as a model for our own families.
- In the family, we grow in our understanding of right and wrong, and learn what's truly important.
- The common good focuses on the needs of the community and people as a whole.
- The Church works to insure that public and political authorities act with truth, justice, freedom, and solidarity for all people.

Matthew 5:33–35, 37, 22:34–40; Psalm 8:1; Luke 2:41–52; John 15:12   CCC: 2134–2140, 2161–2163, 2251, 2252; 1920–1926, 1943, 1944, 1947, 2327–2329, 2458

- Christ makes the Father known to us and makes it possible for us to share in his life.
- Baptism is a celebration of new life in Christ and incorporation into the Church.
- Confirmation seals us with the Gift of the Holy Spirit to live out our journey of faith.
- In the Eucharist we are fed with the Body and Blood of Christ and strengthened for mission.
- In Reconciliation we receive God's forgiveness and return to life with him and the Church.
- The Anointing of the Sick provides the seriously ill and suffering God's grace for strength, courage, and hope.

John 14:1–10; Galatians 3:26–28; Matthew 9:35–38; James 5:14–15   CCC: 1115, 1131; 1275, 1278–1282, 1316–1320, 1408, 1412–1416; 1486, 1490–1497, 1529

- Sunday observance includes participation in Mass, rest, and attention to living a holy life.
- Matrimony strengthens a couple to live out their promises and model the love Christ has for all.
- Through Holy Orders, men are ordained to service in the name of Jesus for the Church.
- Living by the virtues of modesty and chastity strengthens our lives, teaches us faithfulness, and honors human dignity.
- The liturgical year connects our lives more closely to the Paschal mystery of Jesus.
- The Eucharist is at the very heart of what it means to be Catholic.

Ephesians 6:21; John 1:1–11; Ecclesiastes 3:1–8   CCC: 2021–2023, 2190–2195; 1592, 1597, 1600–1664, 2396, 2397, 2400, 2530, 2533; 1193–1195, 1407

- We discern our vocation with the help of family, the Church, and prayer.
- The Church asks us to share our time, talent, and treasure.
- God's kingdom is present but not yet complete.
- As Jesus' followers we are called to end injustice for the sake of God's kingdom.
- Christian hope is based on trusting in God and that we will be united with him forever.
- Jesus will come at the end of time to judge the living and the dead, and the kingdom will be complete.

Luke 2:41–52, 4:14–22, 10:2; Matthew 13:31–32, 25:31–46; John 11:1–44   CCC: 941–944, 1666, 2253, 2694; 550, 2552–2556, 2800; 658, 682,1051,1054–1060

- Sacramentals are holy objects, prayers, and practices that help us respond to God's grace.
- Religious art, especially icons, helps us glorify God and honor the saints.
- The Church is a communion of saints uniting believers in heaven, in purgatory, and on earth.
- The Church honors Mary as the greatest of saints with many feast days and devotions.
- The Church declares some people canonized saints for their lives of heroic virtue and holiness.
- Throughout her history, the Church has strived to live Jesus' message of love, hope, and faith.

Acts 2:42–47; Exodus 20:2–5; Luke 1:26–45; 1 Peter 4:16   CCC: 960, 962, 1053, 1677, 1679, 2141; 973, 974, 1195; 851, 852

PEOPLE OF FAITH

Grade K
Holy Simeon
Moses
Saint Catherine of Siena
Saint John the Baptist
Saint Philip the Apostle
Saint Pier Giorgio Frassati
Saint Thérèse of Lisieux

Grade 1
Blessed Mother Teresa of the Child Jesus
Blessed Pedro Calungsod
Blessed Pope John XXIII
Frederick William Faber
Mary, Mother of God
Michelangelo
Saint Albert the Great
Saint Angela Merici
Saint Dominic
Saint Emily de Vialar
Saint Frances Cabrini
Saint Giuseppina Bakhita
Saint Louise de Marillac
Saint Moses the Black
Saint Nicholas
Saint Patrick
Saint Pedro de San Jose Betancur
Saint Terese of Jesus of the Andes
Saint Thomas of Villanova
Venerable Father Solanus Casey
Zecharaih, Elizabeth, and John

Grade 2
All Saints
Bishop James Augustine Healy
Blessed Julian of Norwich
Blessed Marguerite Bays
Blessed Mariano de Jesus
Blessed Teresa of Calcutta
David
Mary, Mother of God
Pope John Paul II
Saint Anthony Claret
Saint Brigid of Kildare
Saint John Berchmans
Saint Juan Diego
Saint Luke
Saint Paul
Saint Peter
Saint Pius X, Pope
Saint Tarsicius
Saint Teresa Margaret Redi
Saint Victor, Pope
Venerable Pierre Toussaint

Grade 3
Blessed Bartholomew Osypiuk
Blessed Joseph Vaz
Blessed Luigi & Blessed Maria
Jean Donovan
Pierre Teilhard de Chardin
Saint Clement of Rome
Saint Dismas
Saint Elizabeth of Hungary
Saint Francis of Assisi

Saint Genevieve
Saint Gregory the Great
Saint Isaac Jogues
Saint John of Matha
Saint Margaret of Scotland
Saint Mary Ann of Quito
Saint Mary Magdalene
Saint Peter Canisius
Saint Pio (Padre Pio)
Saints Perpetua and Felicity
Sister Thea Bowman
Thomas Merton

Grade 4
Aaron and Miriam
Blessed Frederic Ozanam
Blessed Kateri Tekakwitha
Catherine de Hueck Doherty
Cesar Chavez
Korean Saints and Martyrs
Mary, Mother of God
Naomi and Ruth
Saint Bede
Saint Charles Lwanga
Saint Jane Frances de Chantal
Saint Joan of Arc
Saint John of God
Saint Katharine Drexel
Saint Margaret Mary Alacoque
Saint Martin de Porres
Saint Mary Magdalen Postel
Saint Maximilian Kolbe
Saint Teresa Benedicta
Saints Anne and Joachim
Venerable Matt Talbot

Grade 5
Blessed M. V. Rosal Vasquez
Dorothy Day
Michael the Archangel
Queenship of Mary
Saint Athanasius
Saint Augustine
Saint Benedict
Saint Catherine of Siena
Saint Cecilia
Saint Clare of Assisi
Saint Cyril of Jerusalem
Saint Francis Xavier
Saint Hildegarde of Bingen
Saint Jerome
Saint John Vianney
Saint Marguerite Bourgeoys
Saint Paul Miki
Saint Robert Ballarmine
Saint Stephen, martyred
Saint Thomas Aquinas
Saint Thomas More

Grade 6
Blessed Dorothy C. Orozco
Blessed Fra Angelico
Blessed Peter To Rot
Father John Carroll
Saint Birgitta of Sweden

Saint Charles Borromeo
Saint Elizabeth Ann Seton
Saint Faustina Kowalska
Saint Hilda of Whitby
Saint Ignatius of Loyola
Saint John Baptist de la Salle
Saint John Neumann
Saint John the Baptist
Saint John the Evangelist
Saint Matthias
Saint Monica
Saint Rose Philippine Duchesne
Saint Teresa Benedicta
Saint Teresa of Avila
Venerable Catherine McAuley
Women Martyrs of El Salvador

Grade 7
Archbishop Oscar Romero
Blessed Aloysius Stepinac
Blessed Carlos Manuel Cecilio Rodriguez Santiago
Blessed Kateri Tekakwitha
Blessed Theodore Guerin
Pope Leo XIII
Saint Catherine of Genoa
Saint Frances of Rome
Saint John Bosco
Saint Joseph
Saint Lorenzo Ruiz
Saint Ludmilla
Saint Madeleine Sophie Barat
Saint Margaret Ward
Saint Martin de Porres
Saint Mary MacKillop
Saint Matthew
Saint Peter Claver
Saint Rafqa
Saints Maria Zhao-Guo, Mary Zhao, Rosa Zhao
Venerable Pierre Toussaint

Grade 8
Blessed Cyprian Michael Iwene Tansi
Blessed Damien De Veuster
Blessed Edmund Ignatius Rice
Blessed Elizabeth Catez
Blessed Maria Anna Barbara Cope
Blessed Miguel Pro
Blessed Victoria Rasoamanarivo
Father Eusebius Kino
Mechthild von Magdeburg
Pere (Father) Jacques Marquette
Saint Benedict the Black
Saint Josefina Bakhita
Saint Marcella
Saint Maria del Transito de Jesus Sacramentado
Saint Peter Damien
Saint Prisca and Saint Aquila
Saint Thomas
Saints Perpetua and Felicity
Venerable Louis Martin and Zelie Guerin
Venerable Mariam Thresia Chiramel Mankidiyan
Venerable Samuel Mazzuchelli

Suggestions

- Create an environment for prayer within your classroom. This space can serve as a center to help students understand the beauty, depth, and sublimity of prayer.

- Make the Celebrate step in *Call to Faith* an integral and important part of each lesson.

- Have students memorize certain prayers so that they can pray them spontaneously.

- Use a Bible or the Lectionary when proclaiming Scripture during prayer celebrations.

- **Lectionary Link**—this feature, found on the Celebrate page of each chapter, helps you connect the Sunday readings to life through a process called "Break Open the Word." The readings for each week are found on the Web site.

- **Liturgy Link**—this feature, found on the Celebrate page of each chapter, gives practical tips for engaging students in the closing prayer celebration.

The songs in *Call to Faith* come from the *Singing Our Faith* hymnal.

Visit **www.harcourtreligion.com** for a correlation between *Call to Faith* music track numbers and *Singing Our Faith* song numbers.

Prayer and Worship

Catechesis always leads into prayer. Through prayer, Christians develop a close relationship with Jesus Christ, with God the Father, and with the Holy Spirit. In prayer, believers allow the Lord to touch their hearts, to lead them with his teachings, and to unite them with fellow Christians.

Thus, prayer is essential for anyone growing in faith. It is an important mission of catechesis to help students grow in their appreciation of prayer and to model a life of prayer for them.

Break Open the Word

1. **Prepare minds and hearts to listen to God's word.**
    a. **Light a candle.**
    b. **Move the group to a special environment for prayer.**
    c. **Invite students to quiet their thoughts.**
    d. **Ask students to listen to what God is saying in this reading.**

2. **Proclaim the Gospel.**

3. **Allow for a moment of silent reflection.**

4. **Read the sharing question.**

5. **Share responses to the question.**

GRADE

Five- and Six-year-olds

Suggestions

- The kindergarten years are marked by high levels of curiosity and physical energy. Don't expect the children to sit still for long periods of time.

- Do expect lots of questions. Answer them directly, even if they don't seem to be part of the lesson. A child's curiosity will lead him or her to grow in understanding.

- Your catechesis will be most inviting and effective when you can involve the children intellectually, emotionally, and physically in the lessons and activities.

- Help them develop their motor skills. Kindergarten children often require help to perform precise tasks such as printing, cutting, and gluing. If possible, arrange to have classroom assistance from parents, other catechists, or older children when scheduling fine-motor activities.

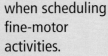

Know The CHILD

Kindergarten is a major threshold in the life of a child. The kindergarten child is making the transition from a home-centered world to the wider universe of school and neighborhood, from play to study, from the preschool years to middle childhood. Sometimes these transitions are not smooth. There will be days when the children behave in ways that are older or younger than their years.

Emotionally, the kindergarten child is generally happy. The children are growing in their ability to name and deal with their feelings, and may "try on" various emotions as they would dress-up clothes. Prolonged sadness or anger in a kindergarten child may indicate emotional problems, reaction to a difficult situation at home, or frustration resulting from learning disabilities. If you notice a child experiencing such problems, follow school or parish policies for offering help.

Whether you've been teaching for many years or are a new teacher or catechist, it's always important to keep in mind the emotional and developmental progress of your children. It helps give you perspective on the work you do with them.

The way of teaching which we learn from the Gospels is called, in the *General Directory for Catechesis*, the "pedagogy of Jesus." It is a gradual learning, in age-appropriate words and actions and prayers, about Christ and the Church. You are participating in this divine pedagogy now. In order for you to succeed, it's important that you *know the child*.

Catholic Social Teachings

For the past 115 years or so, Catholic social teaching has grown to occupy an increasingly important place in catechesis and in Catholic life. Recently, Church leaders have urged all those in the ministry of catechesis to include the social teachings of the Church in all aspects and at all grade levels of religious instruction and faith formation.

Call to Faith is the first elementary religion series to provide a curriculum for Catholic social teachings. Following the recommendations of a task force convened by the U.S. Catholic Bishops in 1995, *Call to Faith* provides a comprehensive, age-appropriate lesson at the end of each unit that correlates to the text.

Following this *Call to Faith* curriculum, students of every age will be deeply motivated by the Catholic social teaching and ready to live it. For parish programs, the complete program is available online at **www.harcourtreligion.com**.

Seven Principles of CATHOLIC SOCIAL TEACHING

- Care for God's Creation
- Life and Dignity of the Human Person
- Rights and Responsibilities of the Human Person
- The Dignity of Work and the Rights of Workers
- Solidarity of the Human Family
- Call to Family, Community, and Participation
- Option for the Poor and Vulnerable

Faith in Action lessons follow a three-step process:

- **Discover** This step describes the Catholic social teaching being presented in the unit and engages the learner in understanding it.

- **Connect** This step gives interesting examples and the witness of people and groups who are living out the teaching.

- **Serve** This step allows students to makes choices about how he or she can practice the principle.

Parish Directors and Coordinators of Religious Education can integrate these lessons into the regular calendar or use them for family or intergenerational sessions.

GO ONLINE The complete Social Justice program is available online at **www.harcourtreligion.com**

Multiple Intelligences

Educational research proves that there are different ways in which people learn. The names of these different ways of learning, or intelligences, follow.

Verbal/Linguistic learning occurs best through reading, writing, telling stories, and discussing ideas.

Musical learning occurs best through singing, listening to music, and remembering melodies.

Logical/Mathematical learning occurs best through solving problems, analyzing, and applying logic.

Visual/Spatial learning occurs best through visualizing, looking at pictures, drawing, and creating.

Bodily/Kinesthetic learning occurs best through physically moving, processing knowledge through bodily sensations, dancing, and acting.

Interpersonal learning occurs best through interviewing people, sharing about one's feelings, and cooperating with others on tasks.

Intrapersonal learning occurs best through working alone and reflecting.

Naturalist learning occurs best through exploring nature and living things.

Dr. Howard Gardner, of Harvard University, revolutionized education with his theory of multiple intelligence. He theorized that there was not only one kind of intelligence. Rather, there were different ways in which people learned. Applying this theory to faith formation shows that there are also many different ways in which people come to know God.

The most common and recognizable form of intelligence is **verbal/linguistic.** People who learn in this way prefer parables, story telling, and creative writing when learning new faith concepts. Those with **musical** intelligence learn best through listening to different kinds of music, making up songs, or singing throughout the lesson.

Those with **logical/mathematical** intelligence enjoy studying the origins of different religions, using clues to identify biblical characters, or examining the true cost of poverty.

Learners with **visual/spatial** intelligence put faith concepts into concrete terms through painting, photography, or unique inventions. The learners eager to act out a story or to dance a prayer are those with **bodily/kinesthetic** intelligence, they who feel comfortable using their bodies to take in information.

Those with **interpersonal** intelligence thrive on community and cooperation, and those with **intrapersonal** intelligence know themselves well and enjoy journaling and reflection.

Those with **naturalist** intelligence use God's creation to learn.

Using Gardner's theory in the faith formation classroom is an opportunity to reach all students, regardless of their learning styles.

Reaching ALL LEARNERS

A student's intelligence is not the only factor in how he or she will learn. Learning is also affected by family situations, learning disorders, and mental or physical impairments. The lessons and teaching methods in *Call to Faith* have been carefully crafted in order to meet the needs of all learners.

A special feature in your Teacher Edition, called "Reaching All Learners," will provide you with tips, suggestions, and proven ways to include students with different learning styles and abilities in your lesson. Some of the suggestions will help you make provisions for physical and mental challenges your children may face, while other suggestions will help you respond to the diverse ways children learn and experience the world.
By varying your teaching strategies, you can help students enhance the range of their learning capabilities.

To accommodate various exceptionalities, consider these general modifications in your classroom management:
- move the child closer to the board or teacher
- allow the child to be a mentor/tutor or to have a mentor/tutor
- designate readers prior to class reading
- provide large print or projected print
- allow the child to use a tape recorder or note-taker
- give oral tests and assessments, and give oral feedback
- allow the child to use a chalkboard, laptop, or an alternate to paper and pencil
- give positive reinforcement for desired behavior and replacement skills for inappropriate behavior
- be swift and consistent with discipline
- have classroom rules displayed, and discuss them frequently
- maintain a routine, and practice daily procedures
- provide multimedia and alternate classroom environments
- give oral directions as well as print directions and explain thoroughly; question students to assess their understanding

The effects of academic deficiencies, learning disabilities, distressed home environments, and poor health can hinder learning. If a child struggles with learning tasks, or shows signs of emotional strain, consider the possible causes and these exceptionalities:

- Large motor or fine motor skill issues can affect movements from walking to handwriting.

- Hearing, speech, visual, and processing issues can obstruct the reception of information as well as alter the ability to follow procedures.

- Emotional issues—like anxiety, withdrawal, and terror—are commonly disguised by outward behaviors like attention seeking, memory loss, and aggression.

- Cognitive issues can result in reading difficulties, loss of impulse control, and distractibility.

"People learn and grow in many different ways"

The Vocation to Teach

Sustaining the vocation to teach as Jesus did takes time and rarely happens without some struggle. At the beginning of each chapter in this Teacher Edition, you will find short essays designed to help you sustain your spirit. These essays will assist you in the ongoing process of assessing the spiritual dimensions of your catechetical commitment, reviewing the expectations that put your vocational commitment at risk, and examining proactive ways of adapting to those challenges.

Perhaps the essence of the grandparent's message was this: The task of sustaining your call is about representing the faith, deeply and authentically, to those you teach.

Visit www.harcourtreligion.com for more Sustaining Your Spirit resources.

Sustaining Your Spirit

Some years ago, a new catechist was struggling to meet the requirements and expectations of effective religious education. Challenged by striving for creative activities and perfectly facilitated classroom discussions, the new catechist felt her commitment beginning to fade.

One day a grandparent arrived early to pick up a student. Instead of waiting in the parking lot, this woman lingered just outside the open door of the classroom, listening to the closing prayer.

Shortly after dismissal, she appeared in front of the catechist and, without a word of introduction, nodded toward the classroom window. The catechist could see students waiting for their rides—the younger children running, playing, and laughing, and the older ones standing in tight circles sharing accounts of the day's events.

It was the landscape of the young—fully alive. The grandparent looked directly at the catechist and said with feeling and certainty: "You may be the only Bible that they ever *really* read."

Your students may not remember all of the material and experiences that you offer them, but they will remember the way that your life and your presence reveal your faith. Your dedication to the commitments and challenges of this ministry will help shape others' lives.

Planning the Year

Consider the Basics

- How many times a week will I teach religion?
- What is the time frame for each lesson?
- How many sessions are scheduled for the year?
- What impact will other parish and school activities—liturgies and assemblies—have on my lesson schedule?

Celebrating the Seasonal Lessons

- Eight lessons and celebrations are tied to the seasons and feasts of the liturgical year.
- The teaching year may be planned to determine where each lesson will fit best.
- Lessons are flexible and can be adapted to meet the needs of children.
- Lessons may be taught individually or may accompany a chapter that discusses the relevant season.
- The Family Faith page is a reproducible master and includes background on the season, a family prayer, and a family activity.

Using Scripture Stories

- Each chapter contains a scripture story.
- In addition, each unit ends with a Scripture Story Booklet related to the unit theme.
- Each Scripture Story Booklet is a pull-out book for students to share in class and at home. Reading these stories at home will reinforce the lesson you have taught in class.

Pacing the Chapters

- *Call to Faith* contains seven units and 21 chapters.
- Each chapter has two activity masters that are fully integrated into the chapter theme and can be used before, during, or after each session.

In parish religious education classes, plan for approximately 60 minutes of class time.

Invite	10 minutes
Explore	40 minutes
Celebrate	10 minutes

In school religious education classes, plan for lesson 5 days per week for about 30 minutes. The lesson can be easily adapted for a 4-day week as well.

Day 1: Invite
Day 2: Explore
Day 3: Explore
Day 4: Explore
Day 5: Celebrate

Benefiting from Prayers and Words of Faith

- The prayers are age appropriate and meaningful to the lives of young children.
- The Words of Faith is a picture glossary that reinforces learning.

Call to Faith COMPONENTS

Student Editions (Grades K–8) help children deepen their faith through compelling stories, activities, prayers, and seasonal celebrations. Family Faith pages help families participate in their children's faith formation. (Available for school, parish, and bilingual programs)

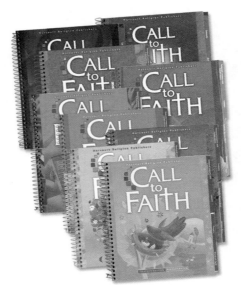

Teacher Editions (Grades K–8) provide all the tools for success—easy-to-use planners, Catechism and GDC connections, a simple three-step catechetical process, a wealth of resources and optional activities, plus activity and assessment reproducibles. (Available for school, parish, and bilingual programs)

Faith at Home: Nurturing Households of Faith features practical suggestions, tips for sharing and celebrating faith at home, and more—all in an engaging magazine.

Call to Faith Music CDs (Grades K–8) offer a repertoire of liturgical music to accompany every chapter and seasonal celebration. Each set includes 30 songs on two CDs.

People of Faith Collection (Grades K–6) includes 133 vibrantly illustrated cards— each with a brief biography and prayer. These cards are excellent tools for encouraging children to learn from examples set by people of faith.

Lectionary Links: Breaking Open the Word visually displays the Sunday lectionary readings along with compelling faith-sharing questions for different ages in an interactive format. Lectionary Links are available for Years A, B, and C.

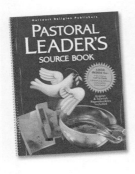

Pastoral Leader's Source Book provides practical resources including professional development articles, implementation models, resources for parish adults, and parent and catechist orientation sessions—plus a separate section for implementing whole community catechesis. Included is a CD-ROM with PowerPoint® presentations that provide tools for training and formation sessions.

Reflect n' Connect Conversation Starter for Intergenerational Gatherings, an inflatable beach ball designed for years of use, offers an active way for connecting people of all ages.

Technology Tools for Your Ministry: No Mousing Around!, by Tim Welch, features wit, wisdom, and above all, clarity, about the technology tools now available to parish ministers. This is a great introduction to the world of technology and a challenging invitation to use every means available today to tell the Story of Jesus Christ-and tell it well.

God Loves Me: Calling Children to Faith Through Song (Grades K–6), by John Burland, features a variety of contemporary songs for children of all ages that align with the **Call to Faith** catechetical themes.

Move! Pray! Celebrate! Music CD and DVD, by John Burland, feature songs of faith that assist in the celebration of Catholic identity with in school and parish communities Includes specific Scripture and Catechism references for each song plus a new Mass Setting.

Big AL LIVE DVDs (Grades K–6) are excellent for beginning a parish meeting, for parent programs of any kind, for intergenerational faith gatherings, or for children to watch by themselves. Each DVD presents ten different Gospel values. The brief and engaging presentations include a short Scripture reading, a reflection from Fr Joe Kempf, a discussion with Big Al, and a prayer.

CALL to FAITH e connect

your online source for lifelong catechesis

www.CalltoFaitheConnect.com

Call to Faith eConnect features a state-of-the-art network that enhances and expands *Call to Faith*. Innovative web tools include multimedia catechetical support, moderated forums, year-round planning tools, online professional development, educational games, podcasts, communication tools…even music and videos for school, parish, and home! Visit *www.CalltoFaitheConnect.com* to try it now.

Kindergarten Contents

UNIT 1
REVELATION

iii

UNIT 2
TRINITY

iv

UNIT 3
JESUS CHRIST

© Harcourt Religion

© Harcourt Religion

© Harcourt Religion

v

vi

Welcome to
Call to Faith!

The following pages provide an opening lesson that will help you and the children get better acquainted with one another and with this textbook. The introductory pages will introduce the children you teach to the text that they will be exploring during the coming year. Together you will form a faith-sharing community with an open, trusting environment and a sense of fun and enthusiasm. Here's a brief look at the components of the opening lesson and how they will help children become more familiar with the catechetical process.

About You

This page, along with the Activity Master that appears on page 5A, will serve as an "ice-breaker" to get your group talking, sharing, interacting, and having fun together.

About Your Faith

The activities and suggestions on this page will help you assess where children are on their faith journeys. Children are called to share what they already know about the Catholic faith, the Bible, and Church Tradition—topics they will build on as they grow in faith with your help and the guidance of the entire Church community.

About Your Book

Both you and the children will get a "sneak preview" of the textbook and become familiar with the features and symbols that will guide you through the lessons, stories, activities, and celebrations included in every chapter.

Call to Faith

During this prayer celebration, you and the children will bond as a community of faith through ritual, Scripture, discussion, prayer, and song.

May **you** and the **children**
find **holiness, joy,** and **many blessings**
during your year of **discovery** and **faith!**

SCHOOL BUS

About You

You, O Lord, are good.
Based on Psalm 86:5

Let's Begin

Welcome Kindergarten is an exciting grade. You will learn many new things. You will also get to know your teacher and your classmates.

Here is a way to help them get to know you.

Draw something you like to do.

1

About You

Objective: To look forward to the year ahead

Let Us Pray

Invite children to join you in the classroom prayer space. In the prayer space, have a crucifix and a Bible opened to the psalm verse. Identify these objects for children.

Lead children in the psalm prayer, having them repeat the psalm verse and response after you.

Let's Begin

- Read aloud the text under Welcome. Tell children that this year is a new beginning for you, too, and that you are looking forward to getting to know them better.

- Read aloud the directions for the drawing activity. Allow time for children to work on their drawings, and then invite volunteers to show and describe their work.

- Point out the variety of responses you receive.

OPTIONAL ACTIVITY

Chart Favorite Things   Ask children about favorite foods, games, and colors.

- Invite children to help you chart the results on the board or on chart paper.

- Encourage children to use counting skills to determine which things in each category are most popular.

Multiple Intelligence: Logical/Mathematical

REACHING ALL LEARNERS

Developmental Diversity   Kindergarten children vary widely in their mastery of the intellectual, physical, and social skills needed in the classroom.

- Provide children with opportunities to practice a wide range of abilities.

- Encourage children by providing positive feedback for trying new skills.

About Your Faith

Invite volunteers to tell about things they like to do with their families.

- Explain that children's families at home and their church family will help them learn about God this year.
- Read aloud the text.
- Ask children to name some things they and their families do with their parish family. Possible responses: pray at Mass, celebrate at picnics and festivals, help people who are in need

Activity

- Read aloud the Think question, and allow time for children to think about it.
- Have children form small groups to talk about their responses.
- Ask children to share their questions about God with you. List them on chart paper or large index cards. Tell children you will be exploring these questions all year.

You will learn many things this year.

You will find out about the world God made. You will hear stories about God's Son, Jesus.

Your family at home and at church will help you.

Activity · Share Your Faith

Think: What is something you know about God?

Share: Talk about how you learned this.

Act: Work with your teacher to make a list of questions you have about God.

QUICK TIP

Assessment Opportunity Responses to the Think question and the list of questions about God will give you some idea of the children's level of understanding.

- Do not correct misinterpretations immediately, but address these points as they arise during lessons.
- Keep the list of questions, and refer to it throughout the year.

???

About Your Book

Your book has many things in it.

It has stories and pictures about God and his Son, Jesus.

It has prayers, songs, and activities, too.

Activity

Connect Your Faith

Seek and Find To get to know your book better, look at the pictures below. Then find an example of each picture somewhere in your book.

3

About Your Book

Read aloud the text.

- Tell children that their textbook is like a map or guidebook that will help them on their journey of faith this year.

Activity

- Introduce the concept of a Seek and Find activity.
- Read aloud the directions.
- Have children work in pairs. Give each pair five sticky notes to mark the pages where they find the pictures. Remind pairs to choose five different pictures to seek and find.
- Invite pairs to hold up their books to show the pages on which they found the pictures. Note that responses will vary because these feature icons are found on many pages throughout the book.
- Explain the concept of book page numbers, and show children where to locate them. Invite pairs to call out the numbers of pages where they found pictures, and have the class turn to these pages.

OPTIONAL ACTIVITY

Scavenger Hunt Expand on the activity in the book, and reinforce children's ability to identify objects associated with faith by having a scavenger hunt in the room.

- Before class, place several objects such as a cross, a statue or picture of Mary, a rosary, and a candle around the room.
- Name the objects for children before having them form teams to find as many objects as they can.

Multiple Intelligence: Bodily/Kinesthetic

CHAPTER BACKGROUND

Textbook Icons

 Indicates opportunities for prayer and celebration.

Directs you to read aloud the text to children.

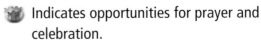 Points out stories or quotations from the Bible.

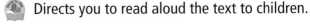 Denotes suggested questions for discussion.

Indicates opportunities for singing together or listening to music.

Call to Faith

 Let Us Pray

Tell children that in this celebration they will hear how Jesus calls people to be his friends and followers.

- Remind children that Jesus is God's Son.
- Teach children the prayer responses.

 Use the *Call to Faith* Kindergarten CD, track 9, to rehearse the song.

Gather

- Invite children into the prayer space. Have them sit comfortably in a circle.
- Follow the order of prayer.
- Invite children to mirror your actions as you pray the Sign of the Cross.
- Leader's prayer:
  God our Father, we are ready to answer the call to be friends and followers of your Son, Jesus Christ.

Listen to God's Word

- Ask children to listen carefully as you proclaim the Gospel.
- Prompt children to respond.

Call to Faith

Gather

Pray the Sign of the Cross together.

Leader: The Lord be with you.

All: **And also with you.**

Leader: Let us pray.

Bow your head as the leader prays.

All: **Amen.**

Listen to God's Word

Leader: A reading from the holy Gospel according to Matthew.

Read Matthew 4:18–22.

The Gospel of the Lord.

All: **Praise to you, Lord Jesus Christ.**

4

 SCRIPTURE BACKGROUND

In Jesus' Time Young children may have a difficult time identifying with the cultural context of the Gospel reading.

- Explain that Jesus lived 2,000 years ago.
- Use a classroom map or globe to help children see the area where Jesus lived.
- Tell children that in Jesus' time, in his home town, many families made their living by fishing, like Simon and Andrew and their father.

LECTIONARY LINK

Break Open the Word Read last week's Sunday Gospel. Talk about how this reading helps us follow Jesus. For children's questions related to the weekly Gospel reading, visit our Web site.

 Visit www.harcourtreligion.com for weekly scripture readings and seasonal resources.

Signing of the Forehead

Come forward as your name is called. The leader will trace the Sign of the Cross on your forehead.

Leader: (Name), may God bless you as you answer Jesus' call to be his friend and follower.

All: Amen.

Go Forth!

Sing together.

We are called to act with justice,

we are called to love tenderly,

we are called to serve one another;

to walk humbly with God!

"We Are Called" © 1988, 2004 GIA Publications, Inc.

5

Signing of the Forehead

- Explain that the cross is the sign of Jesus' followers.
- Call each child forward in turn, and pray the blessing prayer over him or her, tracing a cross on the child's forehead.

Go Forth!

- Have children sing as they leave the prayer space.

LITURGY LINK

The Sign of the Cross The cross is a sign of identity for Christians.

- Remind children that our parish family begins every celebration with the Sign of the Cross.
- Ask children to be on the lookout for crosses and crucifixes displayed at home, in church, and on jewelry, bumper stickers, or books.

Name _____ Date _____

Things I Like

Directions: Circle the things you like to do. Talk about them with a partner.

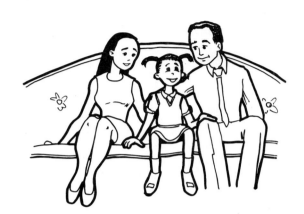

©Harcourt Religion

CALL to FAITH

Seasonal Lessons and Celebrations

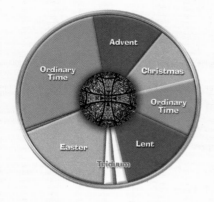

Seasonal Lessons

By means of the yearly cycle the Church celebrates the whole mystery of Christ, from his incarnation until the day of Pentecost and the expectation of his coming again.

Norms for the Liturgical Year and the Calendar, 17

Liturgical Environment

Since these celebrations are meant to have a different tone and flavor than the other lessons, the environment you set for them is important. Factors to include in setting the environment are:

- Color
- Silence
- Music
- Symbols

The heart of these sessions is the celebration. Take time to determine whether your prayer space is appropriate for the ritual or if there is something else, such as moving furniture, adding plants or flowers, or moving to another place that would create a more reflective prayer-filled environment. Use the appropriate liturgical colors for seasons and feasts:

- Green for Ordinary Time
- White or gold for Christmas and Easter
- Purple for Advent and Lent
- White for feasts of Mary
- Red for Pentecost

The use of primary symbols, water, oil, the cross, the Scriptures, and candles is very important. Display them prominently and reverently in your prayer space.

The Role of Music

Besides the music from the *Call to Faith* and *Singing Our Faith* CDs suggested in your teacher edition, use of meditative music at the beginning of a service or during a meditation time will also enhance a prayerful atmosphere for children. Do not be afraid of silence. It is good for students to have time to reflect.

The Church Year

Within the flow of what most people experience as a calendar year, from January first to December thirty-first, there is another year—the liturgical or Church year. This year, which is not dependent on the civil calendar, begins on the first Sunday of Advent or the fourth Sunday before Christmas and ends on the feast of Christ the King, the last Sunday of Ordinary Time. For Christians, as it unfolds each year, the liturgical year is a time of grace and favor because it celebrates and remembers the person of Jesus Christ and the Paschal mystery of his life, death, and Resurrection. Easter, the feast of Jesus' Resurrection, is the most important and principal feast of the Church year. Another significant feast is Christmas—the celebration of the birth of Jesus. These feasts determine the flow of the Church year. Each of them is preceded by a season of preparation: Advent for Christmas and Lent for Easter. Each feast is followed by a number of weeks of celebration called the Christmas Season and the Easter Season. There are also thirty-three to thirty-four Sundays of the Church year called Ordinary Time. Ordinary Time celebrates the events and teachings of Jesus' public life. During the year, as the Church celebrates the mysteries of Christ, it also honors Mary, who is closely linked to the saving actions of her Son, and the saints, who are faithful examples of how to live the Christian life.

In these eight sessions, you will find a celebration for each of the liturgical seasons of the Church year, including the Triduum and a celebration for Mary and one of the saints. Use your class calendar to plan ahead for each of these lessons to coincide with the season or feast during Ordinary Time.

Liturgical Catechesis

These celebrations follow a process of liturgical catechesis which includes forming students in the language, rituals, structure, and order of the liturgy. The process of liturgical catechesis contained in each session includes:

- A reflection about the context of the feast being celebrated.
- A ritual celebration built around a text taken from the Book of Rites or Lectionary. Within the celebration there is always participation in some ritual action.
- An opportunity for reflection and action that flow from the celebration.

The Scriptures

The scripture readings in these sessions are meant to be proclaimed and probed with children. Give them ample time to respond to the dialogue questions. The purpose of the dialogue is to find out what children heard in the proclamation of the word and to explore their thoughts. Always ask open-ended questions and refrain from trying to control the dialogue.

The Students

Elementary grade children bring an innate sense of wonder, awe, and imitation to ritual prayer. They are quieted through the creation of a prayerful environment. They are caught up by the use of signs and symbols and need little explanation of them as long as they are prominently displayed and reverently used. Make your gestures large and inclusive. For example, when you sign children with the Sign of the Cross, sign with large gestures. Use slow and reverent gestures, such as bowing before the Scriptures, and lighting the candle slowly in silence. Children will imitate you and will learn far more by your movements during ritual than by your words.

Special Times

Families share special times together. Some families celebrate birthdays and holidays with food, gifts, and songs.

The Church shares special times together, too. During the Church year, we celebrate the lives of Jesus, Mary, and the saints. We pray when we celebrate these special times. Here are three ways we pray.

We fold our hands in prayer.

6

We bow our heads in silence.

We make the Sign of the Cross.

We say,
In the name of the Father,
and of the Son,
and of the Holy Spirit. Amen.

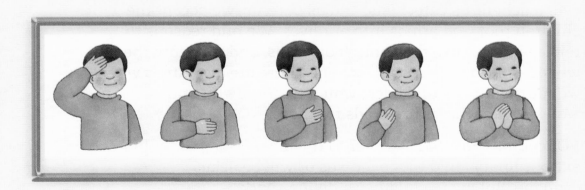

7

Our Mother

As it celebrates the mystery of Christ in the yearly cycle, the Church also venerates with a particular love Mary, the Mother of God and sets before the devotion of the faithful memory of the martyrs and other saints.

General Norms for the Liturgical Year and Calendar, 8

Seasonal Background

Being in charge of children, as a parent, as a catechist, or as a teacher, can sometimes be intimidating. We often ask ourselves, "How will what I do today affect this child's life in the future?"

Mary's approach to her role in Jesus' life can guide our attitude and behavior. The first two chapters of the Gospel according to Luke give us a glimpse of the growth of this young woman. At the Annunciation, Mary accepts God's will with minimal questioning. The beautiful prayer Mary says at the Visitation, the Magnificat, speaks of Mary's astonishment at God's gifts to her. At Jesus' birth, she reveals her child to shepherds and kings. When Jesus is taken to the Temple, she and Joseph are amazed at what they see happening. Finally, after Jesus teaches the elders in the Temple, she stores her observations in her heart, wondering what will come.

As teachers, as catechists, and as parents, we accept the children that God brings into our lives. We find reasons to rejoice in the ways they enrich our lives, and we share the joy we receive from them with others. There are also times when we must simply stand back, watch their growth, and wonder what the future holds for them.

Of course, Mary was Mother to the most extraordinary child that ever was or will be. Jesus is divine. But every child has a divine spark. As you guide the young people in your life, ask Mary to help you find that spark. She is *your* mother, after all!

Reflect ***What can you learn from Mary that will help you be a better person?***

Environment

Materials:

Prayer table
White cloth
Marian statue
Flowers
Bible
***Call to Faith* Kindergarten CD**

- Allow space around the prayer table for children.
- Have several children bring flowers to decorate the prayer table.
- Ask other children to place a white cloth on the prayer table and arrange the flowers.
- Place a statue of Mary on the table.

Ordinary Time

Mary showed us how to be a good parent. She accepted Jesus into her life at the Annunciation, watched over him as he grew, and wondered what would become of him. As our heavenly mother, she claims us as her children, too. We can go to her in prayer for guidance. She can help us gain perspective on the awesome task of creating a happy family.

Birthday celebrations are common in many homes. This lesson celebrates Mary's birth, an event that leads in turn to Jesus' birth. It also recognizes Mary's trust in God the Father and love of Jesus. As a family, work to trust God the Father and love his Son. And remember to honor Mary!

Family Celebration

Celebrate Mary's birthday as you would that of a family member or friend. Have a celebration dinner, perhaps with blue flowers on the table. End the dinner with a special cake, and sing a Marian hymn instead of the birthday song.

As you gather for the meal, set the tone for the celebration by adding the Hail Mary to your usual grace before meals:

> ### Hail Mary
> Hail, Mary, full of grace, the Lord is with you! Blessed are you among women, and blessed is the fruit of your womb, Jesus. Holy Mary, Mother of God, pray for us sinners, now and at the hour of our death. Amen.

Family Activity

Look for ways to honor Mary in your home life. In addition to including special prayers to Mary in your daily devotions, consider celebrating other Marian feasts.

- Consult a liturgical calendar, and mark several feasts that you would like to celebrate with your own family.

- Assign tasks to each family member. One can plan a meal or special dessert. Another can find or write a prayer for the occasion. Another can research the history of the feast and what it teaches us about Mary.

- Finally, gather as a family to enjoy your celebration!

Our Mother

- Point out that everyone has a birthday, and the group will be celebrating a special person's birthday.
- Have children share what they know about Mary. Possible responses: She was Jesus' mother; she did what God asked her to do.
- Call attention to the illustration. Have children describe what is happening in it. Possible response: Mary is caring for Jesus.
- Read the text. Pause occasionally to have children expand on what Mary might have done to help Jesus grow.
- Remind children that Mary is their mother, too, and she will help them grow.

Ordinary Time

Our Mother

Mary was Jesus' mother.

She cared for him.

Mary cares for us, too.

We celebrate Mary's birthday on September 8.

8

Our Mother

 SEASONAL RESOURCES

Books and Videos   Many resources explain Mary's role in our lives.

- *We Learn from Mary* (15 min). St. Anthony Messenger Press. This video teaches children ages 6–10 about Mary's life and meaning to us.
- *Christ's Mother and Ours.* Oscar Lukefahr, CM. (Liguori Publications). This book helps adults explore Mary; it includes references to historic teachings, songs, and devotions.

 CULTURAL CONNECTION

Celebrating Mary   In the Canary Islands, Mary's birthday is part of a two-day festival.

- September 8 is the second day of the festival.
- Islanders celebrate by carrying a statue of the Madonna in procession.
- Fireworks conclude the festivities.

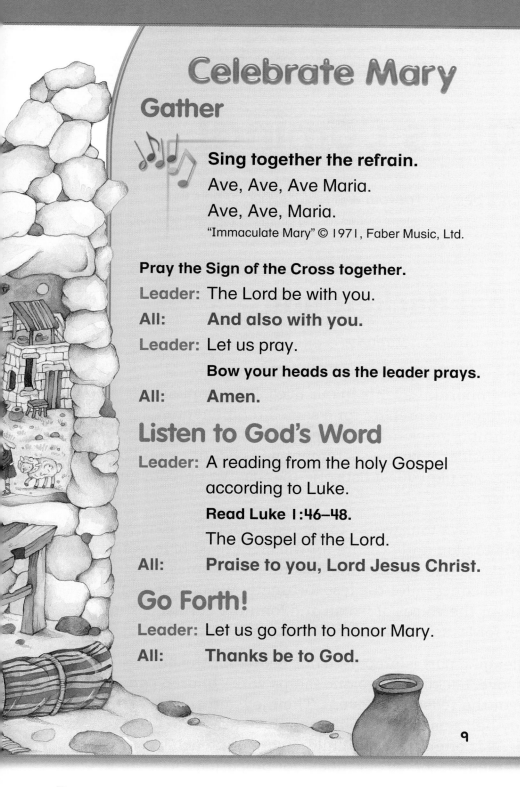

Celebrate Mary

Gather

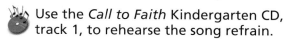 **Sing together the refrain.**

Ave, Ave, Ave Maria.

Ave, Ave, Maria.

"Immaculate Mary" © 1971, Faber Music, Ltd.

Pray the Sign of the Cross together.

Leader: The Lord be with you.

All: And also with you.

Leader: Let us pray.

Bow your heads as the leader prays.

All: Amen.

Listen to God's Word

Leader: A reading from the holy Gospel according to Luke.

Read Luke 1:46–48.

The Gospel of the Lord.

All: Praise to you, Lord Jesus Christ.

Go Forth!

Leader: Let us go forth to honor Mary.

All: Thanks be to God.

9

Celebrate Mary

Gather

- Explain to children that the words *Ave Maria* mean "Hail Mary."

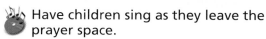 Use the *Call to Faith* Kindergarten CD, track 1, to rehearse the song refrain.

- Teach children the prayer responses.
- Invite children into the prayer space.
- Follow the order of prayer.
- Leader's prayer: **God our Father, thank you for Mary. She watched over Jesus as he grew up. She will watch over us, too.**

Listen to God's Word

- Have children sit.
- Proclaim the Gospel reading.
- Prompt children to respond.
- Have children think quietly about why Mary was blessed.

Go Forth!

- Lead the group in the dismissal rite.

 Have children sing as they leave the prayer space.

 PRAYER

The Magnificat   The Gospel reading is part of the Magnificat, also known as Mary's Canticle.

- This beautiful prayer was Mary's answer to Elizabeth's words of welcome at the Visitation.
- The verses read here express Mary's joy in her decision to follow God's will.
- There are many such versions of this prayer.

LITURGY LINK

Colors and Art   Although blue is the color most often identified with Mary, it is not an approved liturgical color. Therefore, white, which symbolizes purity and joy, is used for Marian feasts.

Mary is depicted in numerous ways in Catholic artwork. Take your group through your parish church to see different representations of her.

Advent

Jesus Is Coming!

Advent is thus a period of devout and joyful expectation.

General Norms for the Liturgical Year and Calendar, 39

Seasonal Background

"I need some time to get ready."

How often have we said or heard that? We want to be prepared for important events in our lives. For a Baptism or First Communion, we prepare for a sacred moment and celebrate its importance to us with a gathering of friends and family. We consider how the sacrament will change us and our relationships. We plan guest lists and menus. We prepare our homes for visitors.

Similarly, we have four weeks to get ready for Christmas. We use this time to plan and prepare for the great feast of love and light. We make or gather gifts and decorate our homes. We show care and concern for the less fortunate. We gather as a Church to hear the voices of Isaiah and John the Baptist ask us to get ready for Jesus' coming. This is the easy part.

The challenging part is preparing our hearts for the burst of Christmas love. Luckily, our relationships with children can help us savor the season of Advent. Their joy and enthusiasm for each day helps us find happiness in the journey to Christmas. As is often the case, children are our teachers. Their excitement becomes our model for preparing for Christmas with joy.

Part of savoring Advent is finding solitude. Ironically, sometimes the best preparation is taking time to do nothing. Give yourself that luxury, if necessary.

Reflect *What can you learn from children about enjoying Advent?*

Environment

Materials:

Prayer table
Purple cloth
Advent wreath
Advent Calendar
Battery operated or electric candles
Bible
***Call to Faith* Kindergarten CD**

- Allow plenty of space around the prayer table, especially if you are lighting the Advent wreath.

- Place a purple cloth on the table along with the wreath.

- Consider decorating the prayer space with seasonal greenery and adding an Advent calendar.

Advent

Christmas is coming! Will you be ready in time? Of course you will! One way or another, you will find time to decorate, gather gifts, and bring joy to others.

Advent is the first four weeks of the Church year. It recalls the time before Jesus was born, when the Chosen People were waiting for the Messiah. When we go to Mass, we hear prayers filled with Old Testament images. We listen to readings about John the Baptist and others who foretold Jesus' life with us.

We are anxious to recall the great step in our salvation, Jesus' birth. However, we must also remember that Advent is a time of waiting. Happily making presents and counting down to Christmas with an Advent wreath or calendar helps families savor the season and listen to its lessons.

Family Celebration

As a family, gather around an Advent wreath or Advent calendar for a prayer celebrating the season. Light the appropriate number of candles on the wreath or do an activity with the calendar. End with this prayer:

> Jesus, Son of God, we are waiting for you to come into our hearts. Help us make a new home for you. Help us be generous and show your love by sharing with others. Amen.

Family Activity

Just as God the Father shared the most precious gift of his Son with us, we are invited to share gifts with others. As a family, consider donating gifts to those who are less fortunate than you.

- Look through closets and dressers to find outgrown clothes, unused toys, and other serviceable household items. Consider donating them to a charity.

- Many parishes and social service agencies, as well as clubs and community organizations, will help families provide Christmas cheer to others. Scan your parish bulletin and local newspapers for opportunities to provide food, clothing, toys, and other gifts.

- Be certain to include your kindergartner in your activities. For example, your child could help you select and wrap gifts for others.

©Harcourt Religion

Jesus Is Coming!

- Have children repeat the word *Advent* after you.
- Ask children what they know about Advent. Possible responses: It comes before Christmas; we count weeks of Advent with a wreath.
- Encourage children to tell how they observe Advent with their families.
- Point out the illustration. Ask what the children in the photograph are doing. celebrating Advent
- Read aloud the text to children.
- Point out that sometimes it is hard to wait. We make our time waiting for Jesus go faster by keeping busy and doing good things for others.

Advent

Jesus Is Coming!

Every year, we remember what life was like before Jesus was born.

We do this during a special time called Advent.

We wait for Jesus and get ready to see him again.

10

 SEASONAL RESOURCES

Books   Many resources are available to supplement your Advent lesson.

- *Celebrating Advent with the Jesse Tree.* Rev. Jude Winkler. (Catholic Book Publishing). This book shows how to use a Jesse Tree to teach Old Testament stories.
- *An Advent Sourcebook.* Thomas O'Gorman. (Liturgy Training Publications). This book includes Scripture, hymns, and homilies.

 CULTURAL CONNECTION

Saint Nicholas   Saint Nicholas was a bishop in the fourth century in what is now Turkey. He was known for his generosity.

- The Dutch preserve the custom of having the saint appear on the eve of his December 6 feast to give small gifts to children.
- Sometimes gifts are left in shoes that the children leave out at night.

Celebrate Advent

Gather

 Sing together the refrain.

Rejoice, Rejoice, Emmanuel

Shall come to you, O Israel.

"O Come, O Come Emmanuel" © 1975, GIA Publications, Inc.

Pray the Sign of the Cross together.

Leader: Blessed be God.

All: **Blessed be God forever.**

Leader: Let us pray.

Bow your heads as the leader prays.

All: **Amen.**

Listen to God's Word

Leader: A reading from the book of Isaiah.

Read Isaiah 40:3.

The word of the Lord.

All: **Thanks be to God.**

Go Forth!

Leader: Let us go to prepare our hearts for Jesus' birth.

All: **Thanks be to God.**

11

Celebrate Advent

Gather

- Review the prayer responses with children.

 Use the *Call to Faith* Kindergarten CD, track 2, to rehearse the song.

- Have children process into the prayer space.
- Light the Advent wreath, or have a child do today's activity with the Advent calendar.
- Have children sing the song.
- Follow the order of prayer.
- Leader's prayer: **God our Father, we are waiting for Jesus. Help us be ready when he comes.**

Listen to God's Word

- Proclaim the Scripture.
- Gesture for children to respond.

Go Forth!

- Lead the group in the dismissal rite.
- Assist children with the response.

 Have children sing as they leave the prayer space.

 **RITUAL**

Procession The children participate in a procession when they enter and leave the prayer area.

- Have children watch the priest and other liturgy participants as they enter and exit weekend liturgies.
- Point out that walking quietly with hands folded shows respect for prayer.

LITURGY LINK

Advent colors The liturgical color for Advent is violet, a shade of purple that is closer to blue than to red.

- This color symbolizes anticipation and penance.
- On the third Sunday of Advent, rose may be used.

Jesus Comes

Next to the yearly celebration of the Paschal mystery, the Church holds most sacred the memorial of Christ's birth and early manifestations. This is the purpose of the Christmas season.

General Norms for the Liturgical Year and Calendar, 32

Seasonal Background

What do we do when a beloved friend arrives for a visit? We welcome the person, see to his or her needs, and settle in to enjoy the company that we have so anticipated. This, too, is what we should do at Christmas. How much time do we really permit ourselves with Jesus in this far-too-busy season?

As with most other things in life, we may feel that we fall short of our goal to make Christ paramount in the Christmas season. The needs that our children, families, and friends present to us are usually more compelling than the friend who has arrived in the guise of the baby in the manger.

So this must be why Christmas comes many times to us. Once a year, we are given the chance to get it right again, to show Christ that we honor his coming. We are asked to lead our friends, families, and children to the manger again, to welcome the quiet child who will change the world for all humankind.

As Christmas approaches again, challenge yourself to accommodate the Christ child. Ask yourself often how a particular activity will lead you and others back to enjoy the company of Jesus. Foster the practices that will permit you to encounter the Christ child in worship, in others, and in yourself. Then give yourself the gift of time to enjoy his company.

Reflect** **How can you make time to meet Jesus again this holiday season?

Environment

Materials:

Prayer table
Gold or white cloth
Battery operated or electric candles
Nativity figures
Christmas flowers or greenery
Bible or Lectionary
Call to Faith Kindergarten CD

- Place a gold or white cloth on the prayer table. Top it with a white candle in a gold or crystal candle holder.

- Have children help you place nativity figures and Christmas flowers or greenery in the prayer space.

Christmas

Families are often together during the Christmas season, but we sometimes neglect to truly connect with one another. Moreover, we often neglect the reason for the season: we take the presence of Christ for granted. But he is the central character of the liturgical season that begins on Christmas and includes the Sunday feasts of the Holy Family, Epiphany, and Baptism of our Lord.

The Christmas feast draws us to our parish church to adore God's son. With your child, explore the nativity set, and think about what a gift we have received.

Family Celebration

This Christmas season, resolve to take time to find Jesus in your child, your Church, and your heart. Plan special family times, such as dinners and evenings together, when you can share the warmth of the holidays. Always dedicate the time together with a prayer, such as the one below.

> Jesus, Son of God, you have come into our hearts and home. Thank you for the special gift of our family and the time we have together. Help us find you in one another. Give us the strength to share your love with everyone we meet. Amen.

Family Activity

As you reflect on the past year, you may want to share photographs and other souvenirs of special moments. Invite family members to view pictures or do a "show and tell" of something special from the past year.

- Encourage each family member to contribute a souvenir and a story to go with it. This can be as simple as a ticket stub or a small gift from another family member.

- If you are far from family and beloved friends, make a point of sharing a holiday photograph, letter, or telephone call to maintain lines of communication.

- Challenge family members to be on the lookout for future memories. As you do things together throughout the year, encourage family members to record favorite memories in a journal. Plan evenings together to share these memories.

Jesus Comes

- Ask children to tell you what they know about Christmas. Reinforce answers that focus on the religious significance of the season.

- Draw children into a circle. Have them bring their books and look at the illustration.

- Ask children to name the people in the illustration. Praise their correct answers.

- Have children close their books as you read the story to them. Invite children to add details to the story.

- Have children suggest ways that they can have a holy Christmas with their families.

Christmas

Jesus Comes

One dark night long ago, a baby was born.

The baby was Jesus.

Mary and Joseph welcomed him into their family.

We welcome Jesus into our family, too.

12

SEASONAL RESOURCES

Books and Videos Many resources are readily available to supplement this lesson.

- *Build Your Own Bethlehem.* Gertrud Mueller Nelson. (Liturgy Training Publications). This activity book contains worksheets for building nativity scenes for telling stories from Christmas to Candlemas.

- *The Mouse in the Manger* (19 min). St. Anthony Messenger Press. This video, meant for young children, tells of a mouse who witnessed the first Christmas.

CULTURAL CONNECTION

La Posada This Mexican tradition reenacts Mary and Joseph's trip to Bethlehem.

- A group of travelers, dressed as Mary and Joseph, sing songs asking for shelter at designated homes.

- They are refused from a succession of shelters. Finally, the pilgrims are invited in for a party at a welcoming home.

Celebrate Christmas

Gather

Sing together the refrain.

Go tell it on the mountain,

Over the hills and everywhere;

Go tell it on the mountain

That Jesus Christ is born.

"Go Tell It on the Mountain" © ND,
Mrs. John W. Work III

Pray the Sign of the Cross together.

Leader: Let us give thanks to God.

All: **Let us give thanks to God.**

Leader: Let us pray.

Bow your heads as the leader prays.

All: **Amen.**

Listen to God's Word

Leader: A reading from the holy Gospel according to Luke.

Read Luke 2:8–11.

The Gospel of the Lord.

All: **Praise to you, Lord Jesus Christ.**

Go Forth!

Leader: Let us share Jesus' love with others.

All: **Thanks be to God.**

13

Celebrate Christmas

Gather

 Use the *Call to Faith* Kindergarten CD, track 3, to rehearse the song.

- Review the prayer responses with children.
- Invite children into the prayer space, and light the Christmas candle.
- Follow the order of prayer.
- Leader's prayer: **God our Father, you sent us your Son. Help us know him. Help us show his love to others.**

Listen to God's Word

- Proclaim the Gospel reading.
- Prompt children to respond.

Go Forth!

- Pray the prayer of dismissal.
- Assist children with their prayer response.

 Have children sing as they leave the prayer space.

PRAYER

Sign of the Cross Tell children that the Sign of the Cross honors God the Father, God the Son, and God the Holy Spirit.

- Point out that the Son mentioned in the prayer is Jesus.
- Encourage children to lovingly pray the Sign of the Cross throughout the Christmas season.

LECTIONARY LINK

Christ Proclaimed This reading is taken from the Gospel for Christmas Midnight Mass.

- The angel's message is the first clue to the waiting world that the Messiah has arrived. The angels did not meet with kings; they told their glad tidings to shepherds. In this way, we realize that Christ has come for everyone.

Saint Francis of Assisi

The saints of universal significance have celebrations obligatory throughout the entire Church.

General Norms for the Liturgical Year and Calendar, 9

Seasonal Background

The season of Ordinary Time has two parts. The first part is between the end of the Christmas season and the beginning of Lent. The second runs from after Pentecost to the beginning of Advent. The feast of Saint Francis of Assisi is in this later time, on October 4.

Francis was born in Assisi in 1181 or 1182. The son of a wealthy merchant, he led a privileged life as a young man. Eventually, however, he sensed the emptiness of his actions. Directed by a voice to "Repair my house," Francis set out to rebuild the deteriorating church of San Damiano.

The rest of Francis' life was dedicated to serving all of God's creatures. He lived in poverty, sharing whatever he had with the poor and the sick. He attracted followers, who dressed like Francis in plain woolen tunics. Like Francis, they also preached God's love and lived on handouts from strangers. This group became the Franciscans, which became an approved order of the Church in 1210.

Francis is best known for his rapport with animals. He was often seen preaching to birds. A famous legend tells of how he made peace between the people of a town and a wolf that had been victimizing them. His deep appreciation of all of creation left us a wonderful legacy.

Reflect   ***How can you foster a love of nature in the children in your life?***

Environment

Materials:

Prayer table
Green cloth
Stuffed animals
Flowers
Bible
***Call to Faith* Kindergarten CD**

- Ask children to bring in their favorite stuffed animals for the prayer service.

- Place a green cloth on the table.

- Decorate the prayer space with flowers.

- Select a place to stand where children will pass you as they leave the prayer space.

Ordinary Time

Saint Francis is one of the most visible saints: we see his image in church, in books, and in gardens. Almost always, birds, small animals, and plants are with him. Francis loved these elements of nature and begged us all to appreciate them. He also had an abiding love for people no one else cared for, including those who were poor or ill. It is not surprising that Francis is the patron of animals, birds, and zoos. He is also patron of Catholic action and ecologists.

Family Celebration

Try to instill some of Saint Francis' love of nature in your family. Go on a family outing to enjoy the beautiful fall weather and leaves. Consider taking along a meal or a snack to make it a picnic. Together, pray these words from Saint Francis' "Canticle of Brother Sun:"

> Most high, all powerful, all good Lord!
> All praise is yours, all glory, all honor, and all blessing.
> To you alone, Most High, do they belong.
> No mortal lips are worthy to pronounce your name.
> All praise be yours, my Lord, through all that you have made.

Family Activity

Saint Francis' feast is an invitation to find ways to preserve the beauty of nature. As a family, look into ways of helping with community ecology projects.

- Learn about local ecological issues. Look for a project where you can make a difference. Perhaps a local park needs attention, or a community garden requires additional funding.

- Decide on a family course of action. Maybe you could work to educate the community about an issue, or write a letter to a civic official or local paper about an ecological issue.

- Follow through on your plans. As you work, pray to Saint Francis for guidance. See what a difference you can make!

Saint Francis of Assisi

- Explain to children that you will be talking about a saint who loved nature.
- Elicit from children how people can show that they love nature. Possible response: by caring for plants, animals, and the earth
- Read aloud the text.
- Explain that Saint Francis wore plain clothes and lived simply so that he could use whatever people gave him to help the poor.
- Examine the illustration with the group. Talk about how it reveals Francis' nature.

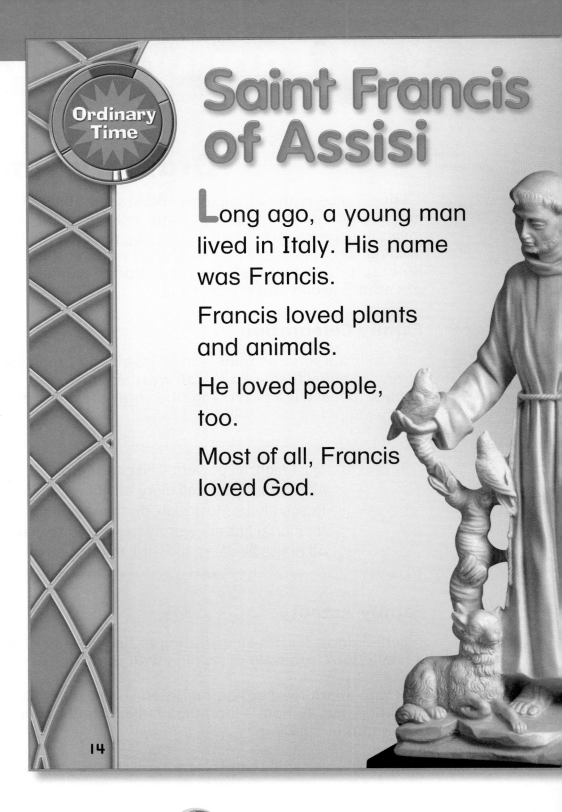

Ordinary Time

Saint Francis of Assisi

Long ago, a young man lived in Italy. His name was Francis.

Francis loved plants and animals.

He loved people, too.

Most of all, Francis loved God.

14

SEASONAL RESOURCES

Books There are many resources that will help children understand Saint Francis' message.

- *Francis: The Poor Man of Assisi*. Tomie dePaola. (Holiday House). Children ages 4–8 will enjoy this illustrated book about Francis' life.
- *The Hymn of the Sun*. Saint Francis of Assisi. (Hymn of the Sun Productions). This is a beautifully illustrated version of Francis' prayer.

CULTURAL CONNECTION

Blessing of Animals In the United States, the Feast of Saint Francis is on October 4.

- This feast is often associated with the blessing of animals.
- Many parishes invite people to bring their pets and agricultural animals to the parish grounds for a blessing ritual.

Celebrate Creation

Gather

 Sing together the refrain.

Sing out, earth and skies!

Sing of the God who loves you!

Raise your joyful cries!

Dance to the life around you!

"Sing Out, Earth and Skies" © 1985,
GIA Publications, Inc.

Pray the Sign of the Cross together.

Leader: Blessed be God.

All: **Blessed be God.**

Leader: Let us pray.

Bow your heads as the leader prays.

All: **Amen.**

Listen to God's Word

Leader: A reading from the book of Psalms.

Read Psalm 104:1, 24, 31.

The word of the Lord.

All: **Thanks be to God.**

Go Forth!

Leader: Let us go forth to enjoy the world.

All: **Thanks be to God.**

15

Celebrate Creation

Gather

 Use the *Call to Faith* Kindergarten CD, track 4, to rehearse the song.

• Teach children the prayer responses.

• Have children bring their stuffed animals into the prayer space.

• Follow the order of prayer.

• Leader's prayer: **God of Love, Saint Francis taught us to enjoy life and your love. Thank you for the world and for Saint Francis.**

Listen to God's Word

• Have children sit quietly with their stuffed animals.

• Read aloud the psalm verses.

• Use a hand gesture to invite children's responses to the psalm.

Go Forth!

• Complete the dismissal rite.

• Lay your hands on each child's head as he or she leaves the prayer space. Point out that you are blessing them because they are part of creation, too.

 Have children sing as they leave the prayer space.

 RITUAL

Laying on of Hands   Many blessings include this gesture.

• Catholics inherited the gesture from the Hebrews, who used it as a signal of granting authority or blessing.

• The gesture is included in the sacraments of Baptism, Reconciliation, Confirmation, Holy Orders, Anointing of the Sick, and Matrimony.

 LITURGY LINK

Colors of the Season   The major color used in Ordinary time is green. It signifies hope and life. We use it in the prayer space during this lesson to honor Francis' love for nature.

On Francis' feast, however, white vestments would be used, as that is the proper color for feasts of saints who were not martyrs.

Changing Ourselves

Lent is a preparation for the celebration of Easter.

General Norms for the Liturgical Year and Calendar, 27

Seasonal Background

Humans are creatures of habit. Many of us have personal rituals that make us feel comfortable and secure. We have a favorite breakfast food, television show, or pair of jeans. We have arrived at a way of doing things, and we want it to stay that way.

Not all of our habits are good ones, as we well know. Perhaps we choose a doughnut instead of a healthy cereal for breakfast, allow entertainment to replace a true conversation with a friend, or neglect our appearance.

Lent is the liturgical season that encourages us to examine our lives, to realize our shortcomings, and to change from within. This is not an easy task.

Fortunately, the Church helps us understand our mission and accept it. Scripture readings include stories of the Transfiguration, the Samaritan woman at the well, the curing of a blind man, and the prodigal son and his forgiving father. Through these readings we find new wonder in what Jesus tells us about how to look at what we do, determine its goodness, and find ways to improve.

Keep your eye on the future. In the same way that winter loosens its grip on nature, Lent will lead into a season of wonder. Prepare yourself for the glory of Easter!

Reflect *What habits of yours have made you complacent? How can you change them?*

Environment

Materials:

Prayer table
Purple cloth
Cross or crucifix
Holy Water
Bible
***Call to Faith* Kindergarten CD**

- Consider decorating the prayer space with children's art about Lent.

- Drape the prayer table with a purple cloth. Add a cross or a crucifix and a bowl of holy water to the table.

Lent

Too often, we look at Lent as a time of sorrow and denial. We think too much of the negative aspects of the change that the Church calls us to make during this season. We focus on finding our weaknesses and feeling unworthy because of them.

This Lent, try to take on the season with a fresher eye. Think of it as a time to spring clean not only your home, but also your life. What needs to change? Which bad habit do you want to replace with a good one?

Don't be discouraged. God knows that you can become more perfect. The sacraments, especially Holy Eucharist and Reconciliation, are wonderful gifts that can help you change. Make a point of using them this season.

Family Celebration

Take a family walk in the woods. As you and your child marvel at the new life in nature, say a short prayer of thankfulness. Make up your own, or say the following:

> God the Father, all around us are signs of change in nature. We thank you for these signs and the joy that they bring us. We also want to change. We want to be better people. We ask this through Jesus and the Holy Spirit. Amen

Family Activity

Find a way to enjoy the new life of the season with your community. Look for projects that will help others prepare for the joy of Easter.

- Many parishes have a time for spring cleaning the church building. Check with the parish office to see if your family can help. Be certain to ask whether there will be jobs appropriate for your child to do.

- Some communities clean up parks and playgrounds during spring. The public is often invited to help. Check your local newspaper or park system bulletin board for these opportunities. Participate as a family.

- As a family, show that you have pride in your home. Do some spring cleaning inside your home, and in your yard.

Changing Ourselves

- Ask children what they know about Lent. Possible responses: It leads to Easter; it is in spring.

- Encourage children to tell how they observe Lent with their families.

- Read aloud the text to children.

- Ask children what changes they have seen in the weather and plants recently. Responses will vary.

Lent

Changing Ourselves

Lent is a special time.

We try to change.

We try to grow in love.

We try to be more like Jesus.

16

SEASONAL RESOURCES

Books   These resources can help you teach about Lent.

- *Forty Days and Forty Nights: A Lenten Ark Moving Toward Easter.* Judy Jarrett and Peter Mazar. (Liturgy Training Publications). This stand-up ark is similar to an Advent calendar.

- *Jesus, Show Us the Way.* Alison Berger. (Twenty Third Publications). This book contains activities and prayers for children ages 5–9.

CULTURAL CONNECTION

Missing Symbols   The Yaqui people of southern Arizona and northwestern New Mexico remove flowers from their churches during Lent.

- Flowers are welcomed back into the church to decorate Jesus' tomb on Good Friday.

- The Yaqui observe Lent with processions and re-enactments of the Passion.

Celebrate Lent

Gather

Sing together the refrain.

Lead me, guide me, along the way,
For if you lead me, I cannot stray.
Lord, let me walk each day with thee.
Lead me, oh Lord, lead me.

"Lead Me, Guide Me" © 1953, Doris M. Akers.
All rights administered by Unichapple Music, Inc.

Pray the Sign of the Cross together.

Leader: The Lord be with you.

All: **And also with you.**

Leader: Let us pray.

Bow your heads as the leader prays.

All: **Amen.**

Listen to God's Word

Leader: A reading from the holy Gospel according to Matthew.

Read Matthew 22:36–39.

The Gospel of the Lord.

All: **Praise to you, Lord Jesus Christ.**

Go Forth!

Leader: Let us grow in God's love.

All: **Thanks be to God.**

17

Celebrate Lent

Gather

 Use the *Call to Faith* Kindergarten CD, track 5, to practice the song.

• Practice the prayer responses with children.

• Ask children to move into the prayer space quietly and bless themselves with holy water.

• Follow the order of prayer.

• Ask children to raise their arms in the orans posture as they make the responses.

• Leader's prayer: **Gracious Father, thank-you for giving us your love. Help us grow stronger in our love for you.**

Listen to God's Word

• Proclaim the Gospel.

• Use a gesture to encourage children to pray the responses.

Go Forth!

• Follow the dismissal rite in the prayer service.

• Assist children with the responses.

Have children sing the song as they leave the prayer space.

 RITUAL

The Orans   The gesture of praying with the hands open and palms up is referred to as the orans.

• Moses used this posture when he prayed during the battle at Rephidim (*Exodus 7:8–16*).

• Many parishes use this posture after the Lord's Prayer is said during the Mass.

 LITURGY LINK

Colors for Penance   Like Advent, Lent's primary color is purple.

• This color denotes sorrow and penance, as well as the preparation for a major feast.

Three Holy Days

The Easter Triduum of the passion and resurrection of Christ is the culmination of the entire liturgical year.

General Norms for the Liturgical Year and Calendar, 18

Seasonal Background

We begin with Holy Thursday. Mass may only be celebrated in the evening this day, making it a special memorial of the institution of the Eucharist. Our celebration is whole-hearted; we are grateful for the gift of the Blessed Sacrament. But our thanks is tempered as we anticipate the events of the next day with the stripping of the altar and the removal of the consecrated bread to the altar of repose. We leave without singing a recessional hymn.

Good Friday dawns with foreboding. We are drawn to the church for prayers and once-a-year services. On this day, we do not celebrate the Eucharist; we share the Communion reserved from yesterday's evening Mass. Our liturgy consists of proclamation of the word, prayers, and Veneration of the Cross. We leave in silence again.

We enter a darkened church on Holy Saturday, trusting that our sadness is over. With the spark of the Easter fire, our hearts leap in surprise. We share the flame of faith. We hear stories of our wandering and redemption. We welcome new members, who remind us of the new life Christ received on Easter. We leave, certain that Jesus has risen. Certain, too, that we will one day rise.

Reflect ***How can you keep the spark of the Easter fire in your faith life throughout the year?***

Environment

Materials:

Prayer table
Crucifix or cross
Battery operated or electric candles
Bible or Lectionary
***Call to Faith* Kindergarten CD**

- Imitate the sparseness of Triduum church decorations by simplifying prayer space decorations.

- Leave the prayer table empty except for a cross or crucifix. Do not cover it.

Triduum

The word Triduum means "three days." We mark the days from sundown to sundown, so we actually celebrate Holy Thursday, Good Friday, Easter Saturday, and Easter Sunday.

On Holy Thursday, we recall the Last Supper, the first Eucharist ever. We feel privileged to carry on this sacred tradition. The next day, we meet during the sacred hours of the afternoon. We remember Jesus' death and honor the cross that led to our salvation.

The Easter Vigil begins on Holy Saturday evening. We hear our family history of salvation. We welcome new members into the Church. We learn of Jesus' new life. We know that we, too, share in salvation. Our journey ends happily.

Family Celebration

During Triduum, meals take on a special significance as we recall the Last Supper and its lasting gift to us.

Gather for a family dinner prior to attending the evening Mass on Holy Thursday. Be certain to have a loaf of bread for all to share. As the meal ends, pray together:

> Jesus, Son of God, thank you for the time we share together. As we commemorate your suffering, death, and rising, help us recognize your gifts to us. Help us appreciate the Eucharist. Help us appreciate the Church. Help us appreciate the companionship of family and friends. We ask this through the Holy Spirit. Amen.

Family Activity

Observe the solemnity of the Triduum with your child. Center your activities around the theme for each day. Make these experiences part of the family holiday preparations.

- On Holy Thursday, bake bread together, and talk about the Eucharist. Point out that your child will be sharing this special meal in a few years.

- On Good Friday, read the story of the Passion from a children's Bible. Talk about how much Jesus must have loved us to suffer for us.

- On Holy Saturday, color eggs together. Talk about how the egg is like Jesus' tomb because it is like a rock. It also gives us life and sustenance because it is food. Use a crayon to draw religious symbols on the eggs before they are dyed, or put religious stickers on them after the dye has dried.

Holy Days

- Ask children to tell you which days are the holiest days of the year. Holy Thursday, Good Friday, Holy Saturday, Easter Suday

- Have children describe the different elements of the illustration.

- Read aloud the text.

- Have children look at the illustration and discuss what is happening. Possible response: Jesus eating with his friends, the Last Supper

Triduum

Holy Days

Holy Thursday, Good Friday, Holy Saturday, and Easter Sunday are special days.

They are the holiest days of the year.

On these days, we remember that Jesus loved us very much.

18

SEASONAL RESOURCES

Books and Videos These resources will help you convey the nature of Triduum.

- *Our Lady of Holy Saturday.* Cardinal Carlo Martini. (Liguori Publications). This book contains reflections on the feelings of Mary and the Apostles during the first Holy Saturday.

- *The Meals of Jesus* (15 min). St. Anthony Messenger Press. This video, intended for grades K–3, helps children discover the Last Supper.

CULTURAL CONNECTION

Food Symbolism Families in Poland spend the Triduum preparing traditional Easter foods which are packed in baskets and blessed on Holy Saturday morning.

- Foods in the basket include boiled and dyed eggs, Polish sausage, bread, and butter shaped to look like a lamb.

- These foods are shared at Easter breakfast.

Celebrate Jesus

Gather

Sing together the refrain.

Jesus, remember me when you come into your Kingdom.

Jesus, remember me when you come into your Kingdom.

"Jesus, Remember Me" © 1981, Les Presses de Taizé, GIA Publications, Inc., agent

Pray the Sign of the Cross together.

Leader: The Lord be with you.

All: **And also with you.**

Leader: Let us pray.

Bow your heads as the leader prays.

All: **Amen.**

Listen to God's Word

Leader: A reading from the book of Philippians.

Read Philippians 2:8–11.

The word of the Lord.

All: **Thanks be to God.**

Go Forth!

Leader: Jesus has done great things for us.

All: **Thanks be to God.**

19

Celebrate Jesus

Gather

- Invite children into the prayer space.
- Explain to the group that the prayer table is empty except for the crucifix or cross because the church is not decorated for most of the Triduum.

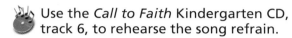 Use the *Call to Faith* Kindergarten CD, track 6, to rehearse the song refrain.

- Practice the prayer responses with children.
- Follow the order of prayer.
- Leader's prayer: **Lord, you have given us so many gifts. We love you for your goodness to us.**

Listen to God's Word

- Proclaim the Scripture.
- Invite children to bow to the crucifix.

Go Forth!

- Lead the dismissal rite.

 Have children sing as they leave the prayer space.

Jesus Is with Us!

The fifty days from Easter Sunday to Pentecost are celebrated in joyful exultation . . . These above all others are the days for the singing of the Alleluia.

General Norms for the Liturgical Year and Calendar, 22

Seasonal Background

Jesus is risen! What could be more astonishing? What could be more predictable?

We have traveled with Jesus through Lent and Triduum. We have heard the stories of Lazarus' return from death. We have listened to the Passion, recalled the First Eucharist, and commemorated Jesus' death on the cross. We know that he was left in the rock-sealed tomb. It has been quite a journey!

But wait! The story is not finished yet!

The Easter Gospels invite us back to the garden. With the women, we find the empty tomb. With Peter, we are puzzled. With Mary Magdalene, we see the Risen Christ in all his glory, and we rejoice with astonishment.

And now with Mary Magdalene and Peter, as well as our friend doubting Thomas, we react with incredulity. We note the new life of the spring season, and the metaphor helps us understand the miracle. If the cold and gray of winter can yield to the lush greenness of spring, then perhaps life can come from death. We begin to grasp that we, too, can be creatures of rebirth and renewal.

Reflect How can you renew yourself in the spirit of the Easter season?

Environment

Materials:

Prayer table
Gold or white cloth
Flowers
Vase
Bible or Lectionary
Call to Faith **Kindergarten CD**

- Bring fresh spring flowers to decorate the prayer space.

- Cover the prayer table with a gold or white cloth. Have an empty vase on the table.

- Allow enough room for children to move around in the prayer space.

Easter

After observing Lent, Holy Thursday, and Good Friday, we share the Apostles' sorrow. But we cannot let the story end with Jesus in the tomb. We know otherwise. At the Vigil liturgy and Easter Sunday Masses, we hear the happy news: Jesus is risen! He is with us again, with new life from the Father.

Because we know this, we have hope for our own lives. We know that if we follow Jesus and show our love for God's creations, we, too, can have life after death. This is the foundation of our faith.

Family Celebration

Easter breakfast is a wonderful time for families to share the joy of the season. Consider having your child tell the Easter story during the meal. Prepare him or her in advance by reading from a children's Bible or other religious book. Talk about how amazing the first Easter must have been. Pray this prayer at the end of the meal:

> God our Father, thank you for the new life Jesus has. We are happy that he is with us once again. Help us follow him so that one day we may have new life, too. Amen.

Family Activity

Easter is not just a day; it is a season that stretches past the Feast of the Ascension and to Pentecost. During these weeks, the earth renews itself, just as our faith does. As a family, find ways to enrich your faith.

- Plan a family garden. Consider growing flowers to decorate your home and growing vegetables for your family and others to eat . Have your kindergartner help you plan the garden, prepare the soil, and plant seeds or nursery plants.

- If you do not have space for a full garden, you and your child can still have the fun of watching plants grow. Consider planting a window box garden or a pot of flowers for your kitchen table.

Jesus Is with Us!

- Have children tell you what they know about Easter. Jesus rose from the dead on Easter.
- Ask children to tell you how their family celebrates Easter. Reinforce the responses that highlight religious ceremonies and cultural customs.
- Read aloud the text.
- Ask children why we are happy at Easter. Possible response: Jesus is with us again.

Easter

Jesus Is with Us!

Easter is a special day.

On Easter, we celebrate that Jesus was raised from the dead.

He had new life. He shares his life with us.

20

SEASONAL RESOURCES

Books   Many resources are available to supplement Easter lessons.

- *The Garden of the Good Shepherd.* Peter Mazar. (Liturgy Training Publications). This book comes with reusable vinyl stickers and a background board for teaching the events of the Easter season.
- *The Rising: Living the Mysteries of Lent, Easter, and Pentecost.* Wendy Wright. (Upper Room Books). This book contains reflections on the Easter season.

CULTURAL CONNECTION

African Easter   In Tanzania, Catholics crowd into the church for the Easter Vigil.

- The church is decorated with butterflies, flowers, and other decorations made of colorful cloth. Drums beat out Easter hymns.
- After the liturgy, traditional dances are performed outside the church.

Celebrate Easter

Gather

 Sing together the refrain.

Alleluia, alleluia, give thanks to the risen Lord.

Alleluia, alleluia, give praise to his Name.

"Alleluia, Alleluia, Give Thanks" © 1973, Word of God Music

Pray the Sign of the Cross together.

Leader: The Lord be with you, alleluia.

All: **And also with you, alleluia.**

Leader: Let us pray.

Bow your heads as the leader prays.

All: **Amen.**

Listen to God's Word

Leader: A reading from the holy Gospel according to Matthew.

Read Matthew 28:5–7.

The Gospel of the Lord.

All: **Praise to you, Lord Jesus Christ.**

Go Forth!

Leader: Let us celebrate Jesus' new life.

All: **Thanks be to God, alleluia.**

21

Celebrate Easter

Gather

 Use the *Call to Faith* Kindergarten CD, track 7, to practice the song refrain.

- Review the prayer responses with children.
- Distribute flowers to children. Have them carry the flowers into the prayer space and put them in the vase.
- Follow the order of prayer.
- Leader's prayer: **Lord, we celebrate your resurrection with great joy. You have shown us that we can live with you forever.**

Listen to God's Word

- Proclaim the Gospel.
- Prompt children to respond.

Go Forth!

- Lead the dismissal rite.

 Have children sing as they leave the prayer space.

 PRAYER

Alleluia! One of the hallmarks of the Easter season is the return of the *Alleluia.*

- This term, meaning "Praise the Lord!" in Hebrew, is absent from our worship during Lent.
- Invite the group to emphasize the term with hand gestures or by repeating it enthusiastically.

 LECTIONARY LINK

The Easter Story These verses from the Gospel of Matthew are contained in the alternate Easter Sunday Gospel during Year A of the lectionary cycle.

- The angel reassures the two Marys and gives them directions, just as an angel reassured Joseph and gave him directions before Jesus' birth.
- In this Gospel, we, too, are directed to share the good news of the Resurrection.

Pentecost

The Holy Spirit

The weekdays after the Ascension until the Saturday before Pentecost inclusive are a preparation for the coming of the Holy Spirit.

General Norms for the Liturgical Year and Calendar, 26

Seasonal Background

Pentecost is the last great feast of the Easter season. The fifty days since Easter have seen the death of winter and the stirring of new life throughout creation. We, too, have been made new and are ripe for our commissioning.

Like Christmas and Easter, Pentecost marks an end and a beginning. We have been through the Easter season, with its joyous beginning. We celebrated the Ascension, standing and looking up with the Apostles, wondering what we will do without Jesus physically present with us.

However, Pentecost marks a fresh beginning for the Church. Commonly called the birthday of the Church, Pentecost calls all of us to maturity. It reinforces the gifts of the Holy Spirit in us and compels us to share what we know of Jesus. Like the Apostles, we can no longer wait in the upper room. We must move out to be with other people. We must make our mark in the world.

As always, God provides us with assistance. Jesus' return to the Father enabled the Holy Spirit to come to us. And he moves among us still, guiding our choices, and imparting gifts of wisdom, understanding, counsel, fortitude, knowledge, piety, and fear of the Lord. All we need to do is ask, and we shall receive them.

Reflect **Which gift of the Holy Spirit should you pray for?**

Environment

Materials:

Prayer table
Red cloth
Battery operated or electric candle
Children's Bible
Bible or Lectionary
***Call to Faith* Kindergarten CD**

- Allow space for children to sit and listen to the Bible story.

- Drape the prayer table with a red cloth. Light a red or white candle on the table.

- Consider decorating the prayer space with red and yellow flowers.

Family Faith

Pentecost

Pentecost is the last feast of the Easter season. It marks the coming of the Holy Spirit to the Apostles and Mary. Appearing like wind and fire, the Holy Spirit fulfilled Jesus' promise to send assistance to the Apostles. Strengthened by the gifts of the Holy Spirit, the Apostles then went out and preached Jesus' message to crowds in Jerusalem.

The Holy Spirit moves among us still, giving us knowledge, wisdom, and other gifts. It is up to us to develop those gifts in ourselves. As you and your child move through the long days of summer, reflect on how you can share Jesus' message with others.

Family Celebration

Pentecost is a celebration of fire and wind. Consider having a family cookout to show some of the benefits of fire. Make certain that an adult monitors any children near the fire.

At the end of the cookout, gather near the fire and read this prayer:

> Holy Spirit, you came to the Apostles like a flame. Teach us to treasure the warmth and light that you bring among us. Help us make good choices and live in God the Father's love. Amen.

Family Activity

Demonstrate that your family wants to share in the gifts of the Holy Spirit and the missionary work of Pentecost. There are many organizations and agencies that would benefit from your assistance. Design a family project that could help one of them.

- Check your parish bulletin to see what types of organizations the parish has. You might also find notices about agencies needing volunteers in your local newspaper.

- Call the agencies to see what types of assistance they need and when. Many agencies can suggest projects that you can easily complete at home, such as making refreshments for meetings or making bag lunches for homeless people. Then you can deliver your project to the agency at your convenience.

- As a family, decide on a project and follow through on it.

- After completing the project, pray a prayer of thanksgiving for the chance to serve others.

The Holy Spirit

- Ask children what they know about Pentecost. Possible responses: It comes in summer; the Holy Spirit came to the Apostles on Pentecost.
- Read aloud a children's Bible version of the Pentecost story to the group.
- Read aloud the text.
- Talk with children about how the Holy Spirit can guide them to be followers of Jesus.

Pentecost

The Holy Spirit

Jesus sent the Holy Spirit to us.

The Holy Spirit helps us make choices.

He guides you to follow Jesus.

On Pentecost, we celebrate that he is with us.

22

 SEASONAL RESOURCES

Books and Videos   These resources may help you present this lesson.

- *Before and After Easter: Activities and Ideas for Lent to Pentecost* . Debbie Trafton O'Neal. (Augsburg Fortress). This book provides crafts for the time between Ash Wednesday and Pentecost.
- *Who Is the Spirit?* (14 min). St. Anthony Messenger Press. This video tells of the workings of the Holy Spirit.

 CULTURAL CONNECTION

Doves on High   In parts of Central and Eastern Europe, carved and painted wooden doves are used as household decorations for Pentecost.

- The doves are suspended over the family table as a reminder of the coming of the Holy Spirit on the first Pentecost.

Celebrate Pentecost
Gather

Sing together the refrain.

Come Lord Jesus, send us your
Spirit, renew the face of the earth.

Come, Lord Jesus, send us your
Spirit, renew the face of the earth.

"Send Us Your Spirit" © 1981, 1982, 1987,
GIA Publications, Inc.

Pray the Sign of the Cross together.

Leader: Blessed be God.

All: **Blessed be God forever.**

Leader: Let us pray.

Bow your heads as the leader prays.

All: **Amen.**

Listen to God's Word

Leader: A reading from the Acts of
the Apostles.

Read Acts 2:1–4.
The Word of the Lord.

All: **Thanks be to God.**

Go Forth!

Leader: The Holy Spirit is with us today.

All: **Thanks be to God.**

23

Celebrate Pentecost

Gather

 Use the *Call to Faith* Kindergarten CD,
track 8, to rehearse the song.

- Review the prayer repsonses with children.
- Light a candle on the prayer table.
- Invite children into the prayer space. Have them stand throughout the service.
- Leader's prayer: **Holy Spirit, thank you for coming to us. We will ask you to help us when we are making choices.**

Listen to God's Word

- Proclaim the Scripture.
- Gesture for children to respond.

Go Forth!

- Lead children in the dismissal rite.

 Have them sing the song as they
return to their places.

LECTIONARY LINK

The Holy Spirit Comes   The scripture reading from this lesson is part of the first reading on Pentecost Sunday.

- It is the story of the coming of the Holy Spirit.
- The story continues by telling how the Holy Spirit's influence enabled the Apostles to share Jesus' story with the rest of the world.

LITURGY LINK

Paschal Candle   The Paschal candle is blessed and lit with the new fire at the Easter Vigil.

- Some parishes decorate it with a cross, the year, and incense grains.
- The candle has been used during Easter at all liturgies. After Pentecost, it will be used primarily at Baptisms and funerals.

Notes

CALL to FAITH

Lessons

Notes

_____

_____

_____

_____

_____

_____

_____

_____

_____

_____

_____

_____

_____

_____

_____

_____

_____

_____

_____

God Made the World
CHAPTER BACKGROUND

 Then the LORD God planted a garden in Eden, in the east, and he placed there the man whom he had formed. Out of the ground the LORD God made various trees grow that were delightful to look at and good for food, with the tree of life in the middle of the garden and the tree of the knowledge of good and bad.

Genesis 2:8–9

Creation Is Good

We cannot help but associate the Creator with what he has created. We can see through his creation that he would like for us to see his goodness all around us.

Just as we ponder and delight in what our ancestors left for us, we share joy and wonder over the gifts God has given us: plants, animals, oceans, continents, sky, planets, and stars. Everything that is on the earth now was put in order, just as Eden was put in order. Creation praised God then, and it will continue to praise him until the end of time.

The Mystery We Share

Part of the joy of creation is that we must work at understanding it. Your kindergartners have observed the order of the climatic seasons and have seen how each one influences plants and animals. The children can see the obvious. But God has also locked secrets away from us, including the workings of our bodies and the mysteries of outer space. We are challenged to work as scientists and artists to discover what is inside us and beyond us, what hidden treasures God willed for us to find and delight us.

Reflect   How can you best share the wonder of creation with children?

Where We Live

God created the world for us to have a place to live. Take this opportunity to introduce maps and globes as a way to raise awareness of the larger world beyond the local community.

- Display a bulletin board of the United States, and place each child's picture in his or her home state.

- Ask children to name states where their family members or friends live.

- Help children find the state and place a pushpin or thumbtack on the state.

What I Like to See

- I like to see myself. Hang my picture in my cubby. Hang a mirror in our classroom.

- I like to see my work. Design multiple bulletin boards to display my work.

- I like to see what the day looks like. Use photos to show the sequence of my routine.

Listening to the Call of Vocation

The word *vocation* comes from the root word *vocare,* which means "to call." Where do you think the call of vocation comes from?

- The call of vocation comes from God. You may try to discern your vocation by praying or submitting your will to the will of God.

- You may also look inward, analyzing your talents and interests to find out what comes naturally for you.

Research indicates that the way you view a vocation directly affects your ability to discern and sustain it.

Reflect **In which direction do you usually turn to hear the call?**

Prayer

Holy Spirit, who sees all in nature and knows that it is good, guide me to see what is good in nature, too. Help me share the beauty of creation with these children. Help me see you in their wonderment and joy. Amen.

Weekly Planner

		Objectives	Materials	Prayer & Scripture
1 Invite	**God Made the World** Page 25	To identify God as the maker of the world	☐ Crucifix ☐ Copies of Activity Master 1, p. 25E ☐ Magazines ☐ Scissors ☐ Glue	Let Us Pray: Psalm 104:24
2 Explore	**God's World** Page 26	To recognize that the world belongs to God	☐ Picture books of animals ☐ Stuffed animals from home	Scripture: Psalm 50: 10–11 Scripture Background: Praising God
	Care for the World Page 27	To demonstrate care for the world	☐ Crayons or markers ☐ Copies of Activity Master 2, p. 30A ☐ Pencils ☐ Scissors	Scripture: Psalm 50: 10–11
	Thank God Page 28	To show thanks in different ways	☐ Paper plates ☐ Crayons or markers ☐ Yarn ☐ Construction paper ☐ *The Beautiful World that God Made*	Scripture: Psalm 50: 10–11
3 Celebrate	**Prayer of Thanks** Page 29	To thank God for the world	☐ Music CD ☐ Bible or Lectionary	Let Us Pray: Prayer of Thanks **Hymn:** All Things Bright and Beautiful

Activities	Enrichment

Let's Begin

Talk about who shares the world with children.

OPTIONAL **Activity Master 1: Cut and Paste, p. 25E**

• **Quick Tip:**
Views of Earth

❓ Discuss things God made.

OPTIONAL Animals, Animals
Multiple Intelligence: Naturalist

Activity

Trace the path, and share ways to take care of the world.

OPTIONAL **Activity Master 2: Make a Place Mat, p. 30A**

• **Reaching All Learners:**
Musical Learners

Activity

Use different animal sounds to thank God.

OPTIONAL Paper Plate Animals
Multiple Intelligence: Visual/Spatial

OPTIONAL Children's Literature
Multiple Intelligence: Verbal/Linguistic

• **Liturgy Link:**
Praise Through Song

• **Lectionary Link:**
Break Open the Word

Pacing the Chapter

Parish
Meets once a week

 In parish religious education classes, plan for approximately 60 minutes of class time.

Invite	10 minutes
Explore	40 minutes
Celebrate	10 minutes

The abundance of activity and enrichment options will allow flexibility in planning for longer sessions if needed.

School
Meets 5 days per week

 In school religious education classes, plan for lesson 5 days per week for about 30 minutes. The lesson can be easily adapted for a 4-day week as well.

Day 1: Invite	**Day 4:** Explore
Day 2: Explore	**Day 5:** Celebrate
Day 3: Explore	

The abundance of activity and enrichment options will allow flexibility in planning for longer sessions if needed.

- Online planning tools include chapter background and planner, activity master, customizable test, and more.
- Enhancement activities for each step of the catechetical process, including alternative prayer experiences and blessings.
- Games, activities, interactive review, alternative assessment, and more for children.

www.calltofaitheconnect.com

Home Connection

Chapter 1 Family Faith, p. 30
Take-home activities, chapter content review, saint features and prayer

 For more family activities
www.harcourtreligion.com

Name _____ Date _____

Cut and Paste

Directions: Make a collage using pictures from magazines.

God's Beautiful World

Chapter 1 — God Made the World

The earth is full of your creation.

Based on Psalm 104:24

Let's Begin

God's Gift

Under the sun and moon,
In a sea of cool, clean air,
Floats the beautiful world
God made for us to share.

● Who shares the world with you?

Responses will vary.

25

Objective: To identify God as the maker of the world

Let Us Pray

Invite children to gather in the prayer space and make the Sign of the Cross. In the prayer space, have a crucifix and a Bible opened to the psalm verse.

Instruct children to join hands and form a circle. Then have them repeat the psalm verse after you.

Let's Begin

God's Gift

- Call attention to the illustration on the page. Talk about what children might see if they were looking back at Earth from space.
- Read aloud the poem.
- Invite children to make up gestures that express the ideas in the poem. For example, they could crouch for "under" and move gracefully for "floats."
- Read aloud the poem again, and have children gesture as you read.
- Invite children to share responses to the question.

OPTIONAL ACTIVITY

Activity Master 1: Cut and Paste Distribute copies of the activity found on page 25E.

- Tell children they will be making a collage.
- Have children cut out pictures from magazines of things in God's world and paste them in the open space.

▲ Activity Master 1

QUICK TIP

Views of Earth The class may enjoy seeing their home planet from different perspectives.

- Consult the NASA Web site or other library resources for photographs of the earth from space.
- Display your findings on a bulletin board or a shelf where children can study them.

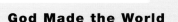

Objective: To recognize that the world belongs to God

God's World

Ask children why they think God made the world. Possible responses: God wanted people to have a place to live; he wanted to show love.

• Read aloud the text. Ask children why everything in the world belongs to God. because God made the world

Animals

• Explain that the Bible is God's holy book.

• Proclaim the Scripture.

• Have children name animals they see in the picture.

• Invite children to name other animals that belong to him.

• Ask volunteers to respond to the question.

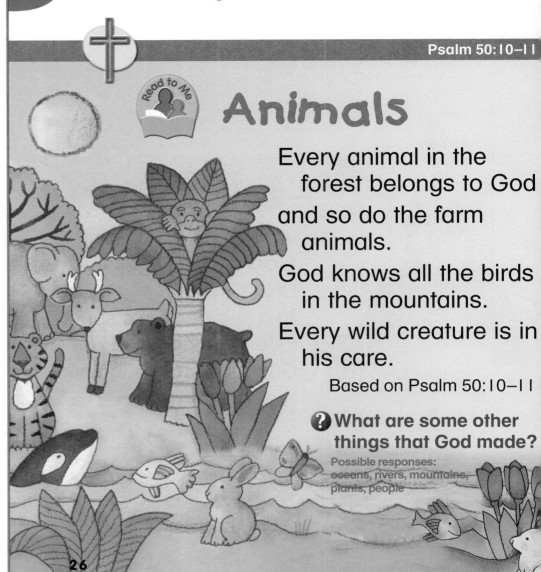

Explore

God's World

The world and everything in it belongs to God.

Psalm 50:10–11

Animals

Every animal in the forest belongs to God and so do the farm animals.

God knows all the birds in the mountains.

Every wild creature is in his care.

Based on Psalm 50:10–11

? What are some other things that God made?

Possible responses: oceans, rivers, mountains, plants, people

26

 SCRIPTURE BACKGROUND

Praising God The verses on this page are part of a psalm that states that God wants us to praise him and obey him.

• The verses assure us that creation is very important to God.

• The remainder of the psalm encourages us to thank God for his favors and praise him when we pray.

Animals, Animals Have children discuss their favorite animals with the class.

• Have animal books available so that children can find illustrations of their favorite animals.

• Invite children to bring a favorite stuffed animal in to show to the group.

Multiple Intelligence: Naturalist

Care for the World

God wants us to take care of the things he made.

— Activity —

Tell how the people in the picture are caring for the world.

27

Objective: To demonstrate care for the world

Care for the World

Remind children that God made the world, and everything in it belongs to him.

- Read aloud the text.
- Ask children where they might find a path like the one in the picture. Possible response: in a park

Activity

- Have children trace the path in the picture with a crayon or marker, starting in the upper left corner. Discuss the pictures in order.
- Pause at each picture and have children describe how that person is taking care of creation. Invite children to share ways they care for creation at home and at school.

OPTIONAL ACTIVITY

Activity Master 2: Make a Place Mat Distribute copies of the activity found on page 30A.

- Tell children they will be making a place mat they can use for snack time.
- Ask them to trace over the letters. Have them decorate their place mats with things God has made.

▲ Activity Master 2

REACHING ALL LEARNERS

Musical Learners Children who learn through song may enjoy singing as they trace the path.

- Teach children this song, to the tune of "This Is the Way We Wash Our Clothes:"

    This is the way we show we care, show we care, show we care, This is the way we show we care For all the things God made.

God Made the World 27

Explore

Objective: To show thanks in different ways

Thank God

Remind children that we thank God for making all creation.

- Point out that all of creation thanks God for his goodness.
- Read aloud the text.
- Tell children they will thank God in a different way.

Activity

- Read aloud the names of the animals.
- Have children suggest other animals and the sounds that they make.
- Assign an animal role to each child. Assemble the group in a circle.
- As you read the text, have the child who is representing that animal step into the center of the circle and act like that animal.
- When you are finished with the text, add additional animals that children choose.

Thank God

We thank God for the world with prayers.

Animals thank God with sounds.

Activity

Pretend you are an animal and use its sound to thank God.

 Bees thank God by buzzing.

 Birds thank God by tweeting.

 Cows thank God by mooing.

 Dogs thank God by barking.

 Lions thank God by roaring.

28

OPTIONAL ACTIVITY

Paper Plate Animals   Have children make paper plate animals.

- Have each child draw an animal face on the plate.
- Have children attach yarn for hair, construction paper beaks for birds, etc.
- Have children hold up the corresponding plate and make animal sounds as you read.

Multiple Intelligence: Visual/Spatial

OPTIONAL ACTIVITY

Children's Literature: Read aloud *The Beautiful World that God Made* by Rhonda Growler Greene (Wm. B. Eerdmans Publishing Co., 2002). This colorfully illustrated story of creation is told in rhyme.

Multiple Intelligence: Verbal/Linguistic

Prayer of Thanks

 Think about the things that make you happy. Say a quiet prayer to thank God for one thing that makes you happy.

 Sing together.

All things bright and beautiful,
All creatures great and small,
All things wise and wonderful,
The Lord God made them all.

All Things Bright and Beautiful

29

Objective: To thank God for the world

 Let Us Pray

Tell children they will thank God with a quiet prayer.

Prayer of Thanks

Prepare

Place things God made in the prayer space.

Use the *Call to Faith* Kindergarten CD, track 1, to rehearse the song.

Gather

Invite children into the prayer space.

- Have children name things they see that God made.
- Ask children to sit quietly.
- Read aloud the instructions for the prayer.

Pray

- Allow time for children to silently thank God for their favorite part of creation.
- Conclude with the song.

 LITURGY LINK

Praise Through Song   Some of the Church's musical tradition has its roots in the psalms of our Hebrew heritage.

- For class celebrations, select songs that reinforce liturgical themes and seasons.
- Work with a music teacher or music minister to help children learn church music.
- Explain that singing is a special form of prayer.

 LECTIONARY LINK

Break Open the Word   Read last week's Sunday Gospel. Talk about how this reading helps us follow Jesus. For children's questions related to the weekly Gospel reading, visit our Web site.

 Visit www.harcourtreligion.com for weekly scripture readings and seasonal resources.

Wrap-Up

Family Faith

Remind children to discuss the Family Faith page at home. Encourage them to talk with family members about what they have learned about how God made the world.

Family Project

- Encourage children to do the activity with their families.

People of Faith

Tell children about Saint Catherine of Siena.

- Saint Catherine of Siena was part of a large Italian family. Many people saw that she was holy, and they wanted to be like her.
- Encourage children to pray the prayer at home with their families.

  Visit **www.harcourtreligion.com** for weekly scripture readings and seasonal resources.

 CHAPTER 1
Family Faith

Catholics Believe

Dear Family,
In Chapter 1, the children learned that God made the world. We share the world with other creatures. We are meant to take care of the creatures in the world. All creatures of the world praise God.

 **SCRIPTURE**

Read Psalm 50:10–11 together with your child.

 www.harcourtreligion.com
For weekly scripture readings and seasonal resources

Family Project

God Made Our World Take a family tr[ip] [to] a local zoo, park, or public garden. With your child, note the variety of birds, anir[mals] and plants that God created. Talk about [how] each one is special. With your child, say [a] prayer thanking God for creation.

People of Faith

Each day Catherine thanked God for giving her the things of the earth.

Saint Catherine ▶ of Siena, 1347–1380

Family Prayer

Gracious God, help us be like Saint Catherine. Help us thank you every day for the gift of creation. Amen.

30 **CCC** *See Catechism of the Catholic Church 339, 358 for further reading on chapter content.*

  HOW DID I DO?

This week was

☐ *one of the best ever!* ☐ *pretty good.* ☐ *in need of improvement.*

In what discussions and activities were children most interested?

_____

What activity did I most enjoy teaching?

_____

In what area do I need to improve?

_____

Name _____ Date _____

Make a Place Mat

Directions: Trace over the letters, then decorate and cut out the place mat.

Thank
you,
God.

God Made You

CHAPTER BACKGROUND

 God created man in his image; in the divine image he created him; male and female he created them.

Genesis 1:27

The Divine Spark

What do all people have in common? It is easy to point to emotional feelings, physical features, and mental abilities. However, we sometimes ignore our most common link: the divine spark that animates our beings.

Too often, we think of that spark as something that only surfaces in our prayer lives. We associate it too strongly with ritual and rules, with formulas and requirements. In truth, the spark or soul is literally what makes us dead or alive. Our bodies depend upon it to fuel our thoughts, to help us feel pleasure, and to appreciate the rest of creation. It sets us apart from other animals, and it prompts communities of humans to form for the purpose of mutual support and adoration of our Creator.

Nurturing the Spark

As a teacher or catechist, you are charged with many mighty tasks. One of the most intimidating is not just maintaining the souls entrusted to your care, but helping them as they grow in knowledge of the Creator. The best way to face this task is with the joy of your own divine spark. As you work with the children in your group, share your joys, reveal to them that you, too, work to know and serve God in your everyday life. Be happy, and share your happiness with them.

Reflect   How do you share your divine spark with those around you?

Senses

Children learn best when using all of their senses. Be creative and incorporate as many sensory explorations as possible in each lesson.

- Be cautious of allergies! Keep a list of all children's allergies handy in your plan book.

- Have children take turns naming smells, tastes, and actions that make them think of their favorite people and places.

Belonging

- I want to belong. Sing welcoming songs upon my arrival.

- I want to feel safe and secure. Provide me with my own space. Put my name and picture on my cubby.

- I want to fit in. Display pictures and books reflecting all ethnic backgrounds.

The Vocation To Teach

The vocation to teach develops differently for each person. Teaching as a vocation has a unique flavor to it. You cannot change its flavor or its taste. Just as root beer and orange soda each taste a certain way, so does the vocation to teach. Some people claim they always knew they would teach. Others never imagined they would be involved in education.

- This vocation comes with the conviction that you can succeed despite economic, domestic, or institutional deficits.

- It also comes with moments of doubt about your effectiveness.

Reflect **Which of these two flavors do you taste more frequently in your catechetical vocation?**

 **Prayer**

Lord God, make me more aware of the joy of your creation and of the divinity within me. Help me remember that the children entrusted to me are filled with you, too. Help me serve you within them. Amen.

Weekly Planner

		Objectives	Materials	Prayer & Scripture
1 Invite	**God Made You** Page 31	To recognize that the senses are gifts from God	☐ Photos children bring from home ☐ Copies of Activity Master 3, p. 31E ☐ Crayons or markers	🌼 **Let Us Pray:** Psalm 139:14
2 Explore	**Made with Love** Page 32	To know that each person is valued by God	☐ *Whoever You Are*	✝ **Scripture:** Genesis 1: 27–28 ✝ **Scripture Background:** God Blesses People
	You Are Special Page 33	To illustrate that differences make each person special	☐ Crayons or markers ☐ Mirrors ☐ Copies of Activity Master 4, p. 36A	✝ **Scripture:** Genesis 1: 27–28
	Our Special Gifts Page 34	To show that talents are special gifts from God	☐ *My Somebody Special*	✝ **Scripture:** Genesis 1: 27–28
3 Celebrate	**Thank You, God!** Page 35	To pray a prayer of thanks	☐ Music CD ☐ Bible or Lectionary ☐ Pictures of the group	🌼 **Let Us Pray:** Thank You, God! 🎵 **Hymn:** All Things Bright and Beautiful

Activities	Enrichment
## Let's Begin Show children that God made them. (OPTIONAL) **Activity Master 3: About Me, p. 31E**	• **Quick Tip:** Treasure Chest
❓ Share ways God blesses people. (OPTIONAL) **Children's Literature** **Multiple Intelligence:** Verbal/Linguistic	
## Activity Draw a picture of yourself. (OPTIONAL) **Activity Master 4: All Are Special, p. 36A**	• **Cultural Awareness:** Diversity
## Activity Act out some things you enjoy doing. (OPTIONAL) **Children's Literature** **Multiple Intelligence:** Verbal/Linguistic	• **Reaching All Learners:** Reluctant Participants
	• **Liturgy Link:** Prayers of Thanks • **Lectionary Link:** Break Open the Word

Pacing the Chapter

Parish
Meets once a week

In parish religious education classes, plan for approximately 60 minutes of class time.

Invite 10 minutes
Explore 40 minutes
Celebrate 10 minutes

The abundance of activity and enrichment options will allow flexibility in planning for longer sessions if needed.

School
Meets 5 days per week

In school religious education classes, plan for lesson 5 days per week for about 30 minutes. The lesson can be easily adapted for a 4-day week as well.

Day 1: Invite   **Day 4:** Explore
Day 2: Explore   **Day 5:** Celebrate
Day 3: Explore

The abundance of activity and enrichment options will allow flexibility in planning for longer sessions if needed.

CALL to FAITH e connect

- Online planning tools include chapter background and planner, activity master, customizable test, and more.
- Enhancement activities for each step of the catechetical process, including alternative prayer experiences and blessings.
- Games, activities, interactive review, alternative assessment, and more for children.

www.calltofaitheconnect.com

Home Connection

Chapter 2 Family Faith, p. 36
Take-home activities, chapter content review, saint features and prayer

For more family activities
www.harcourtreligion.com

Name _____ Date _____

About Me

Directions: Draw a picture of something you enjoy doing.

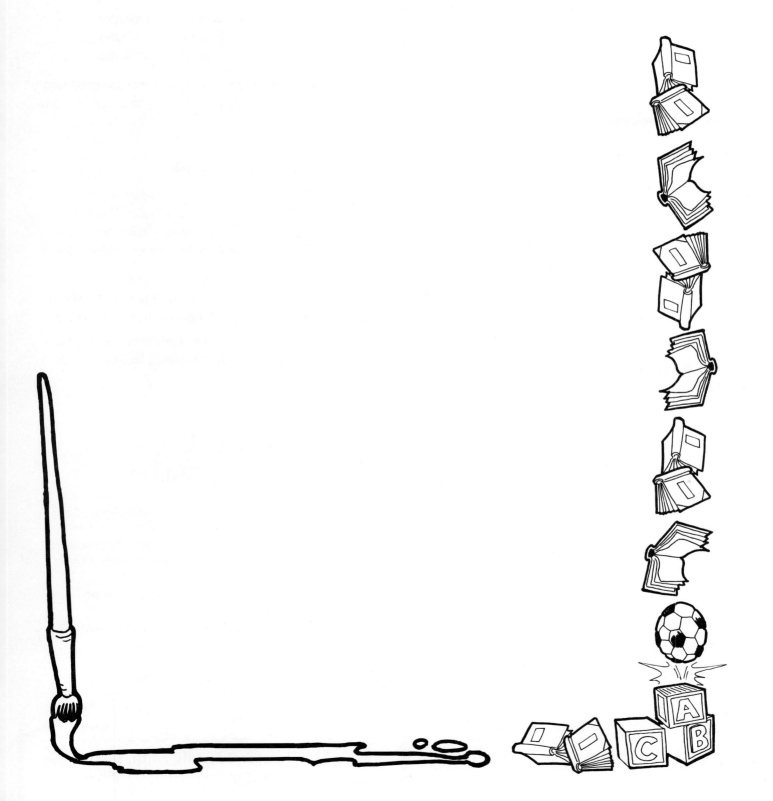

©Harcourt Religion

Chapter 2
God Made You

 I praise you for making me so wonderfully.

Based on Psalm 139:14

Read to Me — Let's Begin

What Do You See?

You look in the mirror,
and what do you see?
Two big eyes staring at me.

You look in the mirror,
and what do you see?
A shiny nose pointing at me.

You look in the mirror,
and what do you see?
Two ruby lips smiling at me.

● What else do you see
in the mirror?

Possible responses: hair, ears, cheeks

31

Invite

1 Invite

Objective: To recognize that the senses are gifts from God

 Let Us Pray

Invite children into the prayer space. Have them place pictures of themselves on the prayer table. Have them repeat the psalm verse after you.

Let's Begin

What Do You See

- Call attention to the photograph of the child and her reflection.
- Read aloud the poem once to familiarize children with it.
- Suggest that children point to their eyes, nose, and mouth as you read aloud the poem again.
- Discuss the question.

OPTIONAL ACTIVITY

Activity Master 3: About Me
Distribute copies of the activity found on page 31E.

- Ask children to describe themselves.
- Have them draw pictures of themselves doing something they enjoy.

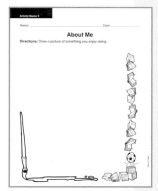

▲ Activity Master 3

QUICK TIP

Treasure Chest Insert a mirror into a box that resembles a treasure chest.

- Tell children that your treasure chest will show them something that is very special to you.
- As children walk past the chest, open it so that each child sees his or her reflection.
- Tell children they are a treasure to you and to God.

God Made You 31

Objective: To know that each person is valued by God

Made With Love

Discuss what makes each person special. Possible responses: God made each person; each person has special looks and talents.

- Point out the illustration of people in the world.
- Call attention to the similarities and the differences between the people.
- Read aloud the text.
- Ask children why God would make so many differences between people. Possible responses: so we can learn from each other, so each person will feel special

Like God

- Proclaim the Scripture.
- Ask the text question.

Explore

Made With Love

God made all people on earth!

You are special because God made you.

 Read to Me

Like God

God made you to be like him.
He made boys and girls.
God blessed you and all people.

Based on Genesis 1:27–28

❓ How does God bless you?

Possible responses: with family and friends, with talent, with beauty

32

✝ SCRIPTURE BACKGROUND

God Blesses People These verses emphasize that men and women are made in God's image.

- In addition to blessing all people and recognizing their goodness, God charged men and women with the task of working the earth to bring forth crops for their food.
- People are also meant to rule the earth kindly, respecting the goodness of all creation.

OPTIONAL ACTIVITY

Children's Literature Read *Whoever You Are* by Mem Fox (Harcourt, 1997) to the class. This book points out differences between languages and lives for people of different cultures. It also emphasizes the similarities among people.

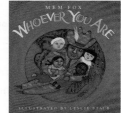

Multiple Intelligence: Verbal/Linguistic

You Are Special

Each person is different.

Each person is special.

Activity

Look at the circle on this page.

Make the person in the circle look like you.

33

Objective: To illustrate that differences make each person special

You Are Special

Point out to children that differences make each person special.

- Ask children what the world would be like if we were all the same. Possible response: We wouldn't be surprised by what anyone did.
- Emphasize that personal differences bring variety to our lives.

Activity

- Read aloud the directions.
- Have a volunteer hand out crayons or markers.
- Instruct children to draw and color hair, eyes, nose, mouth, clothing, and anything else that is special about them.
- Allow children to look in mirrors to help them draw accurately.
- Gather children in a circle, and have each child share what is special in his or her drawing.

OPTIONAL ACTIVITY

Activity Master 4: All Are Special Distribute copies of the activity found on page 36A.

- Tell children they will be coloring a picture.
- Hand out crayons or markers, and have children color the picture of children around the world.

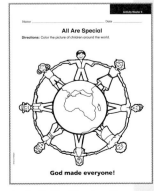

Name _____ Date _____

All Are Special

Directions: Color the picture of children around the world.

God made everyone!

▲ **Activity Master 4**

CULTURAL AWARENESS

Diversity One hallmark of creation is diversity.

- Help children appreciate diversity found within your class and community. Comment occasionally on programs and holidays of diverse cultures.
- Consider displaying photographs from around the world. Label the display *We Are All God's Children*.

Objective: To show that talents are special gifts from God

Our Special Gifts

Tell children that there are many special things about them.

- Read aloud the text.
- Direct attention to the photographs. Explain that the children in the pictures are showing special talents.
- Discuss the ability demonstrated in each photograph.

Activity

- Ask children to think about something special that they do.
- Have children take turns pantomiming something they enjoy doing.
- Challenge the rest of the group to guess what the child is doing.
- The first child to guess correctly may then demonstrate his or her special talent.

Explore

Our Special Gifts

The way we look is not the only special thing about us.

Things we do are special, too.

Activity

What can you do that is special?

Act out one of the special things you do.

34

Children's Literature Read aloud *My Somebody Special* by Sarah Weeks (Harcourt, 2002). At the end of a busy day at school, the last child sits alone with his teacher, growing more and more anxious as he watches the door, waiting and wondering if somebody special will ever come for him.

Multiple Intelligence: Verbal/Linguistic

REACHING ALL LEARNERS

Reluctant Participants Some children in the class may be uncertain of their talents or shy about being in front of a group. Assist these children in the following ways:

- Help children discover their talents by complimenting them on their abilities to draw, sing, jump, clean, and so on.
- Offer to stand with each child to help him or her demonstrate a talent.

Thank You, God!

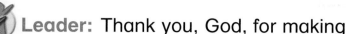

Leader: Thank you, God, for making us like you.

All: **Thank you, God, for making us like you.**

Leader: Thank you, God, for helping us do special things.

All: **Thank you, God, for helping us do special things.**

Sing together.

All things bright and beautiful,
All creatures great and small,
All things wise and wonderful,
The Lord God made them all.

All Things Bright and Beautiful

35

Objective: To pray a prayer of thanks

 **Let Us Pray**

Tell children they will say a prayer of thanks to God.

Thank You, God!

Prepare

Tell children that they will be repeating the prayer after you.

- Place pictures of the group in the prayer space.

Use the *Call to Faith* Kindergarten CD, track 1, to rehearse the song.

Gather

Gather children in the prayer space.

- Have children stand in a circle and hold hands.
- Instruct children to repeat the prayer parts after you.

Pray

- Start the echo prayer, and prompt children as needed.
- Have children raise their joined hands after the prayer.
- Invite children to sing the song.

 LITURGY LINK

Prayers of Thanks   We pray prayers of thanksgiving because we are grateful for all that we have received from God.

- Point out to children that they may include prayers of thanksgiving in their morning and evening prayers.
- Teach children a simple prayer to use before meals to show their thanks for food.

LECTIONARY LINK

Break Open the Word   Read last week's Sunday Gospel. Talk about how this reading helps us follow Jesus. For children's questions related to the weekly Gospel reading, visit our Web site.

GO ONLINE Visit www.harcourtreligion.com for weekly scripture readings and seasonal resources.

Wrap-Up

Family Faith

Remind children to discuss the Family Faith page at home. Encourage them to talk with family members about what they have learned about how God made them.

Family Project

- Encourage children to work on the activity with their families.

People of Faith

Remind children that they learned about Saint Catherine of Siena at the end of the first lesson.

- One of Saint Catherine's special talents was helping other people become holy.
- Encourage children to pray the prayer at home with their families.

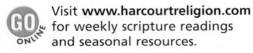 Visit **www.harcourtreligion.com** for weekly scripture readings and seasonal resources.

 Catholics Believe

Dear Family,

In Chapter 2, the children learned that God made all people on the earth. They learned that each person is different from everyone else. They also shared their special talents with each other.

SCRIPTURE

Read Genesis 1:27–28 together with your child.

GO ONLINE www.harcourtreligion.com
For weekly scripture readings and seasonal resources

Family Project

Our Special Family Make a place mat that will remind you of friends and family members who live far away. Glue pictures of the people onto a sheet of construction paper. Label the collage "Our Special Family." After the glue dries, cover the collage with clear adhesive paper. Use the finished place mat during family meals.

People of Faith

Catherine knew that she was special. God made her just like him.

Saint Catherine ▶ of Siena, 1347–1380

Family Prayer

God our Father, help us see you in ourselves. Help us know that we are like you. Amen

36 **CCC** *See Catechism of the Catholic Church 356 for further reading on chapter content.*

HOW DID I DO?

This week was

☐ *one of the best ever!* ☐ *pretty good.* ☐ *in need of improvement.*

In what discussions and activities were children most interested?

_____

What activity did I most enjoy teaching?

_____

In what area do I need to improve?

_____

Name _____ Date _____

All Are Special

Directions: Color the picture of children around the world.

God made everyone!

Faith Focus

■ **God created us because of his love and goodness.** *(CCC 293)*

Catechism Connection

The *Catechism* tells us that God created us so that we could share in his existence, wisdom, and goodness. *(CCC 295)*

NDC Link

The *Directory* points out that God's loving plan for us is expressed in every aspect of catechesis. (See *NDC*, 29B.)

Resources

BOOKS
Discipline Tips. Glavich, Kathleen. Twenty-Third Publications. Provides concrete suggestions for maintaining classroom decorum.

*Let's Celebrate Too!** Burland, John. Includes CD. "God's Love Is . . ." (2:05 min.). Music and gestures reinforce the concept of God's love for us.

*Available at www.harcourtreligion.com

GO ONLINE
Resources
For interactive lesson planner, chapter resources, and activities
www.harcourtreligion.com

In love he destined us for adoption to himself through Jesus Christ, in accord with the favor of his will . . .

Ephesians 1:4–5

God Loves Us

The Church teaches us that human life began as a result of the Creator's love. Hence, we owe our lives to God's love. We did nothing to merit this love, but it comes to us in abundance. We apprehend it through our senses in the beauty of the world and of our fellow creatures. It nourishes us as the spring rains nourish the earth, and we thrive because of this great gift.

We Respond

Although we did nothing to deserve God's love, we cannot help but want to return it, to imitate the great gift we find everywhere. Our own small measure of divinity craves to mirror the one who made us. We do this not because it is demanded of us, but because we are moved by our thankfulness to love others as God loves us.

So we respond by modeling our behavior after God's. We find ways of showing love to one another. We share our earthly goods. We help one another with tasks that are too big for one person. And we do all this gladly, as a way of returning God's gifts to us.

As a person helping to form young minds, you are responding to God's love in a special way. You are working to channel the joy and enthusiasm of youth into an awareness of his love. It is not always easy to do this, but be aware that God is with you in your classroom. His love will guide you as you guide young minds.

Reflect   How do your actions reflect your appreciation for God's gift of love and life?

Word Work

Help children learn the spelling of the word "love".

● Write the word LOVE on the board. Demonstrate how each sound is represented by a letter.

● Teach children to sign L–O–V–E.

● Stress that letters make up words and words make up sentences.

● Recite the sounds of the alphabet, as well as singing the traditional song of the alphabet.

L   O

V   E

Acceptance

● I need acceptance. Give me unconditional love and guidance as God shows toward all people.

● I want to know I'm being understood. Affirm my work and my actions.

Blessed Assurance

Catechesis can be risky. You place yourself before students, parents, and administrators. Some of us become timid and fearful about embracing the possibilities that arise from teaching. Teachers who place themselves in front of students faithfully and with confidence have much to gain.

Many have discovered that this kind of quiet confidence comes from their past. Their confidence came from some person or group that assured them that they were trustworthy and capable.

Now and then, you may need to revisit that person or group to renew your confidence. This will help you recapture and reclaim that blessed assurance.

Reflect **Who comes to mind as one that gave you such a blessed assurance about yourself?**

Prayer

Loving Father, help me remember that your love is the first gift I received. Help me pass this love on to the children in my care. Amen.

Weekly Planner

		Objectives	Materials	Prayer & Scripture
1 Invite	**God Loves You** Page 37	To notice loving behavior among classmates	☐ Copies of Activity Master 5, p. 37E ☐ Pencils ☐ Crayons or markers ☐ Scissors	🙏 **Let Us Pray:** Psalm 86:13
2 Explore	**God's Love** Page 38	To recognize God's love and share it with others		✝ **Scripture:** 1 Corinthians 13:4 ✝ **Scripture Background:** What is Love?
	Show Love Page 39	To demonstrate ways to show love	☐ Crayons or markers ☐ Apple slices ☐ Marshmallow cream ☐ Mini marshmallows ☐ Plastic knife	✝ **Scripture:** 1 Corinthians 13:4
	Learn About God's Love Page 40	To recall God's many gifts	☐ Pencils ☐ Copies of Activity Master 6, p. 42A ☐ Crayons or markers	✝ **Scripture:** 1 Corinthians 13:4
3 Celebrate	**Prayer of Love** Page 41	To pray a responsorial prayer of love	☐ Music CD ☐ Bible or Lectionary	🙏 **Let Us Pray:** Prayer of Love 🎵 **Hymn:** All Things Bright and Beautiful

Activities	Enrichment

Let's Begin

Talk about ways to show love to others

(OPTIONAL) **Activity Master 5: Make a Badge, p. 37E**

(OPTIONAL) Using Manners
Multiple Intelligence: Interpersonal

❓ Discuss how kindness and patience show love.

• **Quick Tip:**
Anytime Valentines

Activity

Draw hearts around pictures that show love.

(OPTIONAL) Smile Snacks
Multiple Intelligence: Bodily/Kinesthetic

• **Justice and Peace:**
Care for Others

Activity

Draw a line to connect the senses.

(OPTIONAL) **Activity Master 6: Go on a Picnic, p. 42A**

• **Reaching All Learners:**
Sensational Senses

• **Liturgy Link:**
Responses

• **Lectionary Link:**
Break Open the Word

Pacing the Chapter

Parish
Meets once a week

In parish religious education classes, plan for approximately 60 minutes of class time.

Invite	10 minutes
Explore	40 minutes
Celebrate	10 minutes

The abundance of activity and enrichment options will allow flexibility in planning for longer sessions if needed.

School
Meets 5 days per week

In school religious education classes, plan for lesson 5 days per week for about 30 minutes. The lesson can be easily adapted for a 4-day week as well.

Day 1: Invite   **Day 4:** Explore
Day 2: Explore   **Day 5:** Celebrate
Day 3: Explore

The abundance of activity and enrichment options will allow flexibility in planning for longer sessions if needed.

- Online planning tools include chapter background and planner, activity master, customizable test, and more.
- Enhancement activities for each step of the catechetical process, including alternative prayer experiences and blessings.
- Games, activities, interactive review, alternative assessment, and more for children.

www.calltofaitheconnect.com

Home Connection

Chapter 3 Family Faith, p. 42
Take-home activities, chapter content review, saint features and prayer

 For more family activities
www.harcourtreligion.com

God Loves You 37D

Name _____ Date _____

Make a Badge

Directions: Write your name on the line. Decorate the badge. Then cut it out and wear it.

promises to show love.

God Loves You

Your love for me is great.
Based on Psalm 86:13

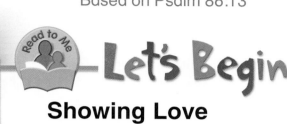

Read to Me — Let's Begin

Showing Love

We show love to others in our kindergarten class.

Antonio helps Benjamin with his coat.

Charles shares a snack with Devon.

Frances paints a picture for Ricky.

George gives a crayon to Harriet.

● How do you show love to others in your class?

Possible responses: by sharing, by saying kind words **37**

Invite

1 Invite

Objective: To notice loving behavior among classmates

Let Us Pray

Teach children hand movements for the psalm verse (point away from self for *your,* draw a heart in the air for *love,* point to self for *me,* and spread your arms apart for *great.*) Read aloud the psalm verse as children perform the actions.

Let's Begin

Showing Love

• Praise children for loving actions you have seen them do.

• Have children inspect the illustration and talk about how children in the picture are helping one another.

• Read aloud the text. Invite children to act out the loving actions listed.

• Discuss the question.

• Ask how children feel when they act out loving actions. Ask how it feels to have others show them love. Responses will vary.

Activity Master 5: Make a Badge Distribute copies of the activity found on page 37E.

• Tell children they will be making a badge to wear.

• Have children write their names on the line, decorate the badge, and cut it out.

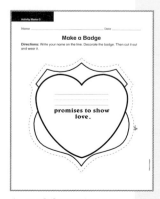

▲ **Activity Master 5**

Using Manners Point out to children that using good manners is a way of showing respect and love.

• Model good manners by using *Please* and *Thank you* as you speak with children.

• Encourage children to use polite expressions, and praise their efforts each day.

Multiple Intelligence: Interpersonal

Objective: To recognize God's love and share it with others

God's Love

Ask children how they know that God loves them. Possible responses: God gave us many gifts; we see God's love in the world.

• Read aloud the text.

What Is Love?

Tell children that the Bible teaches us how to show love.

• Proclaim the Scripture.

• Discuss the question.

Explore

God's Love

God showed love by making everyone on earth.

God loves everyone.

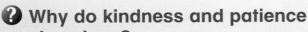

I Corinthians 13:4

What Is Love?

Love is being kind to others.
Love is being patient with each other.

Based on I Corinthians 13:4

? **Why do kindness and patience show love?** Possible response: Kindness and patience show love because they show caring and respect for others.

38

 SCRIPTURE BACKGROUND

What Is Love? This excerpt from a famous passage in *1 Corinthians* shows ways children can show love. Kindness and patience are words they understand. Saint Paul was writing for specific groups within the Corinthian community, but his words ring true for today's readers, primarily because they are a challenge for us to practice, too.

 QUICK TIP

Anytime Valentines Keep a supply of heart-shaped paper doilies or valentine stickers in your desk. Use them to encourage children to show love for others.

• Recognize children who are gentle and loving with friends and classmates.

• Award a doily or "Anytime Valentine" sticker to these children.

Show Love

You show love when you smile at others. Other people show love when they smile at you.

You show love when you wait for others. Others show love when they wait for you.

Activity

✏️ Draw a heart around each picture that shows love.

39

Objective: To demonstrate ways to show love

Show Love

Remind children that you have been discussing ways to show love

• Read aloud the text.

• Ask children for other suggestions of ways to show love. Possible responses: helping at home, asking a new child to join a game

Activity

• Ask a child to show love by handing out crayons or markers to the group.

• Invite children to discuss the illustrations.

• Have children draw hearts around the illustrations that show love.

• Challenge children to explain why they did not put a heart around the remaining illustration.

• Ask for suggestions of other loving actions.

OPTIONAL ACTIVITY

Smile Snacks   These snacks will remind children to smile.

• Give an apple slice, marshmallow cream, and 6–8 miniature marshmallows to each child.

• Have children spread marshmallow cream on one side of each apple slice. Then have them put marshmallows in the cream to make "teeth."

Multiple Intelligence: Bodily/Kinesthetic

✝ JUSTICE AND PEACE

Care for Others   Point out to children that we treat others with respect because all people are created by God.

• We see God's image in the people around us.

• Anything that hurts another person hurts everyone because we all belong to God's family. (See *The Church in the Modern World,* #27.)

Catholic Social Teaching: Life and Dignity

Objective: To recall God's many gifts

Learn About God's Love

Recall that God has given us many gifts because he loves us.

- Ask children to name the senses.
  sight, hearing, smell, taste, and touch
- Read aloud the text to help children connect the senses with God's love for us.
- Discuss how each sense teaches us about the world.

Activity

- Have children tell which part of the body contains each sense.
- Hand out pencils to each child.
- Read aloud the directions, and help children complete the activity.

Explore

Learn About God's Love

God's love is all around us.

We learn about God's love through our senses.

Our senses are gifts from God.

Activity

✏ Draw a line to connect each sense with what it tells us about.

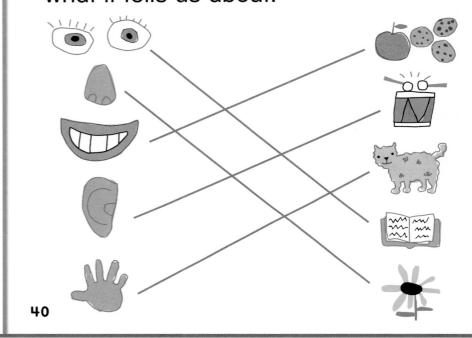

40

★ REACHING ALL LEARNERS

Sensational Senses These activities will help children learn about their senses. (Be mindful of any allergies.)

- Put pinholes in lids of several film canisters. Put an easily recognized scent in each canister. Have children sniff and guess each canister's content.
- Fill other canisters with items that evoke different sounds, such as rice, sand, water, and marbles. Have children shake the canisters and guess what is inside.

OPTIONAL ACTIVITY

Activity Master 6: Go on a Picnic Distribute copies of the activity found on page 42A.

- Tell children they will pretend to go on a picnic and use all their senses.
- Have them draw something they like to see, touch, hear, smell, or taste, and then color the page.

▲ Activity Master 6

Prayer of Love

Leader: God teaches us about his love.

All: We love you, God.

Leader: God helps us show love to others.

All: We love you, God.

Sing together.

All things bright and beautiful,
All creatures great and small,
All things wise and wonderful,
The Lord God made them all.

All Things Bright and Beautiful

Objective: To pray a responsorial prayer of love

 Let Us Pray

Tell children they will pray about God's love.

Prayer of Love

Prepare

• Remind children about the song from earlier celebrations. Ask children to make up actions to go with the song.

Use the *Call to Faith* Kindergarten CD, track 1, to rehearse the song.

Gather

Arrange children in a heart shape in the prayer space.

Pray

• Prompt children to pray after you've read aloud the leader's part.

• Have children act out the song as they sing.

 LITURGY LINK

Responses This prayer celebration relies on the children responding to the leader.

• Similar responses are used throughout Catholic liturgy.

• Consider using Mass greetings, such as "The Lord be with you," occasionally with the children. Teach them the responses.

LECTIONARY LINK

Break Open the Word Read last week's Sunday Gospel. Talk about how this reading helps us follow Jesus. For children's questions related to the weekly Gospel reading, visit our Web site.

 GO **ONLINE** Visit www.harcourtreligion.com for weekly scripture readings and seasonal resources.

Wrap-Up

Family Faith

Remind children to discuss the Family Faith page at home. Encourage them to talk with family members about what they have learned about recognizing God's love.

Family Project

- Encourage children to list their acts of kindness. Have children bring the list to class to share.

People of Faith

Tell children about Saint Catherine of Siena.

- Remind children that Catherine lived in Italy long ago. She loved God very much.
- Catherine was a happy person who made people want to learn from her.
- Encourage children to pray the prayer at home with their families.

Visit **www.harcourtreligion.com** for weekly scripture readings and seasonal resources.

 CHAPTER 3
Family Faith

Catholics Believe

Dear Family,
In Chapter 3, the children learned about God's love for us. They learned that God wants us to show love to other people. They found that their senses tell them about God's love for them.

SCRIPTURE

Read 1 Corinthians 13:4 together with your child.

GO ONLINE www.harcourtreligion.com
For weekly scripture readings and seasonal resources

Family Project

Loving Others Encourage your child to practice acts of kindness. Talk with him or her about how acts of kindness show love. Challenge your child to perform at least one act of kindness each day. Label a sheet of paper "Loving Others" and help your child list the kind acts he or she does each day. At the end of a week, review the list and praise his or her successes.

Loving
Other

People of Faith

Catherine knew that God loved her. She wrote about God's love for her and for others. People still read her book today.

Saint Catherine ▶
of Siena,
1347–1380

Family Prayer

Saint Catherine, help us remember that God loves us. Help us teach one another about God's love. Amen.

42 **CCC** *See Catechism of the Catholic Church 288 for further reading on chapter content.*

HOW DID I DO?

This week was

☐ *one of the best ever!* ☐ *pretty good.* ☐ *in need of improvement.*

In what discussions and activities were children most interested?

_____

What activity did I most enjoy teaching?

_____

In what area do I need to improve?

_____

Name _____ Date _____

Go on a Picnic

Directions: Pretend you are at a picnic. Draw something you like to see, hear, touch, smell, or taste.

©Harcourt Religion

Scripture Story

God Made All Things

(Genesis 1:1–2:4)

Family Note: In class your child has learned that God made all things. Read this Scripture Story together. Then have your child use all the pictures to retell the story. Tell your child that you are happy God has created him or her!

And God made people just like you.

Draw yourself.

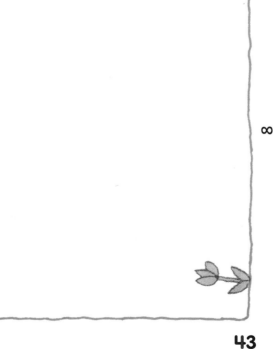

8

43

Scripture Book 1 God Made All Things   4

God made the day.
God said, "Let there be light."

2

Draw plants and animals.

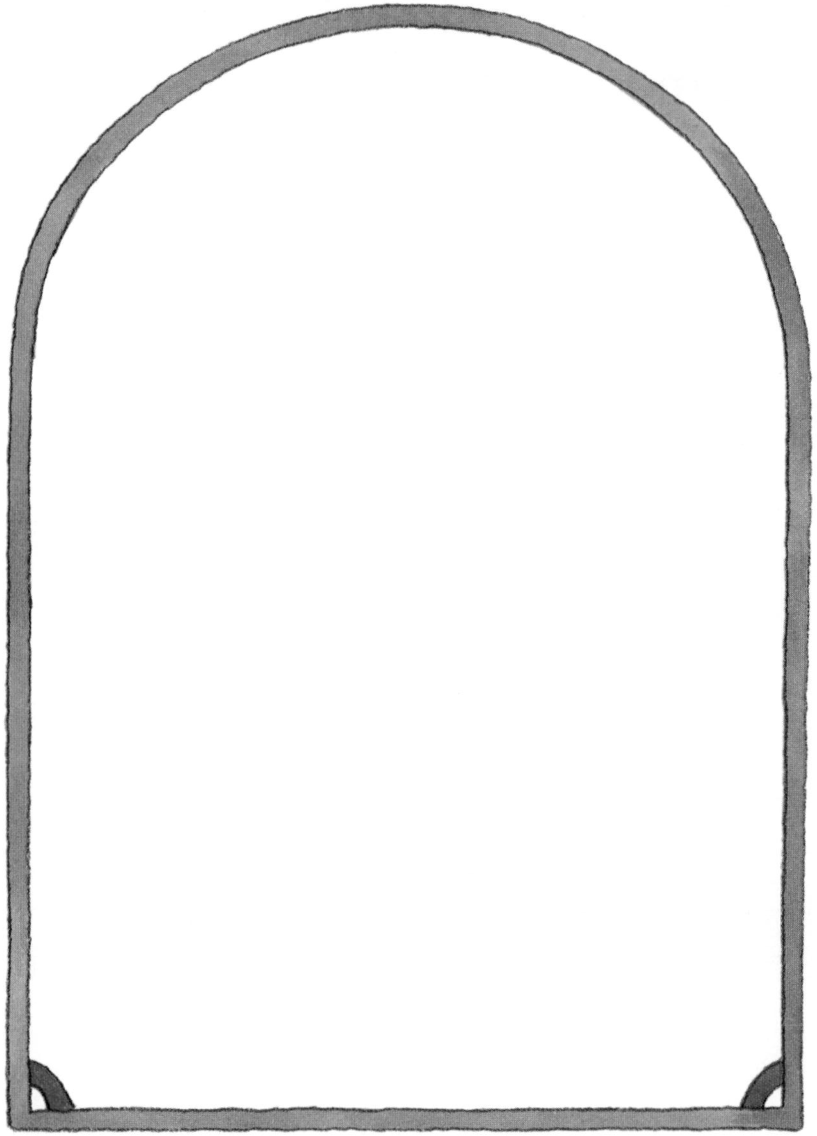

7

44

God made the plants.
God made the animals, too.

6

Draw the sun.

3

45

God made the night.
God made the moon and stars
so bright.

4

Draw the moon and stars.

5

46

Overview

Faith Focus

■ By calling God Father, we profess that he is the source of all things and that he has loving care for all his children. *(CCC 239)*

Catechism Connection

The *Catechism* explains that God is a loving parent to all of us. *(CCC 239)*

NDC Link

The *Directory* reminds us that God is not only the Creator of all things, but a present and loving Father. (See *NDC*, 28A.)

Resources

BOOK
What Catholics Believe. Morris, Joan Pahl. Twenty-Third Publications. A religious educator presents key topics in Catholic beliefs.

DVD/VHS
*Saints Gallery III: Saints for All Seasons** (40 min. total). Oblate Media. One segment recounts the story of Saint Valentine showing love for others.

*Available at www.harcourtreligion.com

Resources
For interactive lesson planner, chapter resources, and activities
www.harcourtreligion.com

 Your Father knows what you need before you ask him.
Matthew 6:8

Loving Father

Although God is referred to with masculine terminology, the Church teaches that he is neither male nor female. God is God.

The constant analogy for God is that of a loving parent. Creation is our evidence that God provides for his children. We see in God's gifts to us that we are loved and cared for, even when we do not understand the way that the world works. Even as adults, we are still children of God.

Parents as God's Workers

Parents play a major role in the lives of their children. The parents or guardians who raise a child know that child's needs and desires. From careful and loving observations, as well as their knowledge of the world, parents learn what is important for their children: to provide for each child's physical and spiritual needs.

All parenthood is modeled after God's parenthood. What this means is that parents and other caregivers imitate his loving care for his children. Being human, earthly parents cannot share in his omniscience or his infinite capacity for love. Mothers and fathers do the best that they can to provide for their children and to make wise decisions on their behalf. But they can fall short. They suffer from their human limits. In their failings, they show in reverse what God is: the perfect parent.

Reflect   How can you model God in your care for the children in your group?

Learning From Others

Start a reading buddies program in your school. Older students mentoring younger students benefit everyone involved.

- Meet on a regular basis. Both groups of children will look forward to their meeting.

- Have younger children pick out books at the school library.

- On nice days, take the two groups to meet outside for a reading on the lawn.

Feelings

- I am full of emotions. Understand me. Teach me with compassion.

- I like to talk. Help me gain language skills by verbalizing my feelings.

- I am starting to notice the feelings of others. Acknowledge and label our feelings out loud. Teach me by example.

Engagement with Others

Blessed assurance in yourself is important. It is also important to experience significant and constructive engagement with others. Doing so enables you to

- see firsthand the goodness of others.

- recognize that sometimes a task is best addressed by a team.

- replenish your level of empathy.

- see that you can still benefit from different styles and approaches.

Engagement with others sustains your spirit by pulling you past your own limitations and by restoring your faith in yourself and others.

	Lone Ranger				Engaged with others
Reflect **Rate yourself**	1	2	3	4	5

 Prayer

Almighty God, long ago you called the world out of nothingness and became our loving creator. Help us feel in all our hearts a childlike love for you. Amen.

Weekly Planner

		Objectives	Materials	Prayer & Scripture
1 Invite	**God the Father** Page 47	To recognize learning from others	☐ Crucifix ☐ Copies of Activity Master 7, p. 47E ☐ Crayons or markers ☐ Pencils	🌸 **Let Us Pray:** Psalm 2:7
2 Explore	**Special People** Page 48	To understand that God teaches how to love	☐ Crayons or markers ☐ Photos children bring from home	
	God Shows Love Page 49	To learn that each person is a child of God	☐ *Big Brown Bear's Up and Down Day*	✝ **Scripture:** 1 John 3: 1 ✝ **Scripture Background:** John's Epistles
	God the Father Page 50	To remember that God the Father loves everyone	☐ Crayons or markers ☐ Copies of Activity Master 8, p. 52A	✝ **Scripture:** 1 John 3: 1
3 Celebrate	**I Believe** Page 51	To celebrate belief in God the Father	☐ Music CD ☐ Bible or Lectionary ☐ Photos children bring from home	🌸 **Let Us Pray:** I Believe 🎵 **Hymn:** All Grownups, All Children

Activities	Enrichment

Let's Begin

Talk about who is special to children.

OPTIONAL **Activity Master 7: Say Thanks, p. 47E**

- **Quick Tip:**
  Different Types of Families

Activity

Draw someone who teaches you.

OPTIONAL Learning Pictures
Multiple Intelligence: Bodily/Kinesthetic

- **Cultural Awareness:**
  Greetings

❓ Share some ways God loves you.

OPTIONAL Children's Literature
Multiple Intelligence: Verbal/Linguistic

Activity

Match actions and words.

OPTIONAL **Activity Master 8: Find the Hidden Word, p. 52A**

- **Reaching All Learners:**
  Shy Children

- **Liturgy Link:**
  I Believe

- **Lectionary Link:**
  Break Open the Word

Pacing the Chapter

Parish
Meets once a week

In parish religious education classes, plan for approximately 60 minutes of class time.

Invite	10 minutes
Explore	40 minutes
Celebrate	10 minutes

The abundance of activity and enrichment options will allow flexibility in planning for longer sessions if needed.

School
Meets 5 days per week

In school religious education classes, plan for lesson 5 days per week for about 30 minutes. The lesson can be easily adapted for a 4-day week as well.

Day 1: Invite	**Day 4:** Explore
Day 2: Explore	**Day 5:** Celebrate
Day 3: Explore	

The abundance of activity and enrichment options will allow flexibility in planning for longer sessions if needed.

- Online planning tools include chapter background and planner, activity master, customizable test, and more.
- Enhancement activities for each step of the catechetical process, including alternative prayer experiences and blessings.
- Games, activities, interactive review, alternative assessment, and more for children.

www.calltofaitheconnect.com

Home Connection

Chapter 4 Family Faith, p. 52
Take-home activities, chapter content review, saint features and prayer

 For more family activities
www.harcourtreligion.com

Name _____ Date _____

Say Thanks

Directions: Draw a picture of someone teaching you something. Then complete the sentence. Give the picture to the person who taught you.

Thank you for teaching me to

_____

- -

_____ .

©Harcourt Religion

Chapter 4

God the Father

God said, "You are my child. I am your father."

Based on Psalm 2:7

Read to Me

Let's Begin

Learn About God's Love

Mr. Rillon's class drew pictures of special people.

- Carlos and his mother plant roses.

- Ivana and her aunt work in the garden.

- Braulio and his dad cook.

- Jean's grandfather reads to her.

What wonderful things have you learned from special people?

Possible responses: how to draw, garden, cook, ride a bike

47

Objective: To recognize learning from others

Let Us Pray

Invite children to gather in the prayer space. In the prayer space, have a crucifix and a Bible opened to the psalm verse.

Teach children the response: "Thank you, God, for caring for me." Read aloud the psalm verse, and have children say the rehearsed response.

Let's Begin

Learn About God's Love

- Talk with children about the picture.

- Read aloud the story.

- For each section of the story, assign the role of the child and the adult. Invite children to act out the text as you read aloud the story again.

- Discuss the question.

OPTIONAL ACTIVITY

Activity Master 7: Say Thanks
Distribute copies of the activity found on page 47E.

- Tell children they will be thanking someone who teaches them.

- Have them draw a picture of someone teaching them.

- Ask them to share the picture with that person.

Activity Master 7

Name _____ Date _____

Say Thanks

Directions: Draw a picture of someone teaching you something. Then complete the sentence. Give the picture to the person who taught you.

Thank you for teaching me to

▲ **Activity Master 7**

QUICK TIP

Different Types of Families Keep in mind children all have different family situations.

- Some may have single parents, some may live with grandparents, others may be adopted.

- Help these children recall other relatives, teachers, or friends who have helped them learn.

Objective: To understand that God teaches how to love

Special People

Ask children how God shows his love for them. Possible responses: by making us, by giving us gifts and talents, by giving us families

Tell children that special people have taught them certain skills.

• Read aloud the text.

• Ask children why people who love them want to teach them new things. Possible responses: to share time with them, to show something that is important, to help children enjoy a hobby

Activity

• Read aloud the directions for the activity.

• Hand out crayons or markers to children.

• Have children share their completed drawings with the class.

Explore

Special People

Moms, dads, grandmas, grandpas, aunts, and uncles are all special.

They love you and teach you many things.

Activity

Draw someone teaching you.

48

CULTURAL AWARENESS

Greetings People from different countries and cultures show respect in different ways.

• French people kiss each other on both cheeks to say hello.

• People in Japan show respect by bowing.

• People in the United States shake hands or hug each other.

OPTIONAL ACTIVITY

Learning Pictures Invite children to bring in photographs of people who have helped them learn.

• Encourage children to name the person in the picture and tell what the person taught them.

• If time permits, have children pantomime what they learned, and have classmates guess the action.

Multiple Intelligence: Bodily/Kinesthetic

God Shows Love

God shows love by giving us people who love us. He shows his love in other ways, too.

I John 3:1

Child of God

See what love God the Father gives you.
You are a child of God because he loves you.

Based on I John 3:1

 How does God love you?
Responses will vary.

49

Objective: To learn that each person is a child of God

God Shows Love

Remind children that God teaches us about love.

- Have children listen for how God shows love for us.
- Read aloud the text.
- Ask children to tell about people who love them. Possible responses: parents, siblings, neighbors, teachers, friends

Child of God

Proclaim the Scripture.

- Ask children what it means to be a child of God. Possible responses: God loves us; he will care for us; we are all brothers and sisters.
- Discuss the question.

 SCRIPTURE BACKGROUND

John's Epistles This scripture verse is from the first letter of John. This letter is written in the style of the Gospel of John and expands on many of the ideas contained in that Gospel.

- This verse affirms our status as children of God, as well as his love for us.
- The verse also challenges us to live in God's love in hope of achieving salvation.

OPTIONAL ACTIVITY

Children's Literature Read aloud *Big Brown Bear's Up and Down Day* by David McPhail (Harcourt, 2003). This book demonstrates the love of friendship and can be a springboard for teaching about God's love for all of us.

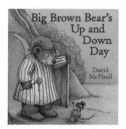

Multiple Intelligence: Verbal/Linguistic

Explore

Objective: To remember that God the Father loves everyone

God the Father

Recall that God loves us.

• Read aloud the text to children.

Activity

• Read aloud the directions for the activity.

• Hand out crayons or markers.

• Read aloud the sentences in the left column.

• Allow time for children to match each sentence with the correct photograph.

God the Father

Everyone is a child of God.

Everyone belongs to God.

God is our Father.

Activity

Match each picture with the best words.

People who love us help us.

People who love us forgive us.

People who love us teach us.

50

REACHING ALL LEARNERS

Shy Children Some children may be uncomfortable talking about love and loving actions.

• Take time to watch for these children in your class.

• Encourage them by working with them individually and using words of affirmation.

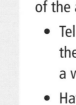

OPTIONAL ACTIVITY

Activity Master 8: Find the Hidden Word Distribute copies of the activity found on page 52A.

• Tell children that by coloring in the dotted pieces, they will find a word.

• Have them color in the pieces and fill in each letter.

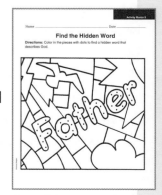

▲ Activity Master 8

I Believe

Leader: God made everything.

All: I believe in God the Father.

Leader: God loves us very much.

All: I believe in God the Father.

Leader: God takes care of us.

All: I believe in God the Father.

Sing together the refrain.

All grownups, all children,
all mothers, all fathers are
sisters and brothers
in the fam'ly of God.

All Grownups, All Children

Objective: To celebrate belief in God the Father

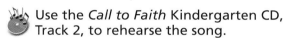 Let Us Pray

Tell children they will say what they believe.

I Believe

Prepare

Decorate the prayer space with family pictures.

• Practice the response with children.

Use the *Call to Faith* Kindergarten CD, Track 2, to rehearse the song.

Gather

Invite children to the prayer space.

• Ask children to hold hands and to bow their heads during the prayer celebration.

Pray

• Read aloud the leader's part, and have children pray the response.

• Allow time for children to tell about their family pictures.

• Conclude with the song.

 LITURGY LINK

I Believe Observant children will note that sometimes a children's Mass prayer begins with "I Believe in God the Father."

• Explain that this prayer tells what Catholics believe about God.

• Challenge children to listen to the Creed at Mass and to tell what they remember about the prayer.

 LECTIONARY LINK

Break Open the Word Read last week's Sunday Gospel. Talk about how this reading helps us follow Jesus. For children's questions related to the weekly Gospel reading, visit our Web site.

 Visit www.harcourtreligion.com for weekly scripture readings and seasonal resources.

Wrap-Up

Family Faith

Remind children to discuss the Family Faith page at home. Encourage them to talk with family members about what they know about God the Father.

Family Project

- Encourage children to do the activity with their families.

People of Faith

Tell children about Pier Giorgio Frassati.

- Pier Giorgio Frassati's life was very similar to the lives of young people today.

- Pier was outgoing and athletic. He liked to climb mountains and to ski.

- He was known for being a person of joy and for spreading that joy to others.

  Visit **www.harcourtreligion.com** for weekly scripture readings and seasonal resources.

CHAPTER 4

Family Faith

Catholics Believe

Dear Family,
In Chapter 4, the children learned that God is the Father of us all. Children may not understand this because we cannot see God. Children learn about God's love from your example.

✝ SCRIPTURE

Read 1 John 3:1 together with your child.

 www.harcourtreligion.com
For weekly scripture readings and seasonal resources

Family Project

Start a Love Note Jar Wash and decorate a jar. As you observe family members showing love for one another, write down what you see and the family member's name. For example, "Ben held the door for a person at church." Place the paper in the jar. Collect papers for a week or so. At a family meal, read aloud the papers. Praise the loving actions, and encourage family members to continue the good work.

Love Notes

People of Faith

Saint Pier Giorgio Frassati lived in Italy. As a young man he went to Mass every day.

Saint Pier Giorgio Frassati, ▶ 1901–1925

Family Prayer

 Pier, pray for us, that we may worship God as you did. Amen.

52 CCC *See Catechism of the Catholic Church 238 for further reading on chapter content.*

? HOW DID I DO?

This week was

☐ *one of the best ever!* ☐ *pretty good.* ☐ *in need of improvement.*

In what discussions and activities were children most interested?

_____

What activity did I most enjoy teaching?

_____

In what area do I need to improve?

_____

Name _____ Date _____

Find the Hidden Word

Directions: Color in the pieces with dots to find a hidden word that describes God.

You Pray

CHAPTER BACKGROUND

 But when you pray, go to your inner room, close the door, and pray to your Father in secret. And your Father who sees in secret will repay you.

Matthew 6:6

The Gift of Prayer

Among the many gifts God has made available to us is prayer. Prayer is our way of sharing our lives with him, of returning our thoughts to the being who is the author of all thoughts. Prayer is a continuation of the oneness we experience with God through Baptism.

As we pray, we humble ourselves by admitting that we are imperfect beings, striving to be worthy of the gifts we have received. We humbly ask for help with situations that are beyond our control, or we give God thanks and praise for his goodness and kindness to us.

The Best Prayers

The Church has many beautiful prayers, such as the Lord's Prayer and the Rosary. As Catholics, it is our duty and right to learn them and appreciate them. Songs, too, are part of the way that Catholics honor God. One of the beauties of teaching is sharing these age-old traditions with young children, to make them aware of our wonderful heritage as Catholics.

But some situations take us beyond the ritual prayers. Some of the most moving and personal prayers are those that come from our hearts, that send our thoughts in our own words to God. God shares critical moments in our lives, both happy and sad. When we share our thoughts with him at such times, it cannot help but be prayer.

Reflect *Do you share your thoughts with God on a regular basis?*

Faith Focus

- **God calls us to pray.** *(CCC 2567)*

Catechism Connection

The *Catechism* urges us to pray. Prayer is the communication that furthers our relationship with God. *(CCC 2565)*

NDC Link

The *Directory* instructs catechists to develop and promote an environment of prayer. (See *NDC*, 20.4.)

Resources

BOOK
The Lord's Prayer. Eerdmans Books for Young Readers. Illustrates the prayer with scenes of a young girl and her father helping a neighbor.

DVD/VHS
What Is Faith? (30 min.). Twenty-Third Publications. This video with Kathleen Chesto examines faith and how we share it.

Resources
For interactive lesson planner, chapter resources, and activities
www.harcourtreligion.com

Important Numbers

Encourage all children to practice reciting important phone numbers. This is an important life skill and one that will serve them well in an emergency situation.

- Help children learn 9-1-1 for emergencies. Ask children to provide examples of emergency situations when calling 9-1-1 is appropriate. Help children understand what a real emergency is.

- Help children see the importance of knowing their own phone number. Allow them to recite their phone number aloud. Praise children for learning such an important skill.

Expressing Myself

- I know what I want. I may not always express myself appropriately. Teach me to use my words well.

- I love to hear stories. Read to me. Establish a take-home library. Help my parents see the importance of reading to me.

Multiple Belonging

People who are comfortable belonging to groups of people possess a wealth of resources. Sustaining the spirit to teach is easier for those who have been raised in one core group of people but have now learned how to move smoothly within another group. The second group may have a different economic or educational level, value system, or ethnicity.

Living within just one core group can lead to a narrow sense of what is important, a poor sense of what is needed, and limited ways of coping with tough times. Belonging to multiple groups can help sustain your spirit by broadening your ability to handle difficulties, communicate, and appreciate what others cherish.

Reflect *How has belonging to multiple groups helped you sustain the spirit to teach?*

 Prayer

Holy Spirit, help me to call on you when I feel sorrow and joy. Let me invite you into my heart to share my thoughts, and help me create an atmosphere of prayer in my classroom. Amen.

Weekly Planner

		Objectives	Materials	Prayer & Scripture
1 Invite	**You Pray** Page 53	To learn to share good news with others	☐ Copies of Activity Master 9, p.53E ☐ Pencils ☐ Crayons or markers	Let Us Pray: Psalm 5:3
2 Explore	**Talking with God** Page 54	To understand that prayer is talking with God	☐ *The Ticky–Tacky Doll*	Scripture: 1 Thessalonians 5: 17–18 Scripture Background: Prayer
2 Explore	**Ways to Pray** Page 55	To know when to pray		Scripture: 1 Thessalonians 5: 17–18
2 Explore	**We Believe** Page 56	To learn about the Holy Trinity	☐ Pencils ☐ Crayons or markers ☐ Copies of Activity Master 10, p. 58A	Scripture: 1 Thessalonians 5: 17–18
3 Celebrate	**The Sign of the Cross** Page 57	To learn to pray the Sign of the Cross	☐ Music CD ☐ Bible or Lectionary ☐ Bowl of holy water	Let Us Pray: The Sign of the Cross **Hymn:** All Grownups, All Children

Activities	Enrichment

Let's Begin

Read and discuss the story.

OPTIONAL **Activity Master 9: Morning Prayer Reminder, p. 53E**

| | • **Quick Tip:** Connect with Relatives |

❓ Discuss when to pray.

OPTIONAL Children's Literature
Multiple Intelligence: Verbal/Linguistic

❓ Share words you use to pray.

• **Cultural Awareness:** Many Ways to Pray

• **Chapter Background:** The Sign of the Cross

Activity

Make signs that remind you to pray.

OPTIONAL **Activity Master 10: Make a Cross, p. 58A**

• **Reaching All Learners:** Tactile Learners

• **Liturgy Link:** Holy Water

• **Lectionary Link:** Break Open the Word

Pacing the Chapter

Parish

Meets once a week

In parish religious education classes, plan for approximately 60 minutes of class time.

Invite	10 minutes
Explore	40 minutes
Celebrate	10 minutes

The abundance of activity and enrichment options will allow flexibility in planning for longer sessions if needed.

School

Meets 5 days per week

In school religious education classes, plan for lesson 5 days per week for about 30 minutes. The lesson can be easily adapted for a 4-day week as well.

Day 1: Invite   **Day 4:** Explore
Day 2: Explore   **Day 5:** Celebrate
Day 3: Explore

The abundance of activity and enrichment options will allow flexibility in planning for longer sessions if needed.

- Online planning tools include chapter background and planner, activity master, customizable test, and more.
- Enhancement activities for each step of the catechetical process, including alternative prayer experiences and blessings.
- Games, activities, interactive review, alternative assessment, and more for children.

www.calltofaitheconnect.com

Home Connection

Chapter 5 Family Faith, p. 58
Take-home activities, chapter content review, saint features and prayer

 For more family activities
www.harcourtreligion.com

Name _____ Date _____

Morning Prayer Reminder

Directions: Put this prayer where your family can pray it every morning.

Dear God, this day is for you.

You Pray

Chapter 5

To you I pray, O LORD.

Based on Psalm 5:3

Read to Me — Let's Begin

Talking with Grandmother

Emily called her grandmother and said, "Good morning, Grandma!"

After school, Emily called her grandmother and said, "I learned to read two new words today!"

At bedtime, Emily called her grandmother and said, "Good night. I love you, Grandma!"

Grandma said, "I love you, too. Thanks for sharing your day with me."

● Why did Emily call her grandmother so often?

Possible response: Emily wanted to share good news with her grandmother. 53

Invite

1 Invite

Objective: To learn to share good news with others

Let Us Pray

Teach children motions for *you* (point away from oneself), *pray* (folded hands), and *Lord* (open arms). Read aloud the psalm. Have children use the motions as you lead the prayer.

Let's Begin

Talking with Grandmother

- Select two children to help you tell the story. Consider using the name of a child in the group rather than *Emily*.
- Read aloud the story as children act out the telephone calls.
- Discuss the question.
- Ask children whom they call when they have special news. Responses will vary.
- Ask why people share good news. Possible responses: to make people happy, to show that they are thinking about others

---

OPTIONAL ACTIVITY

Activity Master 9: Morning Prayer Reminder Distribute copies of the activity found on page 53E.

- Tell children they will make a prayer reminder.
- Ask them to trace the letters, decorate the frame, and display it at home.

▲ **Activity Master 9**

QUICK TIP

Connect with Relatives Be sensitive to individual situations in children's families. Many children live far away from their grandparents or do not have grandparents.

- When family members live far away, suggest that children send drawings or art work to them.
- Parents may also allow children to talk on the phone with far away relatives.

2 Explore

Talking with God

Remind children that we like to talk with people about our lives. Ask children to tell how they can talk with God. Possible response: with prayers

- Read aloud the first two lines of text. Ask children why grandparents like to talk with grandchildren. Possible response: because grandparents love grandchildren

- Draw a parallel between God and grandparents by reading aloud the next three lines. Explain that he is like parents and grandparents and that he loves to hear from his children.

Pray Always

- Proclaim the Scripture.
- Discuss the question.
- Have children look at the pictures. Help children understand that these are both situations in which they can pray.

Explore

Talking with God

Emily's grandmother loves her. She loves it when Emily calls her.

God loves you. He wants you to talk to him. You talk to him when you pray.

I Thessalonians 5:17–18

 Read to Me

Pray Always

One of God's followers told us when to pray. Pray all the time to God. Thank God for everything that happens.

Based on
I Thessalonians 5:17–18

❓ When can you pray to God?

Possible responses: in the morning, at meals, before bedtime

54

✝ **SCRIPTURE BACKGROUND**

Prayer This passage is part of a series of directions Paul wrote to the Christians in Thessalonica.

- Paul explains that prayer is an integral part of a Christian's duties and should be a constant in our lives. This echoes the Parable of the Persistent Widow in *Luke 18:1-5.*

- Prayer shows that we have faith in God and are grateful for his gifts.

OPTIONAL ACTIVITY

Children's Literature Read aloud *The Ticky-Tacky Doll* by Cynthia Rylant (Harcourt, 2002). This story is about problem-solving and communication across generations.

Multiple Intelligence: Verbal/Linguistic

Ways to Pray

Pray to God in your heart with your own words.

● Pray to God when you are happy.

● Pray to God when someone is sick.

● Pray to God when you feel lonely.

 What do you say when you pray?
Responses will vary.

55

Objective: To know when to pray

Ways to Pray

Help children recall that prayer is talking to God.

- Read aloud the text to children.
- As you read, have children point to the photograph that matches the sentence you are reading.
- Ask children why they should talk to God with their own words. Possible response: God wants to know our true feelings.
- Model some prayers that the children in the photographs might pray. For example, the child in the grass might pray, "Thank you for the green grass." Have children make up prayers of their own.
- Discuss the question.

Many Ways to Pray If children in your class speak another language, ask them to teach the class the words to the Sign of the Cross in that language.

- Be certain to connect the correct ritual gestures with the words.
- Point out that God understands all languages and listens to people all over the world.

The Sign of the Cross The Sign of the Cross is the prayer Catholics pray most often. The Sign recalls Christ's death and honors the Trinity with words and actions.

- The Sign has more than one form. We use the triple Sign of the Cross before the Gospel during Mass.
- Eastern Rite Catholics touch their right shoulders first; this is not an incorrect form of the prayer for these believers.

Objective: To learn about the Holy Trinity

We Believe

Recall that we talk with God through prayer.

- Read aloud the text to children.
- Help children understand the concept of the three Persons of the Trinity.

Activity

- Read aloud the directions to children.
- Hand out pencils and crayons or markers.
- Help children name words to put on their signs.
- Help children who have difficulty writing letters.

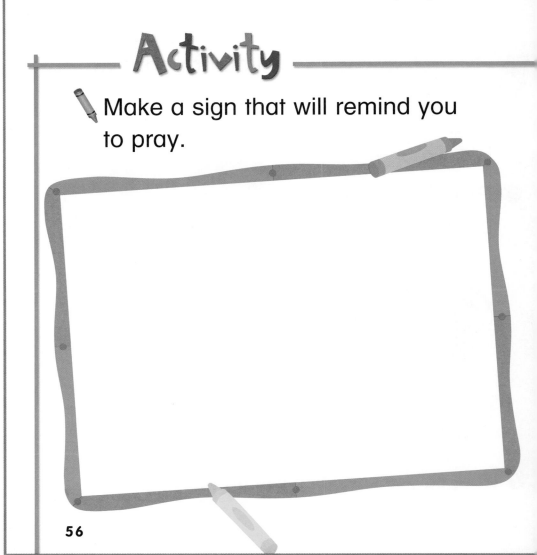

Explore

We Believe

We believe in God the Father.
We believe in Jesus, God's Son.
We believe in God the Holy Spirit.

Activity

Make a sign that will remind you to pray.

56

OPTIONAL ACTIVITY

Activity Master 10: Make a Cross Distribute copies of the activity found on page 58A.

- Tell children they will be making a cross.
- Ask them to connect the dots, color in the shape, and complete the sentence.

Name _____ Date _____

Make a Cross

Directions: Connect the dots. Then color in the shape you made, and complete the sentence.

We begin praying with the Sign of the
Cross.

▲ Activity Master 10

REACHING ALL LEARNERS

Tactile Learners Children who learn through touching will benefit from making crosses of their own.

- Use a hot glue gun to join two craft sticks in a cross.
- Have children wrap colorful yarn around the cross. Secure the yarn ends with a glue gun.
- Display the crosses in your room.

The Sign of the Cross

We begin and end our prayers with the Sign of the Cross.

In the name of the Father,

1

and of the Son,

2

and of the Holy Spirit.

3

4

Amen.

5

Sing together.

All grownups, all children,
all mothers, all fathers are
sisters and brothers
in the fam'ly of God.

All Grownups, All Children

Objective: To learn to pray the Sign of the Cross

 **Let Us Pray**

Tell children they will learn to pray a special prayer.

The Sign of the Cross

Prepare

Place a bowl of holy water in the prayer space.

 Use the *Call to Faith* Kindergarten CD, track 2, to rehearse the song.

Gather

Invite children to the prayer space. Have children make a circle around the holy water.

Pray

- Make the Sign of the Cross as you say the prayer.
- Have children practice making and praying the Sign of the Cross.
- Have children sing the song.
- Suggest that children bless themselves with holy water and pray the Sign of the Cross as they leave the prayer space.

 LITURGY LINK

Holy Water Holy water is placed near the entrance of Catholic churches so that we may bless ourselves as we enter the building.

- Take children to your parish church to show them where the holy water fonts are located.
- Encourage children to bless themselves when they pass a holy water font.
- Consider installing a holy water font in your classroom.

LECTIONARY LINK

Break Open the Word Read last week's Sunday Gospel. Talk about how this reading helps us follow Jesus. For children's questions related to the weekly Gospel reading, visit our Web site.

 GO **ONLINE** Visit www.harcourtreligion.com for weekly scripture readings and seasonal resources.

Wrap-Up

Family Faith

Remind children to discuss the Family Faith page at home. Encourage them to talk with family members about what they have learned about prayer.

Family Project

• Encourage children to complete the activity with family members.

People of Faith

Tell children about Pier Giorgio Frassati.

• Pope John Paul II said that Pier embraced "life's ordinariness."

• Pier lived his faith in his family, in school, and while serving the poor.

• Encourage children to pray the prayer at home with their families.

 Visit **www.harcourtreligion.com** for weekly scripture readings and seasonal resources.

Family Faith

◎ Catholics Believe

Dear Family,
In Chapter 5, the children learned that praying is talking to God. They learned to make the Sign of the Cross to begin and end prayers.

✝ SCRIPTURE

Read I Thessalonians 5:17–18 together with your child.

GO ONLINE www.harcourtreligion.com
For weekly scripture readings and seasonal resources

Family Project

Pray for Others
Make a list of people you want to remember in your family prayers. Have your child decorate the list. Post the list where you can read the names as part of mealtime or evening prayers. Add to the list as needed. Remind your child to begin and end prayers with the Sign of the Cross.

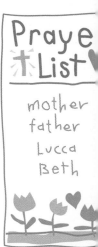

Prayer List
mother
father
Lucca
Beth

People of Faith

Saint Pier Giorgio Frassati liked to ski. He also liked to climb mountains. Pier was cheerful, even when he was sick.

Saint Pier Giorgio Frassati, ▶ 1901–1925

🤲 Family Prayer

Almighty God, help us be like Pier Frassati. Help us to be strong when we are sick or sad. Amen.

58 **CCC** *See Catechism of the Catholic Church 278 for further reading on chapter content.*

❓ HOW DID I DO?

This week was

☐ *one of the best ever!* ☐ *pretty good.* ☐ *in need of improvement.*

In what discussions and activities were children most interested?

_____

What activity did I most enjoy teaching?

_____

In what area do I need to improve?

_____

Name _____ Date _____

Make a Cross

Directions: Connect the dots. Then color in the shape you made, and complete the sentence.

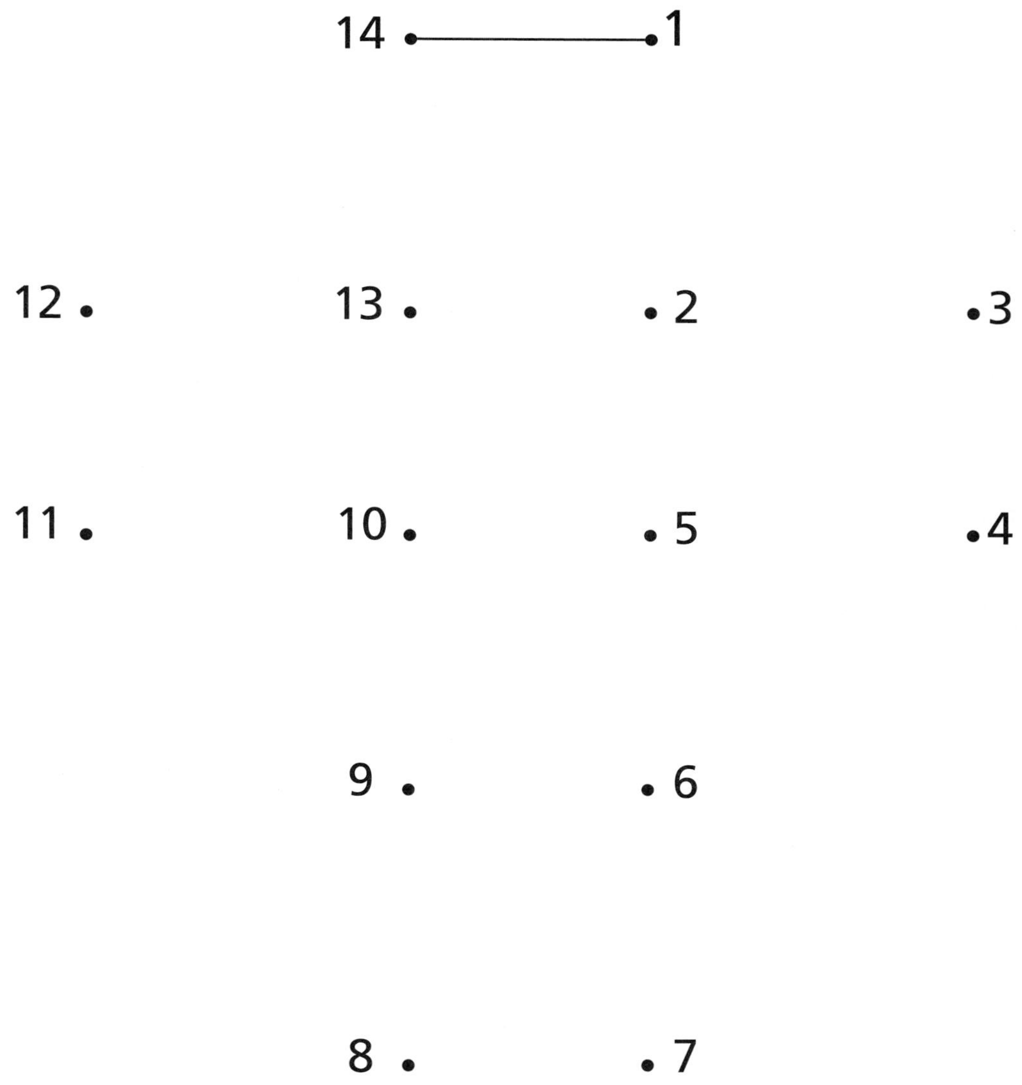

14 •————————• 1

12 •   13 •   • 2   • 3

11 •   10 •   • 5   • 4

9 •   • 6

8 •   • 7

We begin praying with the Sign of the

Cross.

Overview

You Care

CHAPTER BACKGROUND

 The LORD God then took the man and settled him in the garden of Eden, to cultivate and care for it.

Genesis 2:15

God's Helpers

Our heritage is full of wonderful stories of the loving interaction between humans and creation. Saint Francis of Assisi maintained wonderful relationships with animals. Saint Isidore the farmer cared for land and animals. We read these stories and smile, but we often fail to consider how our actions affect the fate of our home planet.

God wants us to use the earth's bounty for our food, clothing, and other necessities. He gave us dominion over the earth. However, we sometimes forget that *dominion* means control, but not ownership. Creation belongs to God; we are but stewards who will be held accountable for how we have managed this treasure.

Taking What We Need

Our culture encourages us to use what we want, then throw it away. Advertisements and peers entice us to get the latest and greatest of everything, whether or not we truly need it. We do not look ahead to the consequences of our actions often enough. The industries that cater to our whims may waste resources and cause pollution, but we are oblivious. However, the earth remembers with her scars.

What we must learn—and teach to our children—is to live lightly and deliberately. We should take only what we need, and whenever possible, replenish what we have taken. Then we will be known as good and faithful servants.

Reflect How do you work to preserve creation?

TIPS FOR TEACHING KINDERGARTNERS

Attention Getters

Children respond well to songs. Develop a routine which includes cues for transitions.

- Have certain songs for gathering, cleaning up, listening, lining up, and dismissal. Transitions will be smoother if students are prompted with a familiar tune.

- Encourage children to learn the songs. Ask children to sing the songs at the appropriate times.

KINDERGARTNERS SAY

Physical Activity

- I like to move. My body needs to be active. Just getting the wiggles out will keep me more focused. My gross and fine motor skills need to develop.

- I like to be challenged. My body is growing and changing. I am rapidly developing new skills.

SUSTAINING YOUR SPIRIT

Marginality

Many who sustain a life committed to the good of others can describe times in which they were ignored or marginalized. You may also feel marginalized as a catechist. You may find that others push you to the margins because of your values, your convictions, your educational level, your financial status, or even your geographic roots.

Marginality, that lonesome place of exclusion and insignificance within a school or parish program, does not have to hamper your ability to sustain the spirit to teach. Resilient people have used occasional experiences of marginalization to reexamine and reaffirm their core values.

Reflect **When have you been marginalized, and has it helped or hindered your ability to sustain the spirit to teach?**

 Prayer

Almighty God, thank you for all of creation, from the mightiest mountains to the smallest of insects. Strengthen me to work to preserve their beauty. Amen.

Weekly Planner

		Objectives	Materials	Prayer & Scripture
1 Invite	**You Care** Page 59	To want to protect nature	☐ Copies of Activity Master 11, p. 59E ☐ Crayons or markers ☐ Scissors ☐ Yarn ☐ Hole Punch ☐ Hangers	🪷 Let Us Pray: Psalm 33:8
2 Explore	**God's World** Page 60	To recognize that God calls us to care for his creation	☐ Nature magazines ☐ Scissors ☐ Glue ☐ Poster board	✝ Scripture: Genesis 1:28 ✝ Scripture Background: Dominion
	Ways to Care Page 61	To learn ways to care for the world	☐ Crayons or markers ☐ Copies of Activity Master 12, p. 64A ☐ Pencils ☐ Scissors	✝ Scripture: Genesis 1:28
	Protect God's World Page 62	To sing about caring for creation		✝ Scripture: Genesis 1:28
3 Celebrate	**Pray with God's Word** Page 63	To listen to what God says about taking care of creation	☐ Music CD ☐ Bible or Lectionary	🪷 Let Us Pray: Pray with God's Word 🔥 Hymn: All Grownups, All Children

Activities	Enrichment
Let's Begin Talk about taking care of living things. OPTIONAL **Activity Master 11:** **A Bug Mobile, p. 59E**	• **Chapter Background:** Christina Rossetti (1830–1894)
❓ Discuss how people care for the things God made. OPTIONAL A Class Collage Multiple Intelligence: Visual/Spatial	
Activity Tell how people care for God's world and draw another way to care. OPTIONAL **Activity Master 12:** **Turn Out the Light, p. 64A**	• **Reaching All Learners:** Fine-Motor Challenges
Activity Sing and act out the song. OPTIONAL Caring for the Classroom Multiple Intelligence: Visual/Spatial	• **Justice and Peace:** Conservation
	• **Liturgy Link:** Quiet • **Lectionary Link:** Break Open the Word

Pacing the Chapter

Parish
Meets once a week

In parish religious education classes, plan for approximately 60 minutes of class time.

Invite	10 minutes
Explore	40 minutes
Celebrate	10 minutes

The abundance of activity and enrichment options will allow flexibility in planning for longer sessions if needed.

School
Meets 5 days per week

In school religious education classes, plan for lesson 5 days per week for about 30 minutes. The lesson can be easily adapted for a 4-day week as well.

Day 1: Invite   **Day 4:** Explore
Day 2: Explore   **Day 5:** Celebrate
Day 3: Explore

The abundance of activity and enrichment options will allow flexibility in planning for longer sessions if needed.

CALL to FAITH e connect

- Online planning tools include chapter background and planner, activity master, customizable test, and more.
- Enhancement activities for each step of the catechetical process, including alternative prayer experiences and blessings.
- Games, activities, interactive review, alternative assessment, and more for children.

www.calltofaitheconnect.com

Home Connection

Chapter 6 Family Faith, p. 64
Take-home activities, chapter content review, saint features and prayer

 For more family activities
www.harcourtreligion.com

Name _____ Date _____

A Bug Mobile

Directions: Color in the bugs. Then cut them out and use them to make a mobile.

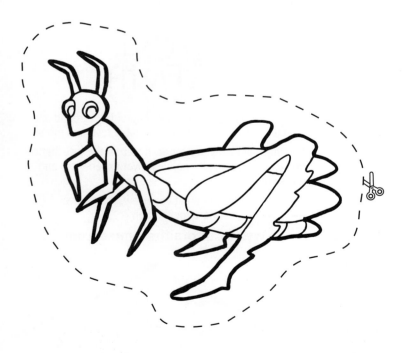

Chapter 6 You Care

Invite

Let all who live in God's world care for it.

Based on Psalm 33:8

Read to Me — Let's Begin

Hurt No Living Thing

Hurt no living thing:
Ladybird, nor butterfly,
Nor moth with dusty wing,
Nor cricket chirping cheerily,
Nor grasshopper so light
of leap,
Nor dancing gnat, nor
beetle fat,
Nor harmless worms
that creep.

by Christina Rossetti

● What living things
do you care for?

Responses will vary.

59

Objective: To want to protect nature

Let Us Pray

Read aloud the psalm verse to children. Have them repeat it after you.

Let's Begin

Hurt No Living Thing

Have children listen as you read aloud the poem. Tell them to try to imagine the creatures as you read.

• Have children name creatures mentioned in the poem. If necessary, reread the poem. Possible responses: butterflies, moths, crickets, grasshoppers, etc.

• Discuss the question.

OPTIONAL ACTIVITY

Activity Master 11: A Bug Mobile Distribute copies of the activity found on page 59E.

• Tell children they will be making a mobile.

• Have them color in the bugs and cut them out. Help them put their mobiles together.

A Bug Mobile

▲ Activity Master 11

CHAPTER BACKGROUND

Christina Rossetti (1830–1894) Christina Rossetti is considered one of England's most distinguished women poets. She was known for her quiet humility and religious devotion. Many of her poems were intended for children. She wrote a book of nursery rhymes that is considered one of the best children's books of the Victorian era.

2 Explore

Objective: To recognize that God calls us to care for his creation

God's World

Ask children why God wants us to care for creation. Possible responses: because God wants us to be happy, because God thinks we are smart

Direct children's attention to the illustration. Discuss how it shows the beauty of the world.

• Read aloud the text.

• Ask children why we must show care for creation. Possible response: because God made it and wants us to show love for his gifts to us

Take Care

• Proclaim the Scripture.

• Ask the discussion question. Allow children to share responses.

God's World

God loves all living things.

When you care for the earth, you show your love for God.

Genesis 1:28

Read to Me

Take Care

God told the first people to take care of the fish in the sea, the birds in the air, and all living things.

Based on Genesis 1:28

❓ **How do people take care of God's creation?** Possible responses: by taking care of ourselves, our pets, and our world

---

✝ SCRIPTURE BACKGROUND

Dominion In this verse and the passage surrounding it, God gives humans responsibility for the earth. God commanded the first people to "fill the earth and subdue it."

• This text is not meant to give humans leeway to do whatever they please.

• Humans are called to respect the environment and their place in it.

OPTIONAL ACTIVITY

A Class Collage Invite children to help you make a collage of beautiful places.

• Distribute brochures or magazines with pictures of natural beauty.

• Have children cut out their favorite pictures and paste them to a piece of poster board.

Multiple Intelligence: Visual/Spatial

Ways to Care

You are old enough to help care for God's world.

Throw trash into the trash can.

Use water wisely.

Put things where they belong.

Activity

Tell how the people in each picture are caring for God's world. Draw a way you can care for God's world.

61

Objective: To learn ways to care for the world

Ways to Care

Remind children that as they get older they can do more and more to care for the world.

• Read aloud the text.

• Ask children to tell how the children in the pictures are caring for the world.

Activity

• Read aloud the directions to children.

• Remind children how the child in each picture is caring for the world.

• Brainstorm other ways of caring for the world: caring for pets, weeding a garden, raking leaves, and so on.

• Hand out crayons or markers to children.

• Direct children to draw one way they can care for God's world.

OPTIONAL ACTIVITY

Activity Master 12: Turn out the Light Distribute copies of the activity found on page 64A.

• Tell children they will be decorating a light switch cover.

• Have them color the cover and trace the reminder on it to turn out unused lights so that we can save the resources God gave us.

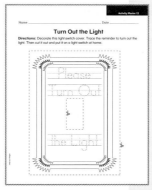

▲ **Activity Master 12**

★ REACHING ALL LEARNERS

Fine-Motor Challenges Many kindergartners may not have sufficient fine motor control to draw well in the relatively small box on this page.

• Supply a separate sheet of drawing paper for these children.

• You may wish to make a box on the paper that is similar to the activity box.

Explore

Objective: To sing about caring for creation

Protect God's World

Tell children that they will sing about caring for creation.

Activity

- Teach children this song to the tune of "Here We Go 'Round the Mulberry Bush."
- Practice the song until children can sing it easily.
- Have children work with a partner to add a line to the song.
- Invite volunteers to sing their line to the class.

Protect God's World

This song will remind you to care for creation.

Activity

Work with a partner. Add one line to the song. Sing the line to the class.

Sing together.

This is the way we protect God's world, so early in the morning.
This is the way we pick up trash, so early in the morning.
This is the way we water God's plants, so early in the morning.
This is the way we save our water, so early in the morning.

62

Caring for the Classroom Children may not always see the classroom as an extension of creation, but it is!

- Point out that the room and the items in it are part of God's world.
- Challenge children to clean their desks and other areas in the classroom.

Multiple Intelligence: Visual/Spatial

JUSTICE AND PEACE

Conservation Humans are meant to have dominion over creation. However, this does not mean that we can do whatever we want with the rest of our world. (See *On Social Concern, #34*.)

- Some natural resources are limited; we should conserve their use.
- Encourage children to think about resources they can conserve.

Catholic Social Teaching: Care for Creation

Pray with God's Word

Leader: Let us listen to God's word.

Read Genesis 1:27–28.

The word of the Lord.

All: **Thanks be to God.**

Sing together.

All grownups, all children,
all mothers, all fathers are
sisters and brothers
in the fam'ly of God.

All Grownups, All Children

63

Objective: To listen to what God says about taking care of creation

 **Let Us Pray**

Tell children they will listen to God's word.

Pray with God's Word

Prepare

- Explain to children that they will pray quietly in their hearts. Explain that they can talk to God without saying the words aloud. He will hear.

- Teach the response, and have children practice saying it.

Use the *Call to Faith* Kindergarten CD, Track 2, to rehearse the song.

Gather

Invite children to the prayer space.

- Have children sit down in a circle.

Pray

- Proclaim the Scripture. Have children respond.

- Allow children to pray quietly. Then say "God our Father, we promise to care for the world."

- Have children stand and sing the song.

 LITURGY LINK

Quiet Children need to experience quiet time. During quiet prayer, they can collect their thoughts and open their hearts to God's messages for them.

- Play quiet music to help children focus their thoughts.

- Children who are very active or easily distracted may benefit from closing their eyes, bending their heads, and holding their hands in their laps.

 LECTIONARY LINK

Break Open the Word Read last week's Sunday Gospel. Talk about how this reading helps us follow Jesus. For children's questions related to the weekly Gospel reading, visit our Web site.

 Visit www.harcourtreligion.com for weekly scripture readings and seasonal resources.

Wrap-Up

Family Faith

Remind children to discuss the Family Faith page at home. Encourage them to talk with family members about caring for the world.

Family Project

• Encourage children to work on the activity with family members.

People of Faith

Remind children that Pier Giorgio Frassati grew up in Italy.

• Pier went to Mass every morning. He believed that since Jesus came to him at Communion each morning, he should visit the poor each day as a sign of his love for others.

• Encourage children to pray the prayer at home with their families.

  Visit **www.harcourtreligion.com** for weekly scripture readings and seasonal resources.

Family Faith

Catholics Believe

Dear Family,

In Chapter 6, the children learned that people are responsible for caring for plants, animals, and other people. The children learned that they can help care for creation, too.

SCRIPTURE

Read Genesis 1:28 together with your child.

GO ONLINE **www.harcourtreligion.com** For weekly scripture readings and seasonal resources

Family Project

Care for the Earth Discuss how recycli[ng] helps save the earth's resources. Particip[ate] in a community recycling program. Encou[rage] your child to help you stack newspapers, cans and bottles in the proper containers, and so on. Point out that these efforts help care for the earth and keep your home an[d] community clean.

People of Faith

Saint Pier Giorgio Frassati tried to make other people happy. He lived his faith at home and at school. He cared for poor people each day.

Saint Pier Giorgio Frassati, ▶ **1901–1925**

Family Prayer

God our Father, help us be like Pier Frassati. Teach us to help the poor. Amen.

64 **CCC** *See Catechism of the Catholic Church 373 for further reading on chapter content.*

HOW DID I DO?

This week was

☐ *one of the best ever!* ☐ *pretty good.* ☐ *in need of improvement.*

In what discussions and activities were children most interested?

_____

What activity did I most enjoy teaching?

_____

In what area do I need to improve?

_____

Name _____ Date _____

Turn Out the Light

Directions: Decorate this light switch cover. Trace the reminder to turn out the light. Then cut it out and put it on a light switch at home.

God promised Noah that water would never again flood the whole earth. God said, "A rainbow is a sign of my promise."

Color the rainbow.

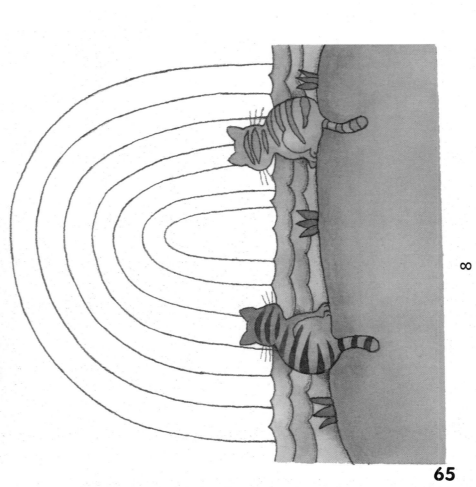

8

Read to Me

Scripture Story
Noah's Ark
(Genesis 6–9)

Family Note: In class your child has learned that God is a loving Father. As you read aloud this booklet, have your child use the pictures to follow along. Then have him or her tell you the story of how God helped Noah.

Long, long, long ago, God told Noah that there would be a flood. "Build a big boat," said God. So Noah built an ark.

2

Then the rain stopped. The sun came out. The water dried up slowly. Noah's family and all the animals left the ark.

7

66

It rained for forty days and forty nights. The water rose higher and higher. Finally, water flooded the whole earth.

6

67

God said, "Take animals with you, Noah. Get two of every kind."

3

Noah led the animals into the ark two by two.

4

5

© Harcourt Religion

68

Faith Focus

- God sent his Son, Jesus, to redeem us. *(CCC 422)*

Catechism Connection

The *Catechism* explains that Jesus is at the heart of all religious teaching. *(CCC 426)*

NDC Link

The *Directory* stresses that Jesus' life and his teachings are central to catechesis. (See *NDC*, 25A.)

Resources

BOOKS
*God Speaks to Us in Feeding Stories.** Getty-Sullivan, Mary Ann. Liturgical Press. "Jesus Feeds People in the Desert." Retells the miraculous story.

The Names of Jesus. Binz, Stephen J. Twenty-Third Publications. Introduces readers to many views of Jesus.

*Available at www.harcourtreligion.com

GO **Resources**
ONLINE For interactive lesson planner, chapter resources, and activities
www.harcourtreligion.com

*And the Word became flesh
and made his dwelling among us,
and we saw his glory,
the glory of the Father's only Son,
full of grace and truth.*

John 1:14

God Among Us

The story is two thousand years old, but we are still amazed by it. God's Son, God himself, became man. Jesus shared our humanity while maintaining his divinity. He lived among us, worked among us, and made friends among us. He taught us what we needed to know most: the Father loves us and has prepared a place for us in heaven!

The story starts humbly, in a stable in Bethlehem. With the children in your group, retell the story. Notice their enthusiasm, and make it your own. Point out that God sent his Son to help us. The children are used to asking for help as well as giving it. They will understand the analogy.

Help from the Son

In Hebrew, the name *Jesus* means "God saves." In the person of Jesus, God saved us from our sins. In teaching his followers, Jesus showed us that God understands our sins. Jesus taught us that God forgives us for our shortcomings and invites us to reunite with him. In his death, Resurrection, and Ascension, Jesus showed his true divinity and saved his human family. The story of his life, no matter how old it is, cannot help but invite wonder and awe.

Jesus' lasting gift to us is the Church. Within her teachings, we find him again, beckoning us to the Father.

Reflect** **What does the Christ of the Bible teach you about God's love?

Bulletin Board Ideas

Displaying the work of young children fosters a sense of belonging and value.

- Explain to children we are all God's children. Take photos of each child, and ask them to write their name on an index card. Place the photos and names of children on a bulletin board labeled "We Are God's Children."

- Display children's artwork by their photos. Allow children time to view other's work on display.

Family

- Family is important to me. Invite and welcome my family to my classroom.

- Establish and maintain relationships with my family. I feel a strong sense of belonging when my home and school worlds connect.

Habits of Mind

Blessed assurance and constructive engagement with others can help you develop good critical thinking habits. Solid thinking skills allow you to think beyond the obvious and to realize what contributes to difficult problems.

Those who sustain their spirit seek different views to enhance, but not compromise, their own. Others seek feedback from anyone familiar with their work, not just from friends. Practicing this kind of thinking—these habits of mind—allows you to harvest richer resources for sustaining your spirit.

Reflect **Circle the habit(s) of mind you would like to cultivate or improve:**

situational analysis   dialogue   seeking feedback

 Prayer

Jesus, Son of God, thank you for being my teacher and my brother. Show me the way to the Father. Help me share your love with the children in my care. Amen.

Weekly Planner

		Objectives	Materials	Prayer & Scripture
1 Invite	**God Sends His Son** Page 69	To understand why parents want their children to help others	☐ Crucifix ☐ Copies of Activity Master 13, p. 69E ☐ Pencils	🙏 Let Us Pray: Psalm 2:7
2 Explore	**God's Son** Page 70	To learn that God sent Jesus to help everyone	☐ Crayons or markers ☐ Copies of Activity Master 14, p. 74A ☐ Scissors	✝ Scripture: Luke 2:1–7
2 Explore	**Jesus Is Born** Page 71	To recall the story of the birth of Jesus	☐ Christmas music CD	✝ Scripture Background: The Nativity
2 Explore	**Who Knew?** Page 72	To realize that Jesus is God's Son	☐ Crayons or markers ☐ Drawing paper	✝ Scripture: Luke 2:1–7
3 Celebrate	**Prayer of Praise** Page 73	To pray a litany of praise	☐ Music CD ☐ Bible or Lectionary ☐ Nativity set	🙏 Let Us Pray: Prayer of Praise 🎵 **Hymn:** Praise to You, O Christ, Our Savior

Activities	Enrichment

Let's Begin

Listen to the story.

(OPTIONAL) **Activity Master 13:
I Can Help, p. 69E**

• **Quick Tip:**
Safety Reminders

Activity

Draw a picture of the baby Jesus.

(OPTIONAL) **Activity Master 14:
Christmas Story Puppet Show, p. 74A**

(OPTIONAL) Cross-Curricular: Music
Multiple Intelligence: Musical

❓ Talk about who took care of God's son.

(OPTIONAL) Add Music
Multiple Intelligence: Musical

Activity

Number the pictures to retell the story of Jesus' birth.

(OPTIONAL) Cross-Curricular: Art
Multiple Intelligence: Visual/Spatial

• **Reaching All Learners:**
Sequencing Difficulties

• **Liturgy Link:**
Litanies

• **Lectionary Link:**
Break Open the Word

Pacing the Chapter

Parish

Meets once a week

In parish religious education classes, plan for approximately 60 minutes of class time.

Invite 10 minutes
Explore 40 minutes
Celebrate 10 minutes

The abundance of activity and enrichment options will allow flexibility in planning for longer sessions if needed.

School

Meets 5 days per week

In school religious education classes, plan for lesson 5 days per week for about 30 minutes. The lesson can be easily adapted for a 4-day week as well.

Day 1: Invite   **Day 4:** Explore
Day 2: Explore   **Day 5:** Celebrate
Day 3: Explore

The abundance of activity and enrichment options will allow flexibility in planning for longer sessions if needed.

CALL to FAITH e connect

- Online planning tools include chapter background and planner, activity master, customizable test, and more.
- Enhancement activities for each step of the catechetical process, including alternative prayer experiences and blessings.
- Games, activities, interactive review, alternative assessment, and more for children.

www.calltofaitheconnect.com

Home Connection

Chapter 7 Family Faith, p. 74
Take-home activities, chapter content review, saint features and prayer

 For more family activities
www.harcourtreligion.com

Name _____ Date _____

I Can Help

Directions: Draw a line from the child to the person or animal who can use the child's help. Then make up a story for each matched set of pictures.

Chapter 7 God Sends His Son

You are my Son.

Based on Psalm 2:7

Read to Me — Let's Begin

Helping

The phone rang.

My dad said proudly, "Yes, my son can help you. He can take in your mail, Mrs. Posey."

Dad said, "Ramon, our neighbor needs you."

"I can help, Dad," I said. "You can send your son."

Dad smiled and hugged me.

● Why was Dad proud to send Ramon to help?

Possible responses: because he knew Ramon could help, because Ramon was willing to help

69

Objective: To understand why parents want their children to help others

Let Us Pray

Invite children to gather in the prayer space and make the Sign of the Cross. In the prayer space, have a crucifix and a Bible opened to the psalm verse.

Have children repeat the psalm verse after you.

Let's Begin

Helping

- Ask children to look at the picture and predict what the story will be about.
- Read aloud the text.
- Ask children why Ramon went to Mrs. Posey's house. to take in her mail
- Talk about how children feel when they help others. Ask children to share how they have helped others.
- Discuss the text question.

OPTIONAL ACTIVITY

Activity Master 13: I Can Help Distribute copies of the activity found on page 69E.

- Have children draw a line from the child to the person or animal that needs help.
- Ask them to make up stories for the pictures.

▲ Activity Master 13

QUICK TIP

Safety Reminders Point out that Ramon only went to help Mrs. Posey after his father gave him permission.

- Remind children that they should never go into a neighbor's home or car without permission.
- Point out that helping others does not mean that we forget about our own safety.

Objective: To learn that God sent Jesus to help everyone

God's Son

Ask children why God sent his Son to help us. Possible responses: because God loved us, because he thought we needed to learn from Jesus

Remind children of how Ramon helped Mrs. Posey.

- Read aloud the first three sentences.
- Ask children what kind of help God's Son can give us. Possible responses: He can teach us to love; he can tell us about God.
- Resume reading aloud the text.
- Ask children what they know about Christmas. Possible response: It is Jesus' birthday.

Activity

- Have children look at the picture.
- Ask children what is missing from the picture. baby Jesus
- Hand out crayons or markers, and have children draw baby Jesus in the manger.

Explore

God's Son

Dad knew that Ramon could help Mrs. Posey.

God the Father knew that his people needed help. He sent his Son to help. Jesus is God's Son.

We celebrate Jesus' birth on Christmas.

Activity

Draw baby Jesus with Mary and Joseph.

70

Activity Master 14: Christmas Story Puppet Show Distribute copies of the activity found on page 74A.

- Tell children they will be making finger puppets.
- Have them color the puppets and the stable, cut them out, and use them to retell the Christmas Story.

▲ Activity Master 14

Cross-Curricular: Music Sing a song. Lead the children in singing the following song to the tune of "Frére Jacques."

God sent Jesus,	Mary was his Mother,
God sent Jesus,	Mary was his Mother,
For everyone,	He's God's Son,
For everyone,	He's God's Son.

Multiple Intelligence: Musical

Read to Me

Jesus Is Born

Joseph and Mary went to Bethlehem.
Clip, clop marched the donkey.

Joseph went to the inn, but there
were no empty rooms.
"No rooms, no rooms," Joseph said.

Joseph and Mary went to sleep in
the stable.
"Good night, good night," said the
animals.

Mary's baby was born.
"Sweet baby, sweet baby," Mary said.

Joseph and Mary
named the baby Jesus.

We are glad you are
here, dear Jesus.

Based on Luke 2:1–7

❓ **Who took care of
God's Son?**
Mary and Joseph

71

Objective: To recall the story of the
birth of Jesus

Jesus Is Born

Remind children that Jesus was God's
Son and lived on earth.

- Prepare children to listen to the
  story by having them sit quietly in a
  circle.

- Proclaim the Gospel reading. Ask
  children where they have heard the
  story before. Possible responses: at
  Christmas, in a story book

- Discuss the text question.

- Ask children to help you retell the
  story. Assign parts for Mary, Joseph,
  the donkey, and the other animals.
  Have the rest of the class repeat the
  last line of each verse.

- Read aloud the story as children act
  it out. Consider inviting parents or
  another class in to view your
  presentation.

✚ SCRIPTURE BACKGROUND

The Nativity The account of Jesus' birth in the
Gospel of Luke comes after the stories of the
Annunciation and Visitation.

- Luke contrasts the earthly rulers who were in
  power at the time with the lowly
  baby who would reign in heaven.

- The joy felt by Mary and
  Joseph is echoed by the angels
  and the shepherds.

OPTIONAL ACTIVITY

Add Music Consider adding songs to the Christmas
story presentation.

- Ask children to tell about
  Christmas songs they know,
  or have your music teacher or
  music minister work with
  children to teach them
  songs of the season.

Christmas Carols

Multiple Intelligence: Musical

Objective: To realize that Jesus is God's Son

Who Knew?

Remind children of the story of Jesus' birth.

- Tell children that Jesus was born into Mary and Joseph's family.
- Read aloud the text.

Activity

Point out the illustrations of the Christmas story.

- Hand out crayons or markers.
- Tell children that the drawings are out of order.
- Have children retell the story. As each element is retold, have children number the illustrations.
- Have children color the pictures.

Who Knew?

Mary and Joseph knew that Jesus was God's Son.

They knew that Jesus would help God's people.

Soon many people learned that Jesus was God's Son.

Activity

Number the pictures to tell the story of Jesus' birth. Then color the pictures.

72

 REACHING ALL LEARNERS

Sequencing Difficulties Some children may have trouble renumbering the Christmas story illustrations. The following process may assist them.

- Photocopy the page.
- Have children cut out the four illustrations.
- As you retell the story, have children pick up illustrations and line them up in order.
- Have children number the drawings.

OPTIONAL ACTIVITY

Cross-Curricular: Art Create classroom cards with children's artwork.

- Have children design cards for your church family and school family. Make cards for different occasions, such as praying for the sick, or a Baptism.

Multiple Intelligence: Visual/Spatial

Prayer of Praise

Leader: We love Jesus.

All: We love Jesus.

Leader: We want to be like him.

All: We want to be like him. Amen.

Sing together.

Praise to you, O Christ, Our Savior,
Word of the Father, calling us to life;
Son of God, who leads us to freedom:
Glory to you, Lord Jesus Christ.

Praise to You, O Christ, Our Savior

73

3 Celebrate

Objective: To pray a litany of praise

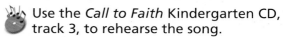 **Let Us Pray**

Tell children they will pray a Prayer of Praise.

Prayer of Praise

Prepare

Place a nativity set in the prayer space. Reserve the baby Jesus figure for the Gather activity.

• Teach children the responses.

Use the *Call to Faith* Kindergarten CD, track 3, to rehearse the song.

Gather

Have a child carrying the baby Jesus figure lead the group as they process into the prayer space.

Pray

• Prompt children to pray after you've read aloud the leader's part.

• In addition to the closing song, sing Christmas carols.

 LITURGY LINK

Litanies A litany is a prayer that contains invocations and responses. The leader prays the invocations, and the group prays the responses.

• Within the Mass, the *Lord Have Mercy* is patterned like a litany.

• The Litany of the Saints is prayed as part of the Easter Vigil service.

 LECTIONARY LINK

Break Open the Word Read last week's Sunday Gospel. Talk about how this reading helps us follow Jesus. For children's questions related to the weekly Gospel reading, visit our Web site.

 GO Visit www.harcourtreligion.com for weekly **ONLINE** scripture readings and seasonal resources.

Wrap-Up

Family Faith

Remind children to discuss the Family Faith page at home. Encourage them to talk with family members about Jesus' birth.

Family Project

• Encourage children to complete the activity with family members.

People of Faith

Tell children about Simeon.

• Simeon and an elderly woman, Anna, greeted baby Jesus when Mary and Joseph took him to the temple.

• Encourage them to pray the prayer at home with their families.

Visit **www.harcourtreligion.com** for weekly scripture readings and seasonal resources.

CHAPTER 7
Family Faith

Catholics Believe

Dear Family,
In Chapter 7, the children learned that Jesus is God's Son. God sent Jesus to help his people. Mary is Jesus' mother. Joseph watched over Jesus and Mary.

SCRIPTURE

Read Luke 2:1–7 together with your child.

GO ONLINE www.harcourtreligion.com
For weekly scripture readings and seasonal resources

Family Project

Acting Like Jesus Point out that Jesus helped Mary and Joseph at home. This week, pick out several jobs that your child can help you with. As you work, praise your child's efforts. Mention that your child is imitating Jesus by helping you.

People of Faith

Simeon was an old man at the time of Jesus' birth. He prayed every day for God to send someone to help God's people.

Holy Simeon, ▶
66 B.C.–3 A.D.

Family Prayer

God the Father, thank you for people like Simeon who give us a good example of prayer. Amen.

74 **CCC** *See Catechism of the Catholic Church 422, 723 for further reading on chapter content.*

? HOW DID I DO?

This week was

☐ *one of the best ever!*   ☐ *pretty good.*   ☐ *in need of improvement.*

In what discussions and activities were children most interested?

_____

What activity did I most enjoy teaching?

_____

In what area do I need to improve?

_____

Name _____ Date _____

Christmas Story Puppet Show

Directions: Color the finger puppets and the stable. Then cut them out. Use them to retell the story of Christmas.

Chapter 8

Overview

Faith Focus

■ Jesus taught us with both words and deeds. *(CCC 547)*

Catechism Connection

The *Catechism* emphasizes that everything Jesus did in his life was done to teach us about God the Father. *(CCC 561)*

NDC Link

Especially in his parables, Jesus used everyday human experiences to teach the faith. (See *NDC*, 28A2.)

Resources

📖 **BOOK**
Alphabet Soup for Christian Living. Coffey. Kathy. Twenty-Third Publications. Offers reflections on how to connect with Jesus.

💿 **DVD/VHS**
*Big Al Live: Gospel Values for Children, Vol 1.** Harcourt Religion Publishers. "Is Jesus Your Shepherd?" (4:34 min.). Explores the meaning of the Good Shepherd image.

*Available at www.harcourtreligion.com

GO ONLINE **Resources**
For interactive lesson planner, chapter resources, and activities
www.harcourtreligion.com

Jesus Teaches
CHAPTER BACKGROUND

 But whoever obeys and teaches these commandments will be called greatest in the kingdom of heaven.

Matthew 5:19

The Foot of the Master

As a teacher or catechist, you have multiple issues to deal with at any given class session. You must arrange the physical classroom, inform parents and administrators of special plans, make certain that materials are available, and, of course, teach. Sometimes it seems as though this last task, the most important one, is the one that gets lost in the shuffle.

When this seems to be the case, it may be time to look again at Jesus' life. He walked around. He talked to people. He taught people what they needed to know. As he taught, he used common examples: the birds of the air, the water needed by all living creatures, the love of a parent for a child. He used parables and psalms to make his points.

Simplify, Simplify

The lesson about teaching that we learn from Jesus is to simplify, to reduce our lesson to its most basic objective. Ask yourself: What do I want the children to learn from this lesson? Write a one-sentence answer to the question. Then find a story or a universal symbol that will help the children discover and apply your objective.

With Jesus as our model teacher, we will find ourselves discovering our children's needs and serving them with simple stories and universal symbols.

Reflect ***How can you best tell the story of Jesus to your group?***

Critical Thinking Skills

A pre-reading discussion will utilize the children's prior knowledge and focus greater attention to the upcoming text.

- Before reading a story, ask children to predict the outcome.

- Show children the cover and some of the pictures inside. Ask them what they think the story will be.

- After reading the story, ask children whose predictions were correct.

Action

- I like to do things. I care more about the doing and not so much about the end product.

- I learn best if things are open-ended and do not always have one right answer.

Vocational Seasons

In *The Courage to Teach*, Parker Palmer suggests that the teaching vocation consists of seasons. In some seasons we may be full of hope and new initiatives. At other times we may be "on low maintenance" and relaxed. Some people may be in a season of deep introspection even as others are experiencing a season of excitement or transitions.

The image of vocational seasons can be of great help in sustaining your spirit. If you are in a season that you don't enjoy, take consolation—the season will pass. Your catechetical vocation isn't over. On the other hand, if you are in a glorious vocational season, enjoy it to the full.

Reflect **Which vocational season are you in at this time: spring, summer, fall, or winter? Explain.**

 Prayer

Jesus, our Savior, you were the finest teacher in the history of the world. You used understandable stories and simple symbols to teach about truth and love. Help me model my teaching after yours so that the children in my care can know God better. Amen.

Weekly Planner

	Objectives	Materials	Prayer & Scripture
1 Invite **Jesus Teaches** Page 75	To learn about different kinds of teachers	☐ Copies of Activity Master 15, p. 75E ☐ Crayons or markers ☐ *Mrs. Spitzer's Garden*	🙏 **Let Us Pray:** Psalm 25:4
2 Explore **How to Live** Page 76	To reflect on what Jesus teaches		✝ **Scripture:** Luke 6:27–36 ✝ **Scripture Background:** Advice for Life
What to Do Page 77	To show that Jesus teaches everyone how to act	☐ Board or chart paper ☐ Pencils ☐ Copies of Activity Master 16, p. 80A ☐ Crayons or markers ☐ Scissors	✝ **Scripture:** Luke 6:27–36
About Jesus Page 78	To explain that the Bible tells stories about Jesus		✝ **Scripture:** Luke 6:27–36
3 Celebrate **Asking Prayer** Page 79	To ask Jesus' help to learn	☐ Music CD ☐ Bible or Lectionary	🙏 **Let Us Pray:** Asking Prayer 🎵 **Hymn:** Praise to You, O Christ, Our Savior

Activities | Enrichment

Let's Begin

Talk about teaching and learning.

(OPTIONAL) **Activity Master 15:**
Learn from Jesus, p. 75E

(OPTIONAL) Children's Literature
Multiple Intelligence: Verbal/Linguistic

? Share what we learn from Jesus.

(OPTIONAL) Show Learning
Multiple Intelligence: Bodily/Kinesthetic

Activity

Circle the words to find what Jesus teaches.

(OPTIONAL) **Activity Master 16:**
Make a Banner, p. 80A

- **Reaching All Learners:**
  Working with Letters

Activity

Guess what Jesus is doing in each picture.

- **Chapter Background:**
  God and Man

- **Quick Tip:**
  Picture Books/Wordless Books

- **Liturgy Link:**
  Processing

- **Lectionary Link:**
  Break Open the Word

Pacing the Chapter

Parish
Meets once a week

In parish religious education classes, plan for approximately 60 minutes of class time.

Invite	10 minutes
Explore	40 minutes
Celebrate	10 minutes

The abundance of activity and enrichment options will allow flexibility in planning for longer sessions if needed.

School
Meets 5 days per week

In school religious education classes, plan for lesson 5 days per week for about 30 minutes. The lesson can be easily adapted for a 4-day week as well.

Day 1: Invite	**Day 4:** Explore
Day 2: Explore	**Day 5:** Celebrate
Day 3: Explore	

The abundance of activity and enrichment options will allow flexibility in planning for longer sessions if needed.

CALL to FAITH
e connect

- Online planning tools include chapter background and planner, activity master, customizable test, and more.

- Enhancement activities for each step of the catechetical process, including alternative prayer experiences and blessings.

- Games, activities, interactive review, alternative assessment, and more for children.

www.calltofaitheconnect.com

Home Connection

Chapter 8 Family Faith, p. 80
Take-home activities, chapter content review, saint features and prayer

 For more family activities
www.harcourtreligion.com

Name _____ Date _____

Learn from Jesus

Directions: Draw a picture of yourself listening to Jesus.

Jesus Teaches

Teach me your paths.
Based on Psalm 25:4

Let's Begin

Many Teachers

You have many teachers in your life.

Teachers share things they know.

Teachers show you how to do things.

Teachers help you learn.

● When have you been like a teacher?

Responses will vary.

75

Objective: To learn about different kinds of teachers

Let Us Pray

Sing the psalm verse to a simple melody. Have children repeat the tune after you.

Let's Begin

Many Teachers

- Tell children about your favorite teacher. Explain why this teacher was special. Tell what you learned from this person.
- Discuss the picture.
- Discuss with children that not all teaching and learning takes place in a classroom.
- Explain that children can teach adults, too. If appropriate, tell what you have learned from members of the class.
- Ask children to name people who teach them.
- Discuss the text question.

OPTIONAL ACTIVITY

Activity Master 15: Learn from Jesus Distribute copies of the activity found on page 75E.
- Tell children they will be drawing a picture.
- Tell them to draw a picture of themselves listening to Jesus.

▲ Activity Master 15

OPTIONAL ACTIVITY

Children's Literature To help children reflect on teachers and teaching, consider reading *Mrs. Spitzer's Garden* by Edith Pattou (Harcourt, 2001). This story celebrates all that teachers do, year after year, to help children grow and blossom. The story complements the themes of this lesson.

Multiple Intelligence: Verbal/Linguistic

Objective: To reflect on what Jesus teaches

How to Live

Ask children to tell the kinds of things that Jesus teaches them. Possible responses: how to show love, that we should be good

Read aloud the first paragraph. Recall with children the discussion of their many teachers.

Jesus Said

Invite children to sit in a circle.

- Tell them to listen to what Jesus says about the Father.
- Proclaim the Gospel reading.
- Discuss the text question.
- Ask children to give an example of how to live Jesus' teachings. Possible responses: We are kind when we take turns; we can share toys.

Explore

How To Live

Many people teach you.
God sent Jesus to teach his people.
Jesus teaches us how to live.
These are some of the things he said.

Luke 6: 27–36

Read to Me

Jesus Said

Love everyone.
Be kind to everyone.
Share what you have.
Be like God the Father.

Based on Luke 6:27–36

? What does Jesus teach you to do? Possible response: to be kind and loving

---

✝ SCRIPTURE BACKGROUND

Advice for Life This scripture passage is contained in the Sermon on the Plain, Luke's counterpart to Matthew's Sermon on the Mount.

- This particular segment of the sermon centers on the love of neighbor.
- The idea of loving one's enemy that is described in verse 27 would have been radical in Jesus' time.

OPTIONAL ACTIVITY

Show Learning Invite children to show ways that others have taught them or ways that they have taught others.

- Have children work in groups of two or three to think of situations in which they have been learners or teachers.
- Have children prepare and act out these situations.

Multiple Intelligence: Bodily/Kinesthetic

What To Do

Jesus teaches you to be kind.
Jesus teaches you to love everyone.
Jesus teaches you that God the Father loves you.

Activity

✏ Circle the words that tell what Jesus teaches.

KIND, LOVE, GOD

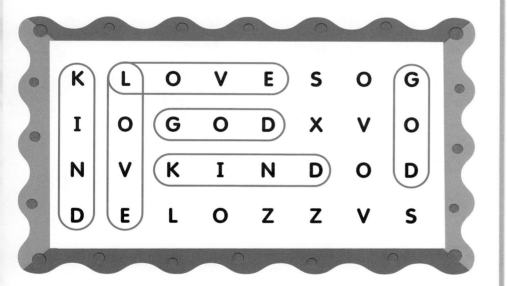

77

Objective: To show that Jesus teaches everyone how to act

What to Do

Remind children that Jesus teaches us what to do.

• Read aloud the text to children.

• Ask children why Jesus would teach us all of these things. Possible responses: He wants us to be happy; he wants everyone to get along.

Activity

• Read the activity directions to children.

• Write KIND, LOVE, and GOD on the board or on chart paper.

• Remind children that words are made of letters. Read aloud the words.

• Have children name the letters in each word.

• Ask children to find a K in the puzzle. Have children look at all of the letters close to the K to find an I. Continue until children have found the entire word.

• Do other words in a similar fashion.

OPTIONAL ACTIVITY

Activity Master 16: Make a Banner Distribute copies of the activity found on page 80A.

• Tell children they will be making a banner.

• Have them color it and cut it out. Tell them to put it somewhere they will see it often.

Make a Banner
Directions: Color the banner. Then cut it out.

Teach me your ways, O Lord. Psalm 25:4

▲ **Activity Master 16**

★ REACHING ALL LEARNERS

Working with Letters A set of magnetic plastic letters can help children work on this puzzle.

• Children who learn by touching will benefit by holding them.

• Visual learners will be helped by seeing the magnetic letters form words in different formations.

Explore

About Jesus

Tell children we learn about Jesus from the Bible, the Church's holy book.

- Point out that people loved to listen to Jesus' stories.
- Mention that we listen to Jesus' stories when we hear stories from the Bible.
- Ask children where they hear stories from the Bible. Possible responses: at home, at school, at church

Activity

- Have children describe what Jesus is doing in each of the pictures, then read aloud the captions.
- Invite children to act out the four pictures. Discuss how people would feel after Jesus fed them or cured them.

About Jesus

The Bible is the Church's holy book. It tells you about Jesus.

Activity

What is Jesus doing in each of these pictures?

- Jesus prayed.

- Jesus healed sick people.

- Jesus fed hungry people.

- Jesus told stories.

78

CHAPTER BACKGROUND

God and Man The pictures on this page reflect that Jesus is both God and man.

- Through miraculous distributions of food and curing the sick, Jesus demonstrated his divinity.
- Jesus reflected his human nature by participating in activities we can do, such as praying and telling stories.

QUICK TIP

Picture Books/ Wordless Books

- Ask a media specialist or librarian to recommend wordless books.
- Encourage children to tell the story using their own words.
- Arrange for children to tell their stories to other classes.

Asking Prayer

Leader: Jesus, teach us to love everyone.

All: **Jesus, teach us to love everyone.**

Leader: Teach us to be kind.

All: **Teach us to be kind. Amen.**

Sing together.

Praise to you, O Christ,
   Our Savior,
Word of the Father,
   calling us to life;
Son of God who
   leads us to freedom:
Glory to you,
   Lord Jesus Christ.

Praise to You, O Christ,
Our Savior

79

Objective: To ask Jesus' help to learn

Let Us Pray

Tell children they will ask Jesus to teach them.

Asking Prayer

Prepare

• Rehearse the responses with children. Point out that they are echoing the leader each time.

   Use the *Call to Faith* Kindergarten CD, track 3, to rehearse the song.

Gather

Invite children to process into the prayer space.

• Have the first child carry in a crucifix and place it on the prayer table.

Pray

• Read aloud the leader's part and prompt children to echo.

• Have children process back to their chairs after singing.

LITURGY LINK

Processing   Processions signal the beginning of community worship.

• Before Mass begins, the priest, deacon and altar servers walk solemnly to the sanctuary.

• Help children model this behavior as they walk quietly to the prayer space. Having a class member carry in the crucifix is a sign that worship is about to begin.

LECTIONARY LINK

Break Open the Word   Read last week's Sunday Gospel. Talk about how this reading helps us follow Jesus. For children's questions related to the weekly Gospel reading, visit our Web site.

GO ONLINE **Visit www.harcourtreligion.com for weekly scripture readings and seasonal resources.**

Wrap-Up

Family Faith

Remind children to discuss the Family Faith page at home. Encourage them to talk with family members about what they have learned about Jesus' teachings.

Family Project

• Remind children that they can be teachers, too.
• Encourage children to teach a skill to someone.

People of Faith

Remind children that Simeon was an old man who prayed in the temple every day.

• *Luke 2:25–26* tells us that God had promised Simeon that he would live to see the Messiah.
• Encourage children to pray the prayer at home with their families.

  Visit **www.harcourtreligion.com** for weekly scripture readings and seasonal resources.

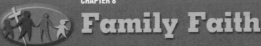

CHAPTER 8
Family Faith

 Catholics Believe

Dear Family,
In Chapter 8, the children learned that Jesus is a great teacher. He teaches all of us to love and to be kind. Most of all, Jesus teaches us to be like God the Father.

 SCRIPTURE

Read Luke 6:27–36 together with your child.

GO ONLINE www.harcourtreligion.com
For weekly scripture readings and seasonal resources

Family Project

Be a Teacher Like Jesus Set up a pla... date with a younger child. Invite your ch... to teach this younger friend a game or a... new skill. Work with the children to assu... that all goes well. Praise both children f... their success in working together.

People of Faith

Mary and Joseph took baby Jesus to the Temple. Simeon recognized that Jesus was sent by God.

Holy Simeon, ▶
ca. 66 B.C.–3 A.D.

Family Prayer

Loving God, help us be like Simeon. Help us recognize Jesus. Keep us in his love. Amen.

80 **CCC** *See Catechism of the Catholic Church 561 for further reading on chapter content.*

? HOW DID I DO?

This week was

☐ *one of the best ever!* ☐ *pretty good.* ☐ *in need of improvement.*

In what discussions and activities were children most interested?

_____

What activity did I most enjoy teaching?

_____

In what area do I need to improve?

_____

Name _____ Date _____

Make a Banner

Directions: Color the banner. Then cut it out.

Teach me your ways, O Lord. Psalm 25:4

You Follow Jesus

CHAPTER BACKGROUND

- Jesus' life is a mystery that teaches us about our own redemption. *(CCC 517)*

Catechism Connection

The *Catechism* tells us that Jesus asks us to follow him in actions, prayer, and acceptance of God's will. *(CCC 519–520)*

NDC Link

The *Directory* notes that in calling his disciples, Jesus invited them to follow his way of life and abandon themselves to God. (See *NDC*, 29B.)

Resources

BOOKS
Pray and Play Bible 2.* Group Publishing. "Jesus Is with Us." Reinforces the story of Jesus' life with activities and prayers.

Pastoral Leader's Source Book.* Chamberlain, Joseph. Harcourt Religion Publishers. "Collaboration on Behalf of the Mission of Jesus Christ." Provides a model for cooperative education within a parish.

*Available at www.harcourtreligion.com

 Resources
For interactive lesson planner, chapter resources, and activities
www.harcourtreligion.com

 Jesus spoke to them again, saying, "I am the light of the world. Whoever follows me will not walk in darkness, but will have the light of life."

John 8:12

We Are Called to Follow

"Follow me!" The phrase has a familiar meaning. We hear it in a store, on a playground, or at work. The words imply knowledge or a skill on the part of the speaker. They also indicate that the speaker is willing to share, to bring us up to his or her level.

The phrase has a special meaning when we hear it from Jesus. It means that he will introduce us to the mysteries of his life, Incarnation, teachings, Passion and death, Resurrection, and Ascension. It means that he will teach us about the Father and the Holy Spirit. It means he wants us to share in his eternal life.

We Respond as Humans

We are drawn to this divine offer, and we try to follow Jesus with love. However, sometimes our sinful nature relegates us to the shadows instead of leading us into the "light of life." We fail to love. We fail to obey. We fail to nurture the divine spark within ourselves and within the people we love.

Because he is human, Jesus understands us and our shortcomings. With the Father, he is willing to forgive us. With the Holy Spirit, he is willing to inspire us to change our lives, to try again to follow him.

So, Jesus' offer is always open. He will always draw us to him and to his companions in the Trinity. We only need to humbly admit our sins and try to do better.

Reflect How do you respond to Jesus' invitation?

TIPS FOR TEACHING KINDERGARTNERS

Leading

Leading and following are ways of the world. God is thankful when we lead in positive ways.

- Allow children to determine examples of leading in a positive way. Help children understand that though they are small, they can serve as positive leaders in big ways.

- Ask children to name people who lead others. Encourage them to consider all levels of leadership including in play and in school.

KINDERGARTNERS SAY

Routine

- I don't tell time yet. I need to be prompted before transitioning between activities.

- I like to help. Use a job chart so that I can contribute to the classroom.

- I learn through play. Provide time for meaningful experiences.

SUSTAINING YOUR SPIRIT

Living with Complexity

Most of us require clarity and consistency from the people around us. However, those who are comfortable with paradox, ambiguity, and complexity are better equipped to sustain the spirit to teach.

None of us should compromise our deepest principles of integrity. To do so would put our vocational spirit at risk. We can work at holding the contradictions in balance and living with the complexity of human imperfection. This will help us sustain the spirit to teach.

Reflect **How would you rate your ability to live with complexity and hold the contradictions in balance?**

Prayer

Jesus, Son of God, I am drawn to your teachings, and I want to follow you. Help me to overcome the barriers that keep me from being a good disciple. As I follow you, let me lead the children in my care to you as well. Amen.

Weekly Planner

		Objectives	Materials	Prayer & Scripture
1 Invite	**You Follow Jesus** Page 81	To demonstrate how people lead one another	☐ Copies of Activity Master 17, p. 81E ☐ Pencils ☐ Crayons or markers ☐ Scissors	🙏 **Let Us Pray:** Psalm 16:11
2 Explore	**Jesus the Leader** Page 82	To understand that Jesus leads us	☐ Crayons or markers	
	Following Jesus Page 83	To learn that Jesus wants everyone to follow him		✝ **Scripture:** Mark 1: 16–19 ✝ **Scripture Background:** Calling the Apostles
	Jesus' Followers Page 84	To realize that followers of Jesus are called Christians	☐ Crayons or markers ☐ Copies of Activity Master 18, p. 86A ☐ Construction paper ☐ Empty pizza boxes ☐ Paint ☐ Marbles and golf ball	✝ **Scripture:** Mark 1: 16–19
3 Celebrate	**Prayer for Help** Page 85	To meditate on following Jesus	☐ Music CD ☐ Bible or Lectionary	🙏 **Let Us Pray:** Prayer for Help 🎵 **Hymn:** Praise to You, O Christ, Our Savior

Activities	Enrichment

Let's Begin

Play "Follow the Leader."

OPTIONAL **Activity Master 17:**
Make Footprints, p. 81E

• **Reaching All Learners:**
Add a Song

Activity

Draw a line from Jesus to the people who follow him.

OPTIONAL Leaders
Multiple Intelligence: Interpersonal

• **Justice and Peace:**
Unity

❓ Discuss why Peter and Andrew followed Jesus.

• **Cultural Awareness:**
Jobs and Work

Activity

Help the Apostles find Jesus.

OPTIONAL **Activity Master 18:**
Follow Jesus, p. 86A

OPTIONAL Cross-Curricular: Art
Multiple Intelligence: Visual/Spatial

• **Liturgy Link:**
Candles

• **Lectionary Link:**
Break Open the Word

Pacing the Chapter

Parish

Meets once a week

In parish religious education classes, plan for approximately 60 minutes of class time.

Invite	10 minutes
Explore	40 minutes
Celebrate	10 minutes

The abundance of activity and enrichment options will allow flexibility in planning for longer sessions if needed.

School

Meets 5 days per week

In school religious education classes, plan for lesson 5 days per week for about 30 minutes. The lesson can be easily adapted for a 4-day week as well.

Day 1: Invite   **Day 4:** Explore
Day 2: Explore   **Day 5:** Celebrate
Day 3: Explore

The abundance of activity and enrichment options will allow flexibility in planning for longer sessions if needed.

• Online planning tools include chapter background and planner, activity master, customizable test, and more.

• Enhancement activities for each step of the catechetical process, including alternative prayer experiences and blessings.

• Games, activities, interactive review, alternative assessment, and more for children.

www.calltofaitheconnect.com

Home Connection

Chapter 9 Family Faith, p. 86
Take-home activities, chapter content review, saint features and prayer

For more family activities
www.harcourtreligion.com

Name _____ Date _____

Make Footprints

Directions: Trace the letter on each footprint. Then color the footprints. Cut out the footprints and use them as decorations at school or at home.

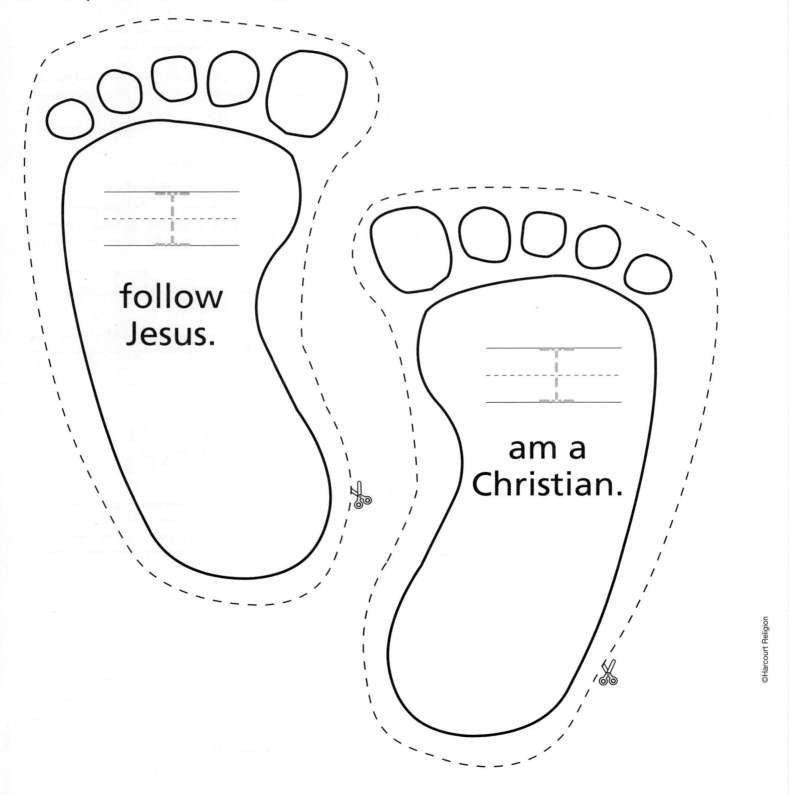

follow Jesus.

am a Christian.

©Harcourt Religion

Chapter 9
You Follow Jesus

You will show me the path to life.

Based on Psalm 16:11

Let's Begin

Follow the Leader

It was playtime.

Mrs. Harper taught the children a game.

One child was the leader.

Everyone followed what the leader did.

Play this game with your class.

● What were some things your class leader did?
Responses will vary.

81

Objective: To demonstrate how people lead one another

Let Us Pray

Brainstorm gestures that demonstrate the psalm. Read aloud the psalm verse. Have children use the gestures as you read aloud the verse.

Let's Begin

Follow the Leader

• Point out the photograph of the children. Ask children to guess what the story will be about.

• Read the text. Praise children who guessed correctly.

• Invite children to play Follow the Leader as a class.

• Demonstrate how to play the game.

• Give every child who wishes to lead the opportunity to do so.

• Have children talk about their experiences.

• Discuss the question.

OPTIONAL ACTIVITY

Activity Master 17: Make Footprints Distribute copies of the activity found on page 81E.

• Tell children they will be making footprints as a reminder to follow Jesus.

• Ask them to trace the letter on each footprint and color them.

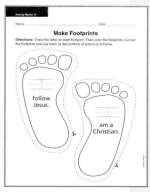

Activity Master 17
Make Footprints
Directions: Trace the letter on each footprint. Then color the footprints. Cut out the footprints and use them as decorations at school or at home.

follow Jesus.

am a Christian.

▲ **Activity Master 17**

REACHING ALL LEARNERS

Add a Song Children who learn through singing may enjoy adding this song to the game. To the tune of "This Is the Way We Wash Our Clothes," sing:

This is the way we follow the leader,
follow the leader, follow the leader.
This is the way we follow the leader
as we play our game.

Objective: To understand that Jesus leads us

Jesus the Leader

Ask children how Jesus leads them. Possible responses: by loving us, by showing us what to do, by telling stories

Read aloud the text to children.

- Pause after each sentence to ask children for examples of how they can be kind, obey, or pray.

- Emphasize the last sentence. Ask children to say how they are followers of Jesus. Possible responses: by praying during Mass, by obeying parents and teachers

Activity

- Hand out crayons or markers.
- Have children tell what is happening in each picture.
- Discuss how the scene shows someone following Jesus.
- When children agree that a picture shows people who are following Jesus, have them draw a line from the scene to Jesus.

Explore

Jesus the Leader

Jesus leads you to be kind.
He leads you to obey.
He leads you to pray.
You are a follower of Jesus.

Activity

 Draw a line from Jesus to the people who are following him.

82

✝ JUSTICE AND PEACE

Unity As followers of Jesus, we are united in solidarity with other Christians.

- This means that we must move from selfishness to concern for the common good. (See *On Social Concern,* Donders, #38.)
- Begin instilling this sense in children by encouraging service projects such as food and clothing drives.

Catholic Social Teaching: Solidarity

OPTIONAL ACTIVITY

Leaders Discuss leadership as a class.

- Elicit from children the qualities of a good leader. Possibilities include: smart, understanding, polite, thoughtful.
- Point out that while leaders may tell us what to do, each of us is responsible for his or her own actions.

Multiple Intelligence: Interpersonal

Following Jesus

The Bible tells many stories about Jesus and his followers.

Mark 1:16–19

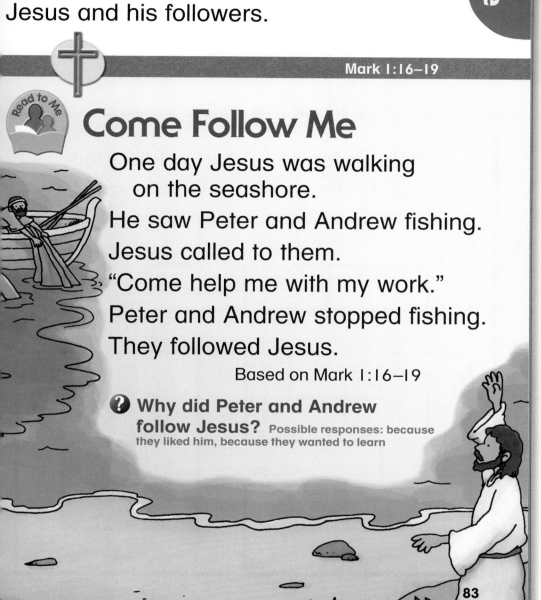

Come Follow Me

One day Jesus was walking on the seashore.
He saw Peter and Andrew fishing.
Jesus called to them.
"Come help me with my work."
Peter and Andrew stopped fishing.
They followed Jesus.

Based on Mark 1:16–19

❓ Why did Peter and Andrew follow Jesus? Possible responses: because they liked him, because they wanted to learn

83

Objective: To learn that Jesus wants everyone to follow him

Following Jesus

Remind children that Jesus leads us.

- Tell children that you will read a story about how Jesus met his followers.

Come Follow Me

- Proclaim the Gospel reading.
- Assign the roles of Jesus, Peter, and Andrew. Read the story again and have children act out the parts.
- Encourage children who are watching the play to stand up and follow Jesus in a parade around the room.
- Discuss the question in the text.

✚ SCRIPTURE BACKGROUND

Calling the Apostles This passage from Mark depicts Jesus calling his first followers. The quick and enthusiastic response that Jesus receives tells us that he was a compelling figure.

- It also shows that the Apostles were willing to leave everything to follow him.
- The story shows that becoming a disciple could cost Jesus' followers both family love and material security.

🌎 CULTURAL AWARENESS

Jobs and Work Children may think of fishing as a hobby. In many parts of the world it is an occupation.

- Tell children that fishing supplies food for much of the world. Suggest that they look at the variety of fish available during their next visit to a grocery store.
- Fishing is a major occupation in coastal areas. Have children look at a globe and find such areas.

Explore

Objective: To realize that followers of Jesus are called Christians

Jesus' Followers

Remind children that we are all followers of Jesus.

- Read aloud the text.
- Ask children why we are followers of Jesus. Possible responses: We want to be like Jesus; he calls to us; we want to be close to God.
- Point out that Jesus has many followers all over the world.
- Explain that Jesus' followers are called Christians because Christ is another name for Jesus.

Activity

- Direct children's attention to the maze.
- Point out that Peter and Andrew are at the start of the maze. Have children find Jesus at the end of the maze.
- Hand out crayons or markers, and have children draw the path in.

Jesus' Followers

Jesus has many followers.
Jesus' followers are called Christians.
You are a Christian.

Activity

Help Peter and Andrew find their way to Jesus.

84

Activity Master 18: Follow Jesus Distribute copies of the activity found on page 86A.

- Tell children they will be drawing a picture.
- Have them draw themselves following Jesus.

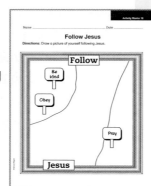

▲ **Activity Master 18**

Cross-Curricular: Art Invite children to make a design.

- Place a round sheet of paper in an empty pizza box.
- Squirt in drops of paint, add marbles and a golf ball. Have children gently shake the box to make a design.

Multiple Intelligence: Visual/Spatial

Prayer for Help

Leader: Jesus, thank you for being
our leader.
Help us be like Andrew and Peter.
Help us hear you calling.
Help us follow you and learn
from you.
Help us be good Christians.

All: Amen.

Sing together.

Praise to you, O Christ,
Our Savior,
Word of the Father,
calling us to life;
Son of God who leads
us to freedom:
Glory to you,
Lord Jesus Christ.

Praise to You, O Christ,
Our Savior

85

Objective: To meditate on following Jesus

Let Us Pray

Tell children they will ask Jesus for help following him.

Prayer for Help

Prepare

• Explain to children they will sit quietly as you lead the prayer.

Use the *Call to Faith* Kindergarten CD, track 3, to rehearse the song.

Gather

Invite children to sit quietly in the prayer space.

Pray

• Read aloud the prayer. Then read it aloud again, and have children repeat each line after you.

• Conclude with the song.

LITURGY LINK

Candles Catholic worship often includes candles. In addition to their beautiful glow, they symbolize Christ as the light of the world.

• The baptismal ritual includes lighting a candle that symbolizes the flame of faith.

• The Paschal candle is lit during the Easter vigil and symbolizes the Resurrection. It is lit at all masses until Pentecost.

LECTIONARY LINK

Break Open the Word Read last week's Sunday Gospel. Talk about how this reading helps us follow Jesus. For children's questions related to the weekly Gospel reading, visit our Web site.

GO ONLINE **Visit www.harcourtreligion.com for weekly scripture readings and seasonal resources.**

Wrap-Up

Family Faith

Remind children to discuss the Family Faith page at home. Encourage them to talk with family members about what they have learned about Jesus as our leader.

Family Project

- Encourage children to do the activity with family members.

People of Faith

Remind children that Simeon met Mary and Joseph in the temple when they took baby Jesus there.

- Simeon's beautiful prayer of thanksgiving is prayed daily as part of the Church's night prayer.
- Encourage children to pray the prayer at home with their families.

  Visit **www.harcourtreligion.com** for weekly scripture readings and seasonal resources.

 CHAPTER 9

Family Faith

Catholics Believe

Dear Family,
In Chapter 9, the children learned that Jesus asks us to follow him. The children heard the story of Jesus calling Peter and Andrew. They learned that followers of Jesus are called Christians.

✝ SCRIPTURE

Read Mark 1:16–19 together with your child.

GO ONLINE www.harcourtreligion.com For weekly scripture readings and seasonal resources

Family Project

Follow the Leader Take turns being leaders and followers. Choose several different activities, such as chores, recreational pastimes, and prayer. Talk with your child about the responsibilities of being a leader. During a family prayer time, pray for the leaders of the parish, community, and country.

People of Faith

Simeon knew Jesus would be a great teacher. Simeon praised God and thanked him for Jesus.

Holy Simeon, ▶
ca. 66 B.C.–3 A.D.

🙌 Family Prayer

Gracious God,
we praise you.
We thank you for
sending Jesus to
lead us. Amen.

86 **CCC** *See Catechism of the Catholic Church 422, 723 for further reading on chapter content.*

❓ HOW DID I DO?

This week was

☐ *one of the best ever!*   ☐ *pretty good.*   ☐ *in need of improvement.*

In what discussions and activities were children most interested?

_____

What activity did I most enjoy teaching?

_____

In what area do I need to improve?

_____

Name _____ Date _____

Follow Jesus

Directions: Draw a picture of yourself following Jesus.

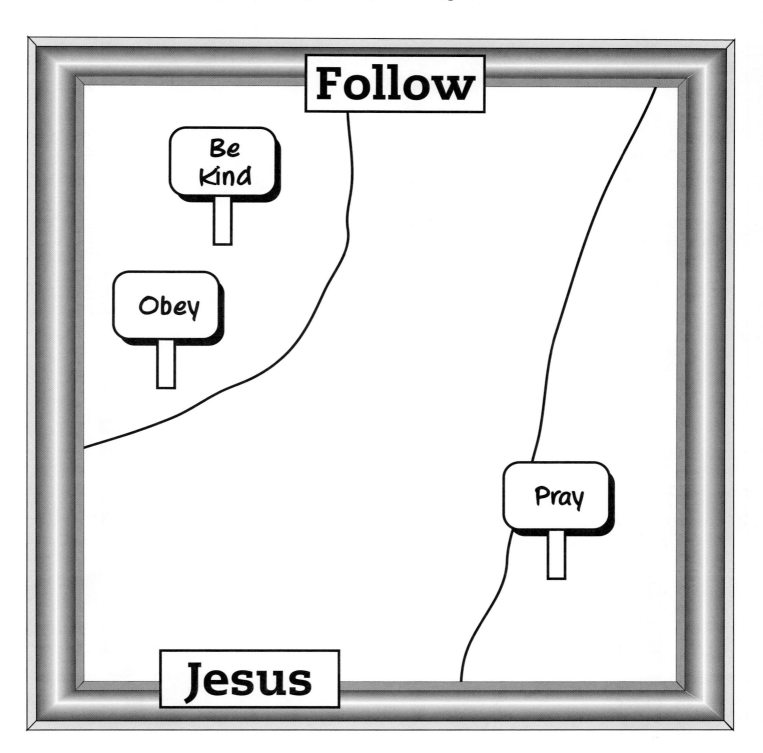

Scripture Story
The Good Neighbor

(Luke 10:25–37)

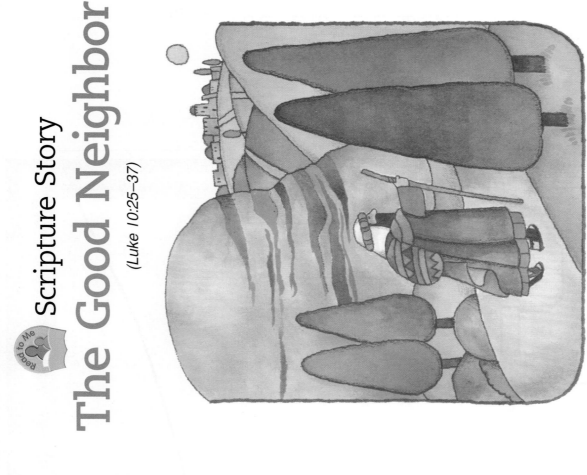

Family Note: In class your child has learned that Jesus taught us to love each other. Read this Scripture Story together. It is the story of the Good Samaritan, a man who loved his neighbor. Ask your child to tell you what the Good Samaritan did.

Jesus said, "Be like the good man. Love your neighbor." Color the heart.

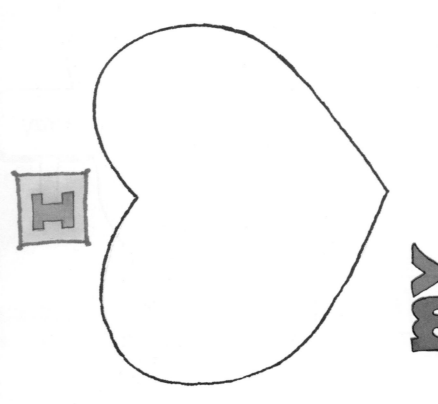

I

my neighbor.

8

87

Long ago, a man asked Jesus,
"How can I be a good neighbor?"

2

Finally, a third man came by.
He stopped and helped.
He was a good man.

7

88

Then, a second man walked by.

He did not stop to help either.

Jesus answered him by telling a story.

Once upon a time, a man was traveling to town.

3

6

89

All of a sudden, some men robbed the man and beat him up! The man was hurt and needed help.

4

A little while later, a man walked by. He did not stop to help.

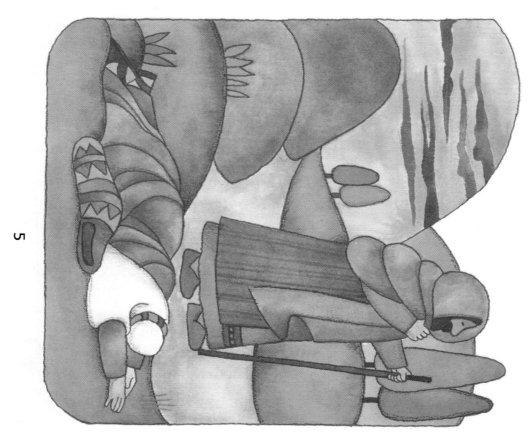

5

90

Overview

Faith Focus

■ The people of God share in Christ's work by being his witnesses in the world. (CCC 785)

Catechism Connection

The *Catechism* explains that we became members of the Church through faith and Baptism. The Church calls all people to become one in the Spirit. (CCC 781–782)

NDC Link

The *Directory* reminds us that education in faith is a lifelong, communal process for all members of the Church. (See *NDC*, 19E.)

Resources

BOOK
Compendium of the Catechism of the Catholic Church. Ratzinger, Joseph. USCCB. Summarizes the content of the *Catechism of the Catholic Church.*

DVD/VHS
Sunday Morning * (19 min.). Oblate Media. Encourages children to learn about worship.

*Available at www.harcourtreligion.com

GO ONLINE **Resources**
For interactive lesson planner, chapter resources, and activities
www.harcourtreligion.com

The Church
CHAPTER BACKGROUND

 But you are "a chosen race, a royal priesthood, a holy nation, a people of his own, so that you may announce the praises" of him who called you out of darkness into his wonderful light.

1 Peter 2:9

We Are the Church

The Church is wonderfully large, spreading well beyond our earthly world. Its membership consists of the living and the dead; we are all joined in the communion of saints. What this means is that we share a bond with others who are marked with the sign of faith. We have all been reborn in belief and in Baptism. We all follow Jesus, and the Holy Spirit assists us in our task of sharing God the Father's word.

The law that members of the Church are enjoined to keep is Jesus' instruction to love others as he loved us. Through thoughts, words, and deeds, we minister to others and give witness to our faith in Jesus. Church members shine Christ's light into the darkest corners of the world, helping those who cannot help themselves. By supporting missions all over the world through prayer and other contributions, we are part of their work.

Unity and Witness

The Church is wonderfully small, too. Even if there are only two or three gathered to pray or do good works, the Church is there. When you assemble your kindergarten group to pray or rejoice, you are a model of the entire Church.

As you teach about the Church, help children know that they share in the tradition and heritage of a wonderful organization. Tell the age-old stories that will show them how Jesus loved us, how his Apostles followed him, and how the early Church flourished. Make them enthusiastic bearers of the word to their friends and families. Help them become priestly people.

Reflect   *How do you announce God's praises?*

TIPS FOR TEACHING KINDERGARTNERS

Spatial skills

Spatial skills are helpful stepping stones for developing skills in mathematics.

- Take children on a walk from the classroom to the church.

- Ask them to draw a map of how to get from the classroom to the church.

- Help children that have difficulty drawing the map or understanding spatial order.

- Ask children to share their maps with a partner.

KINDERGARTNERS SAY

Classroom Ownership

- I like to do "grown-up" chores, such as watering the plants or sweeping up with kid-size brooms.

- I will clean. Teach me how our room is organized. Label shelves with pictures.

- I care for animals. If possible, have a class pet.

SUSTAINING YOUR SPIRIT

Motivations

Many things probably motivated you to enter into the catechetical ministry. At the center of all ministry is a call from God to love and serve him and his Church. The love for Christ and others drives and motivates you to share the good news and work for the kingdom. Take time to think about what else motivated you to become a catechist. The process of naming and claiming the authentic motivations behind your commitment as a catechist can deepen your understanding of your role. Even motivations that may not seem ideal are important to examine.

Reflect **What motivations fuel your spirit to teach?**

 Prayer

Lord God, thank you for creating our Church family. As I teach the children in my care, help me follow you and lead others in making our world a better place. Amen.

Weekly Planner

		Objectives	Materials	Prayer & Scripture
1 Invite	**The Church** Page 91	To understand that people make up the Church	☐ Crucifix ☐ Copies of Activity Master 19, p. 91E ☐ Pencils ☐ Crayons or markers	🪹 **Let Us Pray:** Psalm 27:4
2 Explore	**Church Family** Page 92	To understand how Church family members should act	☐ Paper ☐ Crayons or markers ☐ Pencils	✞ **Scripture:** Colossians 3:15–17 ✞ **Scripture Background:** Acting Together
	All Are Welcome Page 93	To learn that many different people belong to the Church	☐ Crayons or markers ☐ Copies of Activity Master 20, p. 96A ☐ Pencils ☐ Scissors	✞ **Scripture:** Colossians 3:15–17
	The Church Follows Jesus Page 94	To learn ways to follow Jesus as a Church family	☐ *Apple Pie Fourth of July*	✞ **Scripture:** Colossians 3:15–17
3 Celebrate	**Prayer for Others** Page 95	To pray an echo prayer of thanks for the Church family	☐ Music CD ☐ Bible or Lectionary	🪹 **Let Us Pray:** Prayer for Others 🎵 **Hymn:** We Are the Church

Activities	Enrichment

Let's Begin

Perform a finger play.

(OPTIONAL) **Activity Master 19:
Make a Sign, p. 91E**

• **Reaching All Learners:**
Adapting Gestures

❓ Discuss what things Church members do.

(OPTIONAL) Make New Friends
Multiple Intelligence: Interpersonal

Activity

Draw the people you see at Church.

(OPTIONAL) **Activity Master 20:
Fill in the Certificate, p. 96A**

(OPTIONAL) Your Parish
Multiple Intelligence: Visual/Spatial

Activity

Tell how Church members are following Jesus.

(OPTIONAL) Children's Literature
Multiple Intelligence: Verbal/Linguistic

• **Quick Tip:**
Young Helpers

• **Liturgy Link:**
Gestures of Unity

• **Lectionary Link:**
Break Open the Word

Pacing the Chapter

Parish
Meets once a week

In parish religious education classes, plan for approximately 60 minutes of class time.

Invite	10 minutes
Explore	40 minutes
Celebrate	10 minutes

The abundance of activity and enrichment options will allow flexibility in planning for longer sessions if needed.

School
Meets 5 days per week

In school religious education classes, plan for lesson 5 days per week for about 30 minutes. The lesson can be easily adapted for a 4-day week as well.

Day 1: Invite	**Day 4:** Explore
Day 2: Explore	**Day 5:** Celebrate
Day 3: Explore	

The abundance of activity and enrichment options will allow flexibility in planning for longer sessions if needed.

• Online planning tools include chapter background and planner, activity master, customizable test, and more.

• Enhancement activities for each step of the catechetical process, including alternative prayer experiences and blessings.

• Games, activities, interactive review, alternative assessment, and more for children.

www.calltofaitheconnect.com

Home Connection

Chapter 10 Family Faith, p. 96
Take-home activities, chapter content review, saint features and prayer

 For more family activities
www.harcourtreligion.com

Name _____ Date _____

Make a Sign

Directions: Trace the letters on the sign. Then color the sign.

The Church

I want to pray in the Lord's house all the days of my life.

Based on Psalm 27:4

Read to Me

Let's Begin

The Church

Here is the church.
Here is the steeple.
Open the doors,
And see all the people.

● **Name some people you see in your Church.**

Possible responses: friends, relatives, teachers

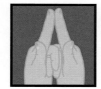 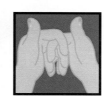

91

1 Invite

Objective: To understand that people make up the Church

Let Us Pray

Invite children to gather in the prayer space and make the Sign of the Cross. In the prayer space, have a crucifix and a Bible opened to the psalm verse.

Brainstorm movements to accompany the psalm verse. Read aloud the psalm verse. Have children do the movements as they repeat the verse.

Let's Begin

The Church

- Show children the pictures, and explain that they go with the poem.
- Some children may know the finger play already; have them help classmates learn it.
- Teach children the finger play. If necessary, explain the term *steeple*.
- Teach children the rhyme and have them practice the rhyme and gestures together.
- Discuss the text question.

OPTIONAL ACTIVITY

Activity Master 19: Make a Sign Distribute copies of the activity found on page 91E.

- Tell children they will be making a sign.
- Ask them to trace the letters and then color the sign in. They can share the sign with their family.

▲ Activity Master 19

★ REACHING ALL LEARNERS

Adapting Gestures If your group has children with fine-motor difficulties, consider adapting the rhyme to use large muscles.

- Church: fingertips together at forehead height and elbows apart at shoulder level
- Steeple: elbows brought together
- Doors: arms open wide
- People: smile and wave

The Church 91

2 Explore

Objective: To understand how Church family members should act

Church Family

Ask children what they think the Church family does. Possible responses: pray together, love God together

Read aloud the text.

- Point out that the people who belong to the parish and Catholics all over the world are your Church family.

How We Live

Proclaim the Scripture.

- Discuss the text question.
- Divide children into three groups.
- Have each group make up gestures to accompany one line in the Scripture.
- As you reread the story, have each group act out its line.

Church Family

The people in the Church are like a family.

Each Sunday your Church family prays together.

Colossians 3:15–17

How We Live

Church family members should love each other.
You should pray and sing to God.
You should thank God.

Based on Colossians 3:15–17

? **What things do you do with your Church family?**

Possible responses: pray, care for parish grounds

92

 ## SCRIPTURE BACKGROUND

Acting Together Biblical scholars believe that Saint Paul wrote this letter when he was imprisoned.

- This passage is part of a longer section in which Paul writes of how Christians should behave.
- Paul emphasizes the love and forgiveness that we have received from Jesus.
- He encourages us to act toward others in the same loving and forgiving way.

OPTIONAL ACTIVITY

Make New Friends If your parish has a sister parish, find out where it is. If not, find out about a parish in another country. Discuss the location of the parish and what life is like for the children.

- Have children draw and label pictures that tell about themselves to send to the other parish.
- As a class, write a letter to the children of the parish and ask them to be pen pals with your class.

Multiple Intelligence: Interpersonal

All Are Welcome

People of different ages are part of the Church.

People of different colors are part of the Church, too.

Everyone is welcome in the Church.

Activity

Draw your Church family.

93

Objective: To learn that many different people belong to the Church

All Are Welcome

Remind children of the variety of people who belong to your parish.

• Read aloud the text.

• Ask children to name some of their Church family friends.

• Ask children to explain why everyone is welcome in the Church family. Possible responses: because we are all God's children, because we want everyone to know about God

• Emphasize that God's love welcomes everyone into the Church.

Activity

• Ask children to describe the outline drawing.

• Hand out crayons or markers.

• Have children draw themselves and their church family.

• Ask children to explain their drawings to the group.

Activity Master 20: Fill in the Certificate Distribute copies of the activity found on page 96A.

• Ask children to write their name and the name of the parish on the correct lines.

• Have them color the certificate, cut it out, and put it in a place where it will be seen often.

▲ **Activity Master 20**

Your Parish Research how your parish was named and its history.

• Get photographs to show children changes over time in the grounds and buildings.

• If your parish has a long history, invite an elderly parishioner to tell what he or she remembers from the early days of the parish.

Multiple Intelligence: Visual/Spatial

The Church 93

Objective: To learn ways to follow Jesus as a Church family

The Church Follows Jesus

Remind children that they belong to the Church family.

- Read aloud the text.
- Ask how the Church family follows Jesus. Possible responses: by praying, by doing what Jesus taught us
- Read aloud articles about service projects from your parish bulletin or your diocesan newspaper. Have children explain how these projects show the people following Jesus.

Activity

- Call children's attention to the pictures on the page.
- Ask children to tell how each picture shows the Church following Jesus.
- Have children make up and act out short skits based on the pictures.

The Church Follows Jesus

Every day, the Church family follows Jesus.

The Church family does what Jesus said to do.

The Church family shows God's love for everyone.

Activity

Tell how each picture shows the Church family following Jesus.

94

OPTIONAL ACTIVITY

Children's Literature Read *Apple Pie Fourth of July* by Janet S. Wong (Harcourt, 2002) to children. This story is about a Chinese-American girl who learns important lessons about community and acceptance.

Multiple Intelligence: Verbal/Linguistic

QUICK TIP

Young Helpers Children may feel that they are too young to be effective members of the Church.

- Reinforce that even small actions can show that they are following Jesus.
- Give examples of parish projects that are the result of many people's efforts.

Prayer for Others

Celebrate

Leader: Loving God, thank you for the people in our Church family.

All: **Thank you for the people in our Church family.**

Leader: They help us follow Jesus.

All: **They help us follow Jesus.**

Leader: They help us show your love.

All: **They help us show your love. Amen.**

Sing together.

I am the Church!
   You are the Church!
We are the Church
   together.
All who follow Jesus,
   all around the world!
Yes, we're the Church
   together.

We Are the Church

95

Objective: To pray an echo prayer of thanks for the Church family

Let Us Pray

Tell children they will thank God for people who help them.

Prayer for Others

Prepare

Prepare the prayer space.

- Tell children that they will be repeating what you say.
- Use the *Call to Faith* Kindergarten CD, track 4, to rehearse the song.

Gather

Invite children to the prayer space.

- Arrange children in a circle.
- Have children hold hands after making the Sign of the Cross.

Pray

- After you pray each prayer aloud, prompt children's response.
- Invite children to raise their clasped hands as they pray "Amen."
- Sing together the song.

LITURGY LINK

Gestures of Unity In many parishes, members of the assembly hold hands during the Lord's Prayer.

- During the final few lines, the clasped hands are sometimes raised to shoulder level.
- These gestures symbolize the unity of the Christian community and the offering of our prayers to God.

LECTIONARY LINK

Break Open the Word Read last week's Sunday Gospel. Talk about how this reading helps us follow Jesus. For children's questions related to the weekly Gospel reading, visit our Web site.

GO ONLINE Visit www.harcourtreligion.com for weekly scripture readings and seasonal resources.

Wrap-Up

Family Faith

Remind children to discuss the Family Faith page at home. Encourage them to talk with family members about what they have learned about the Church family.

Family Project

- Encourage children to do the activity with family members.

People of Faith

Tell children about Saint Philip.

- Saint Philip was one of Jesus' first Apostles; he was called by Jesus after Peter and John were called.
- Encourage them to pray the prayer at home with their families.

Visit **www.harcourtreligion.com** for weekly scripture readings and seasonal resources.

 CHAPTER 10
Family Faith

 ## Catholics Believe

Dear Family,
In Chapter 10, the children learned that they belong to a Church family. The Church family is made up of people of all races and ages. The Church family meets to pray and sing to God. The Church family follows Jesus.

 ## SCRIPTURE

Read Colossians 3:15–17 together with your child.

www.harcourtreligion.com
For weekly scripture readings and seasonal resources

Family Project

The Church Family Participate as a family in a parish activity, such as a dinner, group outing, or community service project. By doing so, you show that you are part of a bigger family—the Church family. After the event, talk with your child about the Church members you met and how they worked together and enjoyed each other's company.

People of Faith

Saint Philip was a special follower of Jesus. He was one of Jesus' first followers.

Saint Philip, first century ▶

Family Prayer

God our Father, help us be special followers of Jesus. Help us be good members of the Church family.

 ## HOW DID I DO?

This week was

☐ *one of the best ever!* ☐ *pretty good.* ☐ *in need of improvement.*

In what discussions and activities were children most interested?

_____

What activity did I most enjoy teaching?

_____

In what area do I need to improve?

_____

96 <u>CCC</u> *See Catechism of the Catholic Church 751, 752 for further reading on chapter content.*

Name _____ Date _____

Fill in the Certificate

Directions: Write your name and your parish name on the lines. Color the certificate, and cut it out.

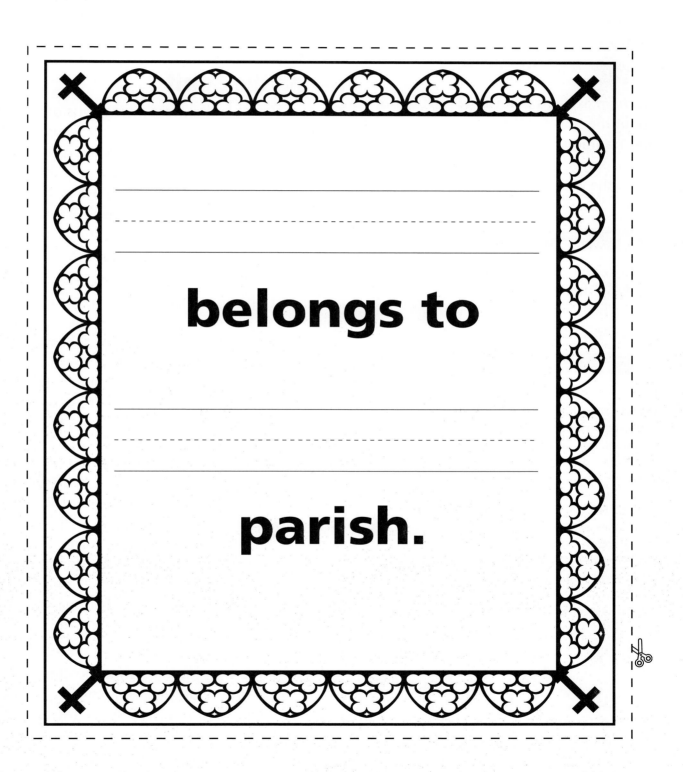

belongs to

parish.

Chapter 11

Overview

Faith Focus

- The Holy Spirit grants us the divine spark of faith. *(CCC 683)*

Catechism Connection

The *Catechism* explains that we learn about the Holy Spirit from Scripture, Tradition, the Church, sacraments, prayer, good works of others, and the witness of saints. *(CCC 688)*

NDC Link

The *Directory* emphasizes the role of the Holy Spirit in catechesis, calling us to bear witness to the truth. (See *NDC*, 28B.)

Resources

BOOK
I Believe: The Nicene Creed. Baynes, Pauline (illustrator). Eerdmans Books for Young Readers. Interprets the Creed with images based on ancient manuscripts.

DVD/VHS
*Spirituality and the Two Halves of Life** (2 hours; three segments). Oblate Media. Noted speaker Ron Rolheiser discusses growth and discipleship.

*Available at www.harcourtreligion.com

Resources
For interactive lesson planner, chapter resources, and activities
www.harcourtreligion.com

 For those who are led by the Spirit of God are children of God.

Romans 8:14

Finding the Spirit

The Holy Spirit is the most mysterious of the three Persons in God. The Father is revealed through Jesus, the Son's, teachings. Jesus is known to us because he walked the earth as a man and teaches us through Scripture. But the Holy Spirit is the most amorphous member of the Trinity. He is mentioned at the Annunciation and is present at Jesus' Baptism. Jesus promises that the Father will send the Holy Spirit, and that promise is fulfilled in wind, flame, and languages on Pentecost.

Ironically, we know the third Person least, but he is the one that is most present to us. He visits us as individuals, granting us inspiration to use our talents every day for the greater glory of God. The Holy Spirit comes in quiet times and in the laughter of children. When you find your heart lifted to God because of sheer joy or great sorrow, it is the Holy Spirit that is directing your thoughts. He is as omnipresent as the wind.

The Church

Within the Church, we encounter the Holy Spirit in sacraments. Most especially, we feel the presence of the Holy Spirit in the Sacraments of Initiation. In Baptism, the Holy Spirit's grace welcomes new members into the Church. In the Eucharist, he helps us meet Christ again. In Confirmation, the Holy Spirit strengthens our faith for the trials that await us.

Over and over again, we brush against the wind and flame that inspired the Apostles to convert thousands. Our mission is to recognize the gifts of the Holy Spirit and to put them to work in our lives.

Reflect *How can you be alert for the presence of the Holy Spirit in your life?*

Storytelling

Retelling a story provides children the opportunity to use their recall skills as well as demonstrate their comprehension of sequence.

- Help children understand every story has a beginning, a middle, and an end.

- Read aloud a story. Then ask children to recall the beginning, the middle, and the end of the story while retelling what happened in each part.

Caring for Things

- I am thoughtful. Teach me ways to care for our planet.

- I am creative. Allow me to recycle. Show me how to reduce waste to protect and preserve God's planet.

- I can care for things. Teach me the ways God cares for us.

Growing from Pain

Catechesis, like all endeavors, can bring you rejection, apathy, ridicule, and even betrayal. Catechists must know that great things are often achieved as a result of painful events.

- Painfulness is the practice of turning pain into a learning experience. As a catechist, you may allow pain to touch you, but you should not get lost in it.

- You can learn to recognize pain in others.

- Pain can help you sustain the spirit to teach if you can predict when your words may cause pain to yourself or others and when some of your past patterns need to be changed.

Reflect   **What painful experience has actually improved your ability to sustain your spirit?**

 Prayer

O Holy Spirit, inspire my lessons. Help me use my own talents to show the children your love for them. Let me lead these sweet minds to see your work in their lives and in the Church. Amen.

Weekly Planner

		Objectives	Materials	Prayer & Scripture
1 Invite	**The Holy Spirit** Page 97	To think about characteristics of the wind	☐ Masking tape ☐ Tree branch or vine ☐ Copies of Activity Master 21, p. 97E ☐ Crayons or markers ☐ Hole Punch ☐ Yarn or string	🌺 Let Us Pray: Psalm 23:3
2 Explore	**The Spirit Comes** Page 98	To learn that the Holy Spirit comes to help	☐ Copies of Activity Master 22, p. 102A ☐ Crayons or markers ☐ Scissors ☐ Glue ☐ String	✝ Scripture: Acts 2:1–4 ✝ Scripture Background: The First Pentecost
	A Helper Page 99	To recognize the work of the Holy Spirit in the Church	☐ Bubbles ☐ Balloons ☐ Kites ☐ Wind socks or streamers	✝ Scripture: Acts 2:1–4
	The Holy Trinity Page 100	To learn about the Holy Trinity	☐ Crayons or markers	✝ Scripture: Acts 2:1–4
3 Celebrate	**Helping Prayer** Page 101	To meditate on the role of the Holy Spirit	☐ Music CD ☐ Bible or Lectionary	🌺 Let Us Pray: Helping Prayer 🔔 **Hymn:** We Are the Church

Activities	Enrichment
Let's Begin Act like the wind is blowing. OPTIONAL **Activity Master 21: Make a Pennant, p. 97E**	• **Chapter Background:** Christina Rossetti (1830–1894)
Discuss how the Holy Spirit came to Jesus' friends. OPTIONAL **Activity Master 22: Make a Dove, p. 102A**	
Activity Tell how the Holy Spirit is guiding the people in the pictures. OPTIONAL Wind Toys **Multiple Intelligence:** Naturalist	• **Quick Tip:** The Holy Spirit
Activity Talk about the Holy Trinity and color the picture.	• **Reaching All Learners:** Thinking in Threes • **Chapter Background:** Symbols of God
	• **Liturgy Link:** Invocation • **Lectionary Link:** Break Open the Word

Pacing the Chapter

Parish

Meets once a week

60 minutes per lesson

In parish religious education classes, plan for approximately 60 minutes of class time.

Invite 10 minutes
Explore 40 minutes
Celebrate 10 minutes

The abundance of activity and enrichment options will allow flexibility in planning for longer sessions if needed.

School

Meets 5 days per week

30 minutes per lesson

In school religious education classes, plan for lesson 5 days per week for about 30 minutes. The lesson can be easily adapted for a 4-day week as well.

Day 1: Invite
Day 2: Explore
Day 3: Explore
Day 4: Explore
Day 5: Celebrate

The abundance of activity and enrichment options will allow flexibility in planning for longer sessions if needed.

CALL to FAITH econnect

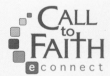

- Online planning tools include chapter background and planner, activity master, customizable test, and more.
- Enhancement activities for each step of the catechetical process, including alternative prayer experiences and blessings.
- Games, activities, interactive review, alternative assessment, and more for children.

www.calltofaitheconnect.com

Home Connection

Chapter 11 Family Faith, p. 102
Take-home activities, chapter content review, saint features and prayer

GO ONLINE **For more family activities www.harcourtreligion.com**

Name _____ Date _____

Make a Pennant

Directions: Decorate the pennant. Then cut it out and punch the holes out.

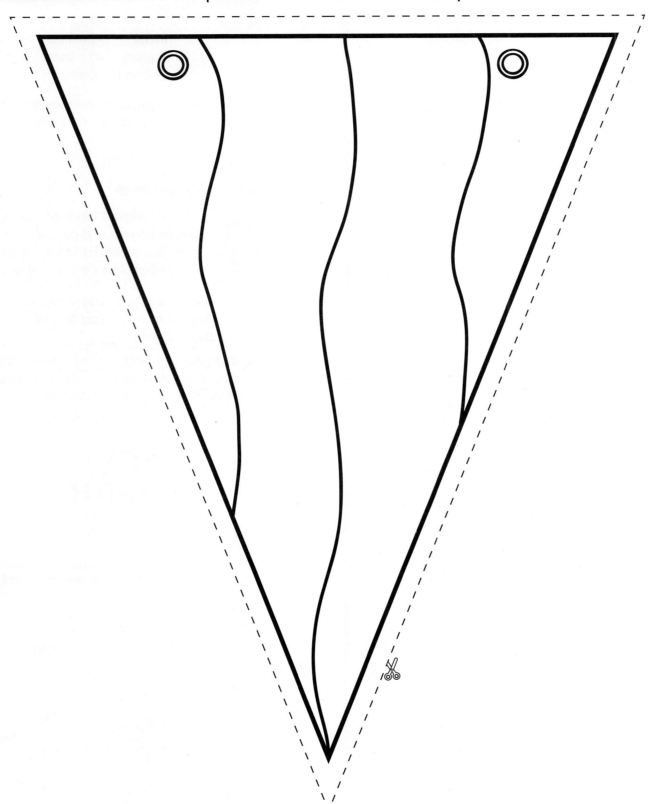

Chapter 11 The Holy Spirit

You guide me along the right path.

Based on Psalm 23:3

Who Has Seen the Wind?

Who has seen the wind?
Neither I nor you:
But when the leaves hang
    trembling,
The wind is passing through.
Who has seen the wind?
Neither you nor I:
But when the trees bow
    down their heads,
The wind is passing by.

by Christina Rossetti

● How do you know the wind is near you?

Possible responses: We feel it on our bodies; we see clouds move; we hear it go through trees.

97

1 Invite

Objective: To think about characteristics of the wind

Let Us Pray

Make a path around the room with masking tape. Read aloud the psalm verse. Have children walk along the "path" as they repeat the psalm.

Let's Begin

Who Has Seen the Wind?

Read aloud the poem once to familiarize children with it.

- Assign a child to wave a vine or tree branch to simulate the sound of wind passing through.
- Have other children act like trembling leaves and bowing trees.
- Read aloud the poem again.
- Ask children the text question.
- Have children act out other signs of the wind.

OPTIONAL ACTIVITY

Activity Master 21: Make a Pennant Distribute copies of the activity found on page 97E.

- Ask children to decorate the pennant and cut it out.
- Punch the holes out, and use yarn or string to hang the pennants in the classroom.

▲ Activity Master 21

CHAPTER BACKGROUND

Christina Rossetti (1830–1894) Christina Rossetti was known for writing poems that centered on religious themes. She was one in a family of poets; her brother Dante Gabriel Rossetti is also well known. She was known for her humility as well as for her sense of humor and observation of the world around her.

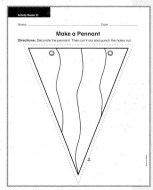

Objective: To learn that the Holy Spirit comes to help

The Spirit Comes

Remind children of how they know the wind is at work.

- Explain that you will read a bible story about how the Holy Spirit came to Jesus' friends.

- Proclaim the scripture story.

- Explain that the story took place after Jesus had returned to his Father. Jesus' friends missed him and were sad.

- Have children make the sound of wind at the appropriate point in the story.

- Ask children how Jesus' friends must have felt about the coming of the Holy Spirit. Possible responses: happy, full of energy, strong

- Discuss the text question with the group.

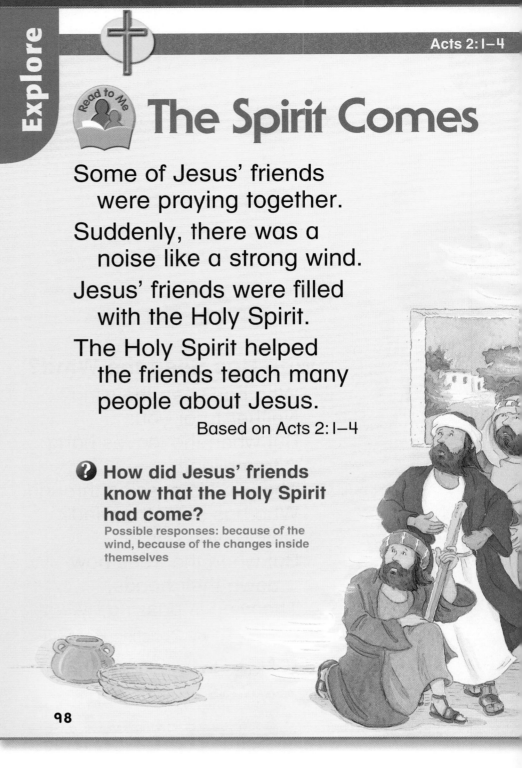

Explore

Acts 2:1–4

Read to Me — The Spirit Comes

Some of Jesus' friends were praying together.

Suddenly, there was a noise like a strong wind.

Jesus' friends were filled with the Holy Spirit.

The Holy Spirit helped the friends teach many people about Jesus.

Based on Acts 2:1–4

❓ How did Jesus' friends know that the Holy Spirit had come?
Possible responses: because of the wind, because of the changes inside themselves

98

OPTIONAL ACTIVITY

Activity Master 22: Make a Dove: Distribute copies of the activity found on page 102A.

- Tell children a dove is a sign of the Holy Spirit.

- Have them decorate the parts, cut them out, and glue them together.

- Help them tape a string to the dove's back.

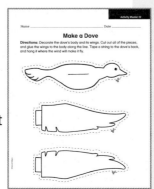

Name _____ **Date** _____

Make a Dove

Directions: Decorate the dove's body and its wings. Cut out all of the pieces, and glue the wings to the body along the line. Tape a string to the dove's back, and hang it where the wind will make it fly.

▲ Activity Master 22

SCRIPTURE BACKGROUND

The First Pentecost This story from *Acts* retells the events of the first Pentecost.

- With wind and tongues of flame, the Holy Spirit inspired the Apostles to begin their ministry. They were given the gift of tongues; all their listeners were able to understand their preaching.

- This gift symbolizes the mission of the Church to share the Gospel with all nations.

A Helper

The Holy Spirit came like the wind to the Church.

Jesus sent the Holy Spirit to be with his friends.

He helps the Church family follow Jesus.

He guides the Church.

Activity

How is the Holy Spirit guiding the people in the pictures?

99

Objective: To recognize the work of the Holy Spirit in the Church

A Helper

Remind children that the Holy Spirit guides us.

- Read aloud the text.
- Ask children how the Holy Spirit might help a child. Possible responses: by helping the child pray, make good friends, learn about God, be kind

Activity

- Discuss how the Holy Spirit is guiding the people in the pictures to do God's work in the world.

OPTIONAL ACTIVITY

Wind Toys Have a "wind fair" with toys that are based on wind principles.

- Blow bubbles or toss balloons to see what contained air can do.
- Construct and fly kites.
- Make and run with wind socks or streamers.

Multiple Intelligence: Naturalist

QUICK TIP

The Holy Spirit Some children may think of a spirit as a ghost. They may be fearful of the idea of the Holy Spirit.

- Create a positive feeling about the Holy Spirit by explaining that he watches over us night and day and keeps us safe.
- Explain that he can help us make good choices if we ask for help.

Explore

Objective: To learn about the Holy Trinity

The Holy Trinity

Remind children that the Holy Spirit is God.

- Ask children what names they have heard for God. Possible responses: Father, Son, Jesus, Holy Spirit

- Read aloud the text.

- Explain that God is three Persons in one.

- Repeat the names of the Persons of the Trinity, and have children say them after you.

Activity

- Explain that the drawing is a sign that stands for the Holy Trinity.

- Point out that the three circles are separate but connected. The circles are the same size. They remind us of the three Persons of the Trinity.

- Read aloud the activity directions.

- Hand out crayons or markers.

The Holy Trinity

There are three Persons in God.

God the Father made us.

God the Son is Jesus. He teaches us.

God the Holy Spirit helps God's people

God the Father, God the Son, and God the Holy Spirit together are the Holy Trinity.

Activity

 These circles remind you of the Holy Trinity.

Color each circle.

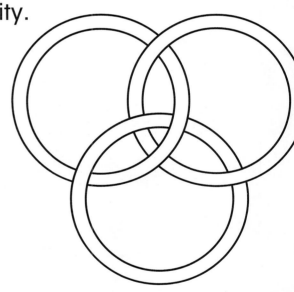

100

Thinking in Threes Legend attributes using the shamrock's three leaves for teaching about the Trinity to Saint Patrick. You can use this same plant to help children see three-in-one, or use these other examples:

- A hard-boiled egg has a shell, a white, and a yolk
- An apple has skin, flesh, and seeds
- A tree has roots, a trunk, and leaves

Symbols of God These symbols are often used as reminders of the Trinity.

- The Trinity: equilateral triangle, three interwoven circles, three fishes
- God the Father: all-seeing eye, hand of the Creator
- Jesus: lamb, Good Shepherd, vine, cross
- Holy Spirit: descending dove, flame, seven-pointed star

Helping Prayer

Leader: Holy Spirit, Jesus sent you to his friends. You helped them do God's work. Please come to us now. Help us be friends to Jesus. Help us do God the Father's work. Thank you.

All: Amen.

Sing together.

I am the Church! You are
the Church!
We are the Church
together.
All who follow Jesus,
all around the world!
Yes, we're the
Church together.

We Are the Church

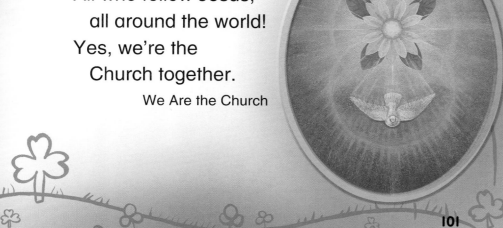

101

Objective: To meditate on the role of the Holy Spirit

 Let Us Pray

Tell children they will Pray to the Holy Spirit.

Helping Prayer

Prepare

Cover prayer table with a red cloth.

Use the *Call to Faith* Kindergarten CD, track 4, to rehearse the song.

Gather

Calm children and invite them to sit comfortably in the prayer space.

- Tell children that you will read a quiet prayer.
- Ask children to think about the Holy Spirit as you pray.

Pray

- Pray aloud the leader's prayer.
- Invite children to stand in a circle. Have them raise their hands in praise as they sing.

 LITURGY LINK

Invocation As a sign of blessing, a priest or deacon often extends one or more arms, palms down, toward the group or individual being blessed.

- This gesture invokes the power of the Holy Spirit.
- Encourage children to observe when the priest makes this gesture during Mass. Have them listen for the words he says when he makes this gesture.

 LECTIONARY LINK

Break Open the Word Read last week's Sunday Gospel. Talk about how this reading helps us follow Jesus. For children's questions related to the weekly Gospel reading, visit our Web site.

GO **Visit www.harcourtreligion.com for weekly scripture readings and seasonal resources.**

Wrap-Up

Family Faith

Remind children to discuss the Family Faith page at home. Encourage them to talk with family members about what they have learned about the Holy Spirit.

Family Project

- Encourage children to complete the activity with family members.

People of Faith

Remind children that Saint Philip was a follower of Jesus.

- Philip followed Jesus during much of his public life. He was present for the miracle of the loaves and fishes.
- Encourage children to pray the prayer at home with their families.

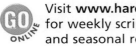 Visit **www.harcourtreligion.com** for weekly scripture readings and seasonal resources.

 Catholics Believe

Dear Family,

In Chapter 11, the children learned about the Holy Spirit. The Holy Spirit guides the Church family. They learned that the Holy Spirit is God. God the Father, Jesus, and the Holy Spirit make up the Holy Trinity.

✝ SCRIPTURE

Read Acts 2:1–4 together with your child.

 www.harcourtreligion.com
For weekly scripture readings and seasonal resources

Family Project

The Holy Spirit As a reminder that the Holy Spirit is with your family, make or buy a wind sock or wind chimes. Tell family members that they cannot see the wind, but they can see and hear it working. Point out that the Holy Spirit is like the wind. We cannot see him, but we can see the results of his work in the world. Suggest that family members say a prayer to the Holy Spirit whenever they hear the chimes or see the wind sock move.

People of Faith

Saint Philip was among Jesus' friends when the Holy Spirit came like the wind.

Saint Philip ▶
the Apostle,
first Century

🎁 Family Prayer

Come Holy Spirit, fill our hearts with your love. Help us serve God and others. Amen.

102 CCC *See Catechism of the Catholic Church 253, 791 for further reading on chapter content.*

❓ HOW DID I DO?

This week was

☐ *one of the best ever!* ☐ *pretty good.* ☐ *in need of improvement.*

In what discussions and activities were children most interested?

_____

What activity did I most enjoy teaching?

_____

In what area do I need to improve?

_____

Name _____ Date _____

Make a Dove

Directions: Decorate the dove's body and its wings. Cut out all of the pieces, and glue the wings to the body along the line. Tape a string to the dove's back, and hang it where the wind will make it fly.

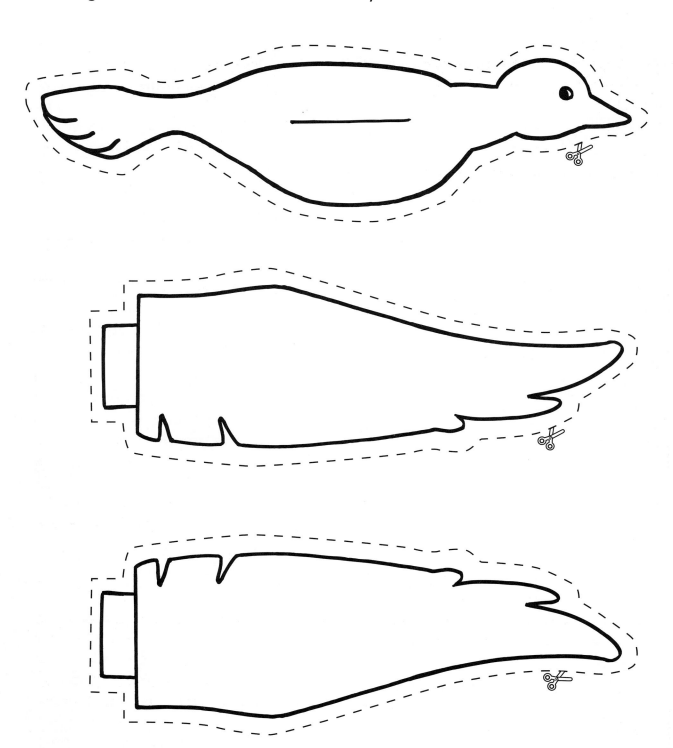

Overview

Helping Others

CHAPTER BACKGROUND

Faith Focus

■ Jesus' life was spent serving others. *(CCC 786)*

Catechism Connection

The *Catechism* exhorts us to incorporate the Works of Mercy into our interactions with our neighbors. *(CCC 2447)*

NDC Link

In response to God's love for us, we are called to reach out to others in love. (See *NDC*, 40.)

Resources

📖 **BOOKS**
Little Red Hen Gets Help. Spengler, Kenneth. Harcourt Children's Books. Shows the need for cooperation.

The Catholic Source Book, fourth edition.* Klein, Peter (editor). ACTA Publications. Contains essential teachings of the Church and addresses many Church-related topics.

*Available at www.harcourtreligion.com

Resources
For interactive lesson planner, chapter resources, and activities
www.harcourtreligion.com

 Do not neglect to do good and to share what you have; God is pleased by sacrifices of that kind.

Hebrews 13:16

Many the Gifts

As Catholics of the twenty-first century, we have much for which to be thankful. Science and industry have provided us with many comforts and conveniences. We live in a prosperous country and have great freedom. We are greatly blessed.

The burden that can come with such blessings is, unfortunately, complacency. It is all too easy to see that our own immediate surroundings are sufficient for our needs. Why should we look further if we might not like the view?

We must look further to see how other members of the Body of Christ are faring. If they have any need, we must work to alleviate that need.

Many the Works

We assist our neighbors by performing Works of Mercy. Individually and as part of the Church, we help others when we provide food, clothing, shelter, and medical care. By supporting Church groups, private agencies, and government services for the poor, we are serving God through his people.

On an individual level, we help Christ by consoling and advising the people we encounter in our daily lives. When you dry one of your kindergartners' tears or sit with a grieving neighbor, you are performing Works of Mercy. You are promoting the kingdom of God on earth through your service.

Reflect   What Works of Mercy can you perform to serve others?

Safety Rules

Help children understand that following safety rules is an important practice.

- Have a reverse field trip. Ask a firefighter, police officer, or paramedic to come to your class and explain safety habits with your group.

- Ask children to invent safety rules for the group. Make a chart, entitled "Our Safety Rules," listing the rules children come up with. Place the chart in a conspicuous area so that all children can see it.

The Real World

- I love to imitate. Provide real-world props for me to play with.

- I love to go places. Take field trips. Just walking outdoors is an adventure.

- I learn through my senses. If I can see it, smell it, touch it, hear it, or taste it, then I can really understand it.

Holy Urgency

Sometimes advice to wait your turn, calm down, and be patient decreases the passion fueling your catechetical commitment. Sustaining your spirit seems to require a mixture of perspective, passion, humility, and self-importance.

Those who sustain their commitments know that their contribution may not compare to other great works but that it is their most important contribution. They will stop at nothing to do it well, and they will not lower their expectations. In maintaining this holy urgency about their work, they protect themselves from the kind of passivity that extinguishes the fire of the spirit to teach.

Reflect **How much passion do you have for your catechetical efforts? What fuels it? What weakens it?**

 Prayer

Jesus, Son of God, show me that you are in the needy people of the world. Help me find ways of serving you through the Church and in my personal encounters with others. Let my example teach others how to be servants. Amen.

Weekly Planner

		Objectives	Materials	Prayer & Scripture
1 Invite	**Helping Others** Page 103	To discuss the effect of good deeds	☐ Copies of Activity Master 23, p. 103E ☐ Crayons or markers	🌼 **Let Us Pray:** Psalm 11:7
2 Explore	**The Church Serves** Page 104	To show that Jesus wants his followers to serve others		✝ **Scripture:** Matthew 25:35–36 ✝ **Scripture Background:** Works of Mercy
	You Can Serve Page 105	To learn ways to help others	☐ Copies of Activity Master 24, p. 108A ☐ Crayons or markers ☐ Scissors ☐ Glue	✝ **Scripture:** Matthew 25:35–36
	Choosing to Serve Page 106	To become aware of the ways people serve others	☐ Drawing paper ☐ Crayons or markers	✝ **Scripture:** Matthew 25:35–36
3 Celebrate	**Asking Prayer** Page 107	To ask for help in serving others	☐ Music CD ☐ Bible or Lectionary ☐ Musical instruments	🌼 **Let Us Pray:** Asking Prayer 🎵 **Hymn:** We Are the Church

Activities	Enrichment
Let's Begin Look at the picture and read the story. ⟨OPTIONAL⟩ **Activity Master 23:** **Draw a Caring Basket, p. 103E**	• **Justice and Peace:** Living in Community
❓ Discuss how children serve others.	• **Cultural Awareness:** Universal Needs
Activity Trace the path and act out ways to serve people along the way. ⟨OPTIONAL⟩ **Activity Master 24:** **Make a We Serve Heart, p. 108A**	• **Quick Tip:** Mission Projects
Activity Talk about people who serve others. ⟨OPTIONAL⟩ Do a Kind Deed **Multiple Intelligence:** Interpersonal	• **Reaching All Learners:** Future Servers
	• **Liturgy Link:** Serving at Worship • **Lectionary Link:** Break Open the Word

Pacing the Chapter

Parish
Meets once a week

In parish religious education classes, plan for approximately 60 minutes of class time.

Invite	10 minutes
Explore	40 minutes
Celebrate	10 minutes

The abundance of activity and enrichment options will allow flexibility in planning for longer sessions if needed.

School
Meets 5 days per week

In school religious education classes, plan for lesson 5 days per week for about 30 minutes. The lesson can be easily adapted for a 4-day week as well.

Day 1: Invite   **Day 4:** Explore
Day 2: Explore   **Day 5:** Celebrate
Day 3: Explore

The abundance of activity and enrichment options will allow flexibility in planning for longer sessions if needed.

- Online planning tools include chapter background and planner, activity master, customizable test, and more.

- Enhancement activities for each step of the catechetical process, including alternative prayer experiences and blessings.

- Games, activities, interactive review, alternative assessment, and more for children.

www.calltofaitheconnect.com

Home Connection

Chapter 12 Family Faith, p. 108
Take-home activities, chapter content review, saint features and prayer

 **For more family activities**
www.harcourtreligion.com

Name _____ Date _____

Draw a Caring Basket

Directions: Here is an empty basket. Draw what you would put into it to show someone that you care about him or her.

©Harcourt Religion

Helping Others

The Lord loves good deeds.
Based on Psalm 11:7

Read to Me — **Let's Begin**

The Kindness Basket

Denise was sick. She missed a lot of school. Her classmates wanted to cheer her up. They made cards for her. They made her favorite cookies. They put the things in a basket. Miss Shay took the basket to Denise. Denise was happy to see the basket.

● What made Denise happy? **Responses will vary.**

103

Objective: To discuss the effect of good deeds

 Let Us Pray

Read aloud the psalm verse. Have children repeat it after you.

Let's Begin

The Kindness Basket

- Call attention to the photograph. Have children describe what they see in the photograph.
- Ask children to guess what the story will be about.
- Read aloud the story.
- As you discuss the text question, emphasize that the material goods made Denise happy, but the love that the basket represented probably meant even more to her.

OPTIONAL ACTIVITY

Activity Master 23: Draw a Caring Basket Distribute copies of the activity found on page 103E.

- Tell children they will be drawing things that show they care.
- Have children fill the empty basket with their drawings.

▲ **Activity Master 23**

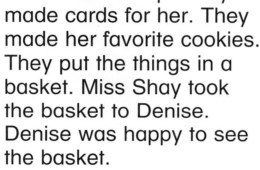
JUSTICE AND PEACE

Living in Community People live in communities. They share their lives with one another.

- We promote justice and love by giving to others.
- We can do this through personal interactions or through public and private organizations (*The Church and the Modern World*, #30).

Catholic Social Teaching: Call to Family and Community

Explore

Objective: To show that Jesus wants his followers to serve others.

The Church Serves

Recall the story of the basket.

- Explain that serving others means to help them and not expect anything in return.
- Read aloud the text.
- Ask why serving others shows love. Possible response: because it makes us look at what others need and give it to them

Ways to Serve

Tell children you will read to them what Jesus says about serving.

- Proclaim the Gospel reading.
- Ask children to describe what Jesus taught.
- Discuss the text question.

The Church Serves

Miss Shay's class wanted to show love to Denise.
Your Church family shows love by serving others.

Matthew 25:35–36

Read to Me

Ways to Serve

Feed people who are hungry and thirsty.
Give clothes to people who need them.
Be friendly to new people
Based on Matthew 25:35–36

❓ How can you serve?
Possible responses: by obeying parents, by giving things to people in need, by following Jesus

104

SCRIPTURE BACKGROUND

Works of Mercy This passage occurs as Jesus is teaching about the rewards of the just at the Last Judgment.

- It lists six of the seven Corporal Works of Mercy.
- The passage reinforces the idea that Jesus is among us in people who need food, clothing, drink, and companionship.

CULTURAL AWARENESS

Universal Needs Children may benefit from considering what each person needs for a comfortable existence.

- Tell children that everyone needs food, clothing, shelter, medical care, and education.
- Using library or Internet resources, find examples of how these needs are met in a variety of societies. Discuss the examples with children.

You Can Serve

You show love when you serve others.
You can choose different ways to serve.

Activity

Pretend you are walking to church with a friend and your family.

Act out what you see on the way.
Show how you can serve others.

105

Objective: To learn ways to help others

You Can Serve

Recall that Jesus wants us to serve others.

• Explain that each of us has many chances to serve others every day.

Activity

• Read aloud directions for the activity.

• Have children begin at the house where the two children are.

• Instruct children to trace the path to the church with their fingers.

• When children come to a place in the path where there is an opportunity to serve, have them describe the situation and act out ways to respond.

• Caution children to remember their personal safety. Reinforce safety rules about unknown people and unfamiliar animals. Point out that notifying police and other safety workers is a way of helping, too.

• Ask children about other situations in which they have helped in the past. Responses will vary

---

OPTIONAL ACTIVITY

Activity Master 24: Make a We Serve Heart Distribute copies of the activity found on page 108A:

• Tell children they will be making a heart.

• Help children follow directions for coloring and gluing the hearts.

▲ Activity Master 24

QUICK TIP

Mission Projects Ask a missionary to speak to your class about his or her work.

• Ask him or her to share about helping people in need and spreading Jesus' good news.

• Explain that your church family helps people right in your neighborhood.

• Tell children that they can be missionaries by doing simple things to help others.

Objective: To become aware of the ways people serve others.

Choosing to Serve

Remind children that Jesus wants us to serve others.

- Point out that you are happy to serve children by teaching them, and that many adults have jobs that permit them to serve others.
- Read aloud the text.

Activity

- Point out the pictures on the page.
- Read aloud the directions.
- Ask children the ways that each profession serves others.
- Ask children if there are other professions that serve others.
  Possible responses: teachers, lawyers, police officers

Choosing to Serve

Everyone can serve in some way. Some grownups serve others every day.

Activity

Tell how each person in the picture serves others.

106

 REACHING ALL LEARNERS

Future Servers Children can have an opportunity to demonstrate their commitment to future service through a show-and-tell about professions.

- Have children dress up as if they were adults in a helping profession.
- Ask each child to tell the group how members of the profession serve others.

OPTIONAL ACTIVITY

Do a Kind Deed Many parishes have programs for visiting home-bound or hospitalized members. If your parish has one, consider a class project to support it.

- Have children make greeting cards for visitors to take when they visit.

Multiple Intelligence: Interpersonal

Asking Prayer

Leader: Dear Jesus, help us serve people.

All: **Help us follow you.**

Leader: Help us be kind to each other.

All: **Help us follow you.**

Leader: Help us share with one another.

All: **Help us follow you. Amen.**

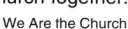 **Sing together.**

I am the Church!
   You are the Church!
We are the Church together.
All who follow Jesus,
   all around the world!
Yes, we're the Church together.

We Are the Church

107

Objective: To ask for help in serving others

 Let Us Pray

Tell children they will pray to be good followers of Jesus.

Asking Prayer

Prepare

- Tell children that they will say the same response to each of your prayers. Rehearse the response.

- Point out that musicians serve. Hand out musical instruments for children to accompany the song.

  Use the *Call to Faith* Kindergarten CD, track 4, to rehearse the song.

Gather

Invite children to play instruments as they come into the prayer space.

Pray

Have children stand during the celebration.

- Read aloud the leader's part, and have children pray the response.

- Have children use the musical instruments as they sing.

LITURGY LINK

Serving at Worship   Children may not realize that the people who help at Mass are serving God's people.

- Point out that these people serve by reading aloud, playing music, carrying up the gifts, and so on.

- Ask children to notice the ways that people serve at next Sunday's Mass. At the next class, have the children discuss what they saw.

LECTIONARY LINK

Break Open the Word   Read last week's Sunday Gospel. Talk about how this reading helps us follow Jesus. For children's questions related to the weekly Gospel reading, visit our Web site.

GO ONLINE Visit www.harcourtreligion.com for weekly scripture readings and seasonal resources.

Wrap-Up

Family Faith

Remind children to discuss the Family Faith page at home. Encourage them to talk with family members about what they have learned about serving others.

Family Project

• Encourage children to participate in the project with family members.

People of Faith

Remind children that Saint Philip knew Jesus.

• After Jesus' death, Philip traveled to Greece to serve Jesus and others by sharing Jesus' story.

• Encourage children to pray the prayer at home with their families.

Visit **www.harcourtreligion.com** for weekly scripture readings and seasonal resources.

Family Faith

Catholics Believe

Dear Family,
In Chapter 12, the children learned that Jesus wants us to serve by feeding the hungry, giving drinks to the thirsty, and giving clothing to the needy. The children also learned that members of the Church family serve in different ways.

SCRIPTURE

Read Matthew 25:35–36 together with your child.

GO ONLINE www.harcourtreligion.com
For weekly scripture readings and seasonal resources

Family Project

Serve Your Community Gather toys and clothes that your child has outgrown. Talk with your child about how these items are no longer useful to him or her. Explain that these clothes and toys would be useful to children who need them. With your child, take the items to a Saint Vincent de Paul Center or another organization that will distribute them to the needy. Praise your child's service to others.

People of Faith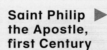

With the Holy Spirit's help, Saint Philip told people how to follow Jesus.

Saint Philip the Apostle, first Century ▶

Family Prayer

Saint Philip, you told people how to follow Jesus. Help us know how to follow Jesus, too. Amen.

108 CCC *See Catechism of the Catholic Church 910, 2447 for further reading on chapter content.*

HOW DID I DO?

This week was

☐ *one of the best ever!*   ☐ *pretty good.*   ☐ *in need of improvement.*

In what discussions and activities were children most interested?

_____

What activity did I most enjoy teaching?

_____

In what area do I need to improve?

_____

Name _____ Date _____

Make a We Serve Heart

Directions: Color the pictures that show ways to serve. Cut out the colored pictures, and glue them into the heart. Then decorate the heart.

Scripture Story

Paul's Message

(Colossians 1:24–25; 3:2, 8–11, 13–17)

Family Note: In class your child has learned that members of the Church are to live good lives. After reading this Scripture Story together, ask your child to tell you some of Saint Paul's suggestions for living good lives. The next time you attend Mass together, listen for more advice on living good lives.

8

Sing and pray to God.

Most of all, thank God for his love.

Do these things in Jesus' name.

That is what Paul told us to do.

Draw yourself following Paul's advice.

109

Long ago, a man named Paul loved God.
Paul taught about Jesus.
He traveled to many places to teach.

2

Jesus wants us to live in peace.
Try to keep Jesus' peace in your heart.
Teach other people about Jesus.

7

110

Paul wrote letters to the people he had taught.

He told them how to behave.

We still read his letters today.

They are part of the Bible.

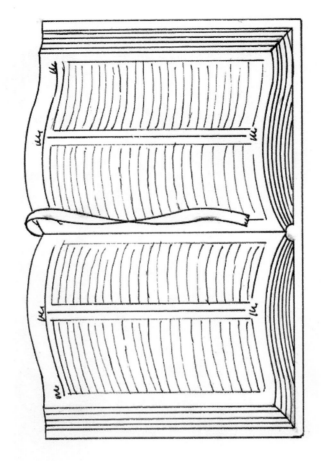

Color the Bible.

3

Forgive each other.

Remember, Jesus forgave people who hurt him.

That is why you must forgive people who hurt you.

6

III

This is what Paul wrote to some Christians in a place called Colossae.

I send you happiness from God the Father.

Jesus is with everyone who is in the Church.

4

Think about what God wants you to do.

Be nice to everyone.

Don't be angry or tell lies.

Remember that Jesus loves everyone.

5

112

Overview

Faith Focus

■ God made humans with free will. *(CCC 1730)*

Catechism Connection

The *Catechism* teaches that we have the freedom to make our own choices and the responsibility to make choices that are in accord with God's will. *(CCC 1731-1734)*

NDC Link

We are called to live the Good News by following Jesus' commandment of love of God and neighbor. (See *NDC*, 25G.)

Resources

BOOK
Circles of Hope.* Williams, Karen Lynn. Eerdmans Books for Young Readers. A brother's love is tested as he tries to honor his baby sister.

DVD/VHS
The Patients of a Saint* (115 min.). San Damiano Foundation. Tells the story of an American doctor who cares for poor children in Peru.

*Available at www.harcourtreligion.com

Resources
For interactive lesson planner, chapter resources, and activities
www.harcourtreligion.com

 As I have loved you, so you also should love one another.
John 13:34

Freedom

The world and our human limitations present us with many situations that require us to make choices. Some are relatively innocuous: white bread versus whole wheat, walking or riding a bus; making a telephone call now or later. Other choices, however, reveal our true nature and show what we value most: Do I pay a fair price or try to make a deal that favors me? Will I skip Sunday Mass so that I can be at the beach early? Should I work late or attend a child's big game?

The free will that God endowed each of us with is a wonderful blessing, but it is also a burden. It forces us to be responsible for our actions because it allows us to choose between what will bring us closer to God and what will take us away from him.

Of course, God and the Church recognize that personal responsibility for an action is lessened by a lack of knowledge, duress, fear, and other factors. However, those actions that are consciously willed can make or break our relationships with others and with God.

The Ultimate Example

Love is the ultimate choice demanded of us. Happily, Jesus provides the ultimate example of love for us to follow: he loved us enough to die for us. Few of us need to make that great sacrifice. But we are called to make smaller sacrifices, to exercise our freedom appropriately, to further the kingdom of God on earth.

Reflect   How do your personal choices reflect your values?

Hug-a-thon

Emphasize that being nice and caring for others is a way of showing love. Tell children that just giving someone a hug is a way to be caring and loving.

- Invite children to hug as many classmates as possible. Be mindful that some children are shy and this assignment may cause them to feel uncomfortable.

- Remind children that God wants them to be kind and loving to everyone because he is kind and loving to them.

Respect

- I am a unique individual. Learn my name quickly, and work hard to pronounce it correctly.

- I like to talk. Allow me time to talk. Value what I have to say.

Keeping Company

Sustaining your spirit requires a community of voices. Some voices cheer you on and unconditionally support you. Other voices ask you to reevaluate and extend your thinking.

We tend to let our relationships and networks develop naturally. If instead you intentionally keep company with colleagues, friends, and family who provide challenging and supportive voices, you gain the confidence to sustain your spirit.

Keeping company with prophets and cheerleaders, mystics and managers, sergeants and social workers allows you to create and maintain a kind of invisible community that is pulsating instead of passive.

Reflect **Does the company you keep comfort and challenge you? If so, list three voices and the roles they play in sustaining your spirit.**

 Prayer

Gracious God, I am thankful for the freedom to choose in my life. Help me always make choices that move me closer to you. Amen.

Weekly Planner

		Objectives	Materials	Prayer & Scripture
1 Invite	**You Show Love** Page 113	To understand how to treat others kindly	☐ Crucifix ☐ Copies of Activity Master 25, p. 113E ☐ Pencils ☐ Crayons or markers ☐ Scissors ☐ Drawing paper	Let Us Pray: Psalm 33:5
2 Explore	**Be Kind** Page 114	To understand that kind actions please others and God	☐ *Bless This House*	Scripture: John 15: 9, 12 Scripture Background: Loving
	Love as Jesus Loves Page 115	To learn to show love to others as Jesus did	☐ Crayons or markers ☐ Copies of Activity Master 26, p.118A ☐ Pencils ☐ Scissors	Scripture: John 15: 9, 12
	Love Others Page 116	To demonstrate how to show love to others	☐ Pencils	Scripture: John 15: 9, 12
3 Celebrate	**Prayer of Praise** Page 117	To meditate on loving others	☐ Music CD ☐ Bible or Lectionary	Let Us Pray: Prayer of Praise **Hymn:** Love One Another

Activities	Enrichment

Let's Begin

Read the poem, and act it out.

OPTIONAL **Activity Master 25:**
A Helping Hand, p. 113E

OPTIONAL Poetry Book
  Multiple Intelligence: Visual/Spatial

❓ Discuss how Jesus wants you to love others.

OPTIONAL Children's Literature
  Multiple Intelligence: Verbal/Linguistic

Activity

Look at the pictures, and draw a heart around the pictures that show love.

OPTIONAL **Activity Master 26:**
A Loving Choices Heart, p. 118A

• **Quick Tip:**
  Catch a Child!

Activity

Help finish the rhymes, and match them with the pictures.

OPTIONAL Sign Language
  Multiple Intelligence: Bodily/Kinesthetic

• **Reaching All Learners:**
  Sharing Languages

• **Liturgy Link:**
  Asking Forgiveness

• **Lectionary Link:**
  Break Open the Word

Pacing the Chapter

Parish
Meets once a week

In parish religious education classes, plan for approximately 60 minutes of class time.

Invite	10 minutes
Explore	40 minutes
Celebrate	10 minutes

The abundance of activity and enrichment options will allow flexibility in planning for longer sessions if needed.

School
Meets 5 days per week

In school religious education classes, plan for lesson 5 days per week for about 30 minutes. The lesson can be easily adapted for a 4-day week as well.

Day 1: Invite	**Day 4:** Explore
Day 2: Explore	**Day 5:** Celebrate
Day 3: Explore	

The abundance of activity and enrichment options will allow flexibility in planning for longer sessions if needed.

• Online planning tools include chapter background and planner, activity master, customizable test, and more.

• Enhancement activities for each step of the catechetical process, including alternative prayer experiences and blessings.

• Games, activities, interactive review, alternative assessment, and more for children.

www.calltofaitheconnect.com

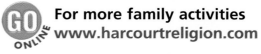

Home Connection

Chapter 13 Family Faith, p. 118
Take-home activities, chapter content review, saint features and prayer

GO ONLINE **For more family activities**
www.harcourtreligion.com

Name _____ Date _____

A Helping Hand

Directions: Write your name on the line. Then color in the hand and cut it out.

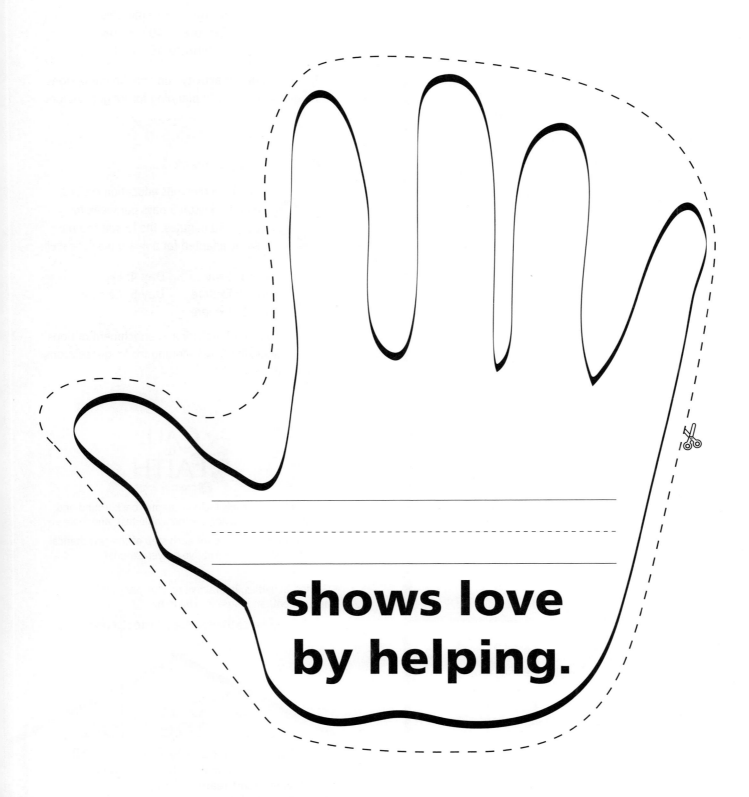

shows love by helping.

You Show Love

The Lord loves justice and right.

Psalm 33:5

Read to Me — Let's Begin

The Big Circle

Sara helped Troy by opening the door for him.

Troy picked Pam's paper up from the floor.

Pam shared her snack with Mary Joy.

Then Mary Joy made Sara a special toy.

What a loving group!

● What happens when one person is kind to another?
Responses will vary.

113

Objective: To understand how to treat others kindly

Let Us Pray

Invite children to gather in the prayer space and make the Sign of the Cross. In the prayer space, have a crucifix and a Bible opened to the psalm verse.

Read aloud the psalm verse. Have children repeat it after you.

Let's Begin

The Big Circle

• Read aloud the poem.

• Help children notice that each child is both a giver and a receiver of help.

• Discuss the text question.

• Select several children to act out the poem. Read aloud the poem again as children perform.

OPTIONAL ACTIVITY

Activity Master 25: A Helping Hand   Distribute copies of the activity found on page 113E.

• Tell children they will be making a hand.

• Help children follow directions for making the hand.

Activity Master 25
A Helping Hand
Directions: Write your name on the line. Then color in the hand and cut it out.

shows love by helping.

▲ **Activity Master 25**

OPTIONAL ACTIVITY

Poetry Book   Read aloud the poem, and point out the rhyming words.

• Ask children to come up with other rhyming words.

• Make up rhymed couplets about showing kindness.

• Write each couplet on paper, and combine them in a book.

Our Class Poems

Multiple Intelligence: Visual/Spatial

Objective: To understand that kind actions please others and God

Be Kind

Recall the poem and how the children helped one another in it.

Ask children why we should treat other people kindly. *Possible responses: because it feels good, because Jesus wants us to, because we want them to be happy*

• Read aloud the text.

• Ask children how they can be kind and show love. *Possible responses: by sharing toys, by helping at home, by helping others learn at school*

Love Others

• Tell children that they will hear what Jesus teaches about kindness and love.

• Proclaim the Gospel reading.

• Discuss the text question.

Explore

Be Kind

The children in the classroom were kind to one another.

Jesus teaches you to be kind.

He wants you to show love.

John 15:9, 12

 Read to Me

Love Others

I love you just like God the Father loves me.
This is what you should do:
Love one another as I love you.

Based on John 15:9, 12

❓ **How does Jesus want you to love others?**
as he loves me

114

✝ SCRIPTURE BACKGROUND

Loving This passage comes near the end of Jesus' description of himself as the vine and his followers as the branches.

• Our love is demonstrated by our commitment to each other and our loyalty to the commandments.

• Through the example of Jesus and the Father, we come to know love and are able to share it with others.

OPTIONAL ACTIVITY

Children's Literature Read *Bless This House* by Leslie Staub (Harcourt, 2000). This book contains a simple, tender, and gently humorous bedtime prayer that celebrates family, home, and all the creatures of the earth.

Multiple Intelligence: Verbal/Linguistic

Love as Jesus Loves

Jesus showed love in many ways.
He obeyed his parents.
He prayed to God the Father.
He visited the sick.

Activity

Draw a ♡ around the pictures that show love.

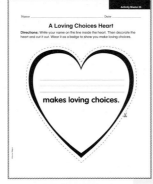

115

Objective: To learn to show love to others as Jesus did

Love as Jesus Loves

Ask a child to recall the Gospel reading. Possible responses: We should love others as Jesus loves us; Jesus loves us as the Father loves him.

- Read aloud the text.
- Point out that every day, we can make loving or unloving choices.

Activity

- Read aloud the activity directions.
- Hand out crayons or markers.
- Have children complete the activity on their own or in small groups.
- Ask children to share their answers with the group.
- Discuss the answers.

OPTIONAL ACTIVITY

Activity Master 26: A Loving Choices Heart Distribute copies of the activity found on page 118A.

- Tell children they will be making a heart.
- Help children follow directions for decorating and cutting out the heart.

Name _____ Date _____

Activity Master 26

A Loving Choices Heart

Directions: Write your name on the line inside the heart. Then decorate the heart and cut it out. Wear it as a badge to show you make loving choices.

_____ makes loving choices.

▲ Activity Master 26

QUICK TIP

Catch a Child! As the school year progresses, children begin to feel comfortable in your group. They feel safe as a result of your positive attention.

- When you see a child performing a kind act, praise and affirm that child.
- Call or send notes home to tell parents or guardians about a child's kindness.

Explore

Objective: To demonstrate how to show love to others

Love Others

Tell children that this lesson is about loving others.

- Ask children how they feel when they do loving actions. Possible responses: happy, pleased
- Read aloud the text.
- Reinforce the connection between feeling loved by God and passing that love on to others.

Activity

- Read aloud the activity directions.
- Hand out pencils.
- Point out the ryhmes in the left column. Tell children that they will help you finish each ryhme. Then they will match the ryhme with a picture in the right column.
- Complete the activity as a group.

Explore

Love Others

When you love other people, you do good things for them. This makes them happy. It makes you happy, too.

Activity

Listen to the beginning of each rhyme. Help your teacher finish the rhyme. Then connect the rhyme with its picture.

Taylor did not have a treat, so John gave her a peach to ___eat___.

Molly had a sad, sad, look, so Seamus read her favorite ___book___.

116

★ REACHING ALL LEARNERS

Sharing Languages If you have a child who is proficient in another language, ask the child to teach some phrases to the group.

- Possible phrases include: "Let's be friends" and "Let me help you."
- Have children think of other phrases and ask (in a courteous fashion) to learn them.
- Encourage children to use the phrases in classroom situations.

OPTIONAL ACTIVITY

Sign Language Explain that there are many different ways to show love and to tell people how you love them.

- Teach children some simple sign language for phrases such as "I love you" and "peace."
- Explain that hugs and smiles are also another way to show love.

Multiple Intelligence: Bodily/Kinesthetic

Prayer of Praise

Leader: Jesus, you give us a wonderful gift. You give us your love. You show us how to love and forgive others. We praise you and love you when we love others.

All: Amen.

Sing together.

Love one another,
Love one another,
as I have loved you.

Care for each other,
Care for each other,
as I care for you.

Love One Another

117

Objective: To meditate on loving others

 Let Us Pray

Tell children they will praise Jesus for his love.

Prayer of Praise

Prepare

Quiet the group.

Use the *Call to Faith* Kindergarten CD, track 5, to rehearse the song.

Gather

Invite children to move quietly into the prayer space.

Pray

- Slowly read aloud the prayer, and prompt children for the response.
- Pause for reflection at the end of the meditation.
- Have children conclude with the song.

 LITURGY LINK

Asking Forgiveness   Tell children that each Mass begins with the Penitential Rite.

- At this time, we have a chance to think about how we have hurt others.
- We privately tell God we are sorry for making unloving choices. Then, together, we ask God to forgive us.

 LECTIONARY LINK

Break Open the Word   Read last week's Sunday Gospel. Talk about how this reading helps us follow Jesus. For children's questions related to the weekly Gospel reading, visit our Web site.

GO ONLINE   **Visit www.harcourtreligion.com for weekly scripture readings and seasonal resources.**

Wrap-Up

Family Faith

Remind children to discuss the Family Faith page at home. Encourage them to talk with family members about what they have learned about loving others.

Family Project

- Encourage children to do the activity with family members.

People of Faith

Tell children about Moses.

- Point out that Moses was one of the great leaders of God's people in the time before Jesus was born.
- God asked Moses to help his people and Moses said "yes."
- Encourage children to pray the prayer at home with their families.

Visit **www.harcourtreligion.com** for weekly scripture readings and seasonal resources.

Catholics Believe

Dear Family,
In Chapter 13, the children learned that Jesus wants them to love others as he loves them. They talked about loving actions and how these actions make people happy.

✝ SCRIPTURE

Read John 15:9,12 together with your child.

GO ONLINE www.harcourtreligion.com
For weekly scripture readings and seasonal resources

Family Project

Make a Star Chart Encourage loving actions by making a chart. "Catch" your child being good. Put a gold star on the chart every time he or she is kind, helpful, patient, generous, etc. Praise your child when the chart is full of stars.

People of Faith

Moses was a great leader long before Jesus was born. God chose Moses to be a leader of his people. Moses helped God's people.

**Moses,
12th Century B.C.** ▶

Family Prayer

Almighty God, help us follow your rules for us. Help us show love and care to others. Amen.

118 **CCC** *See Catechism of the Catholic Church 1825 for further reading on chapter content.*

? HOW DID I DO?

This week was

☐ *one of the best ever!* ☐ *pretty good.* ☐ *in need of improvement.*

In what discussions and activities were children most interested?

_____

What activity did I most enjoy teaching?

_____

In what area do I need to improve?

_____

Name _____ Date _____

A Loving Choices Heart

Directions: Write your name on the line inside the heart. Then decorate the heart and cut it out. Wear it as a badge to show you make loving choices.

makes loving choices.

Overview

Faith Focus

- Human actions can be judged as good or evil. *(CCC 1749)*

Catechism Connection

The *Catechism* explains that humans must act to develop a good conscience. *(CCC 1783)*

NDC Link

The *Directory* explains that catechesis helps people apply timeless moral principles to the circumstances of today. (See *NDC*, 44.)

Resources

BOOK
Hand Commands: The Ten Commandments for Little Ones. Dunagan, Ann. Kregel Publications. Provides a way to remember the commandments using finger plays.

DVD/VHS
Walking the Bible (168 min.). WGBH (Oblate Media). Describes a walk through the Holy Land, including a visit to Mount Sinai.

Resources
For interactive lesson planner, chapter resources, and activities
www.harcourtreligion.com

You guide me along the right path for the sake of your name.

Psalm 23:3

The Conscience

The conscience is the voice that helps us discern right from wrong. Our consciences have been developed by personal experiences, through formal religion lessons, and by guidance from the Holy Spirit and from people we admire.

Most adults think that their consciences have been fully formed for many years, but that is not the case. The conscience grows and changes with every human experience. Its formation continues throughout life, so even adults have some time left to perfect it!

Proper Formation

Teachers and catechists play a vital role in forming the consciences of children in their care. You have a choice to either train children with love and good example or to make them behave out of fear and intimidation. Either method may keep your classroom quiet, but you must also consider which method will help the children know what to do in the future. Jesus clearly tells us how to behave toward anyone: act with love.

So, act with love you must. Pray for guidance from the Holy Spirit, and align yourself with companions who will help you make good choices. As you work to form the consciences of children, remember that you are a work in progress yourself!

*Reflect **What can you do to further develop your conscience?***

Word Friendly Classrooms

Make your classroom a place where reading is encouraged.

- Display poems, songs, and verses throughout the room at children's eye level.
- Maintain a classroom library where children can freely read books of their choice.

Choices

- I like to express myself. Teach me appropriate ways to get my point across.
- I am learning right from wrong. Teach me to make good choices as Jesus would have me do.
- I am eager to please. Show me that God gave me free will. Help me to make good choices.

Keeping Sabbath

Keeping Sabbath means taking time to worship and rest. Our fast-paced secular world puts pressure on us and makes it easy to feel overwhelmed. Sometimes we lose sight of the values and virtues we hold most sacred.

Sustaining your spirit requires more than keeping the right company, living with complexity, and turning pain into thoughtfulness. It requires rest and worship that allow us to remember who we are and whose we are. Keeping Sabbath through worship and rest allows us to reflect on and renew our relationship with God, our moral life, and the spiritual resources available to us as children of God in a community of faith.

Reflect *How can you improve the way you worship and rest?*

 Prayer

God, our Father, I am still learning and forming my own conscience. What an awesome task it is to be responsible for working with so many young consciences as well! Help me guide them along the right path to you. Amen.

Weekly Planner

		Objectives	Materials	Prayer & Scripture
1 Invite	**Good Choices** Page 119	To consider how rules keep everyone safe	☐ Copies of Activity Master 27, p. 119E ☐ Crayons or markers	🌸 **Let Us Pray:** Psalm 19:8
2 Explore	**Help with Choices** Page 120	To realize that people help us make good choices	☐ Pencils ☐ Large jar ☐ Small slips of paper	
	God's Rules Page 121	To learn what Jesus tells everyone about God's rules		✝ **Scripture:** Matthew 19:18–19 ✝ **Scripture Background:** Rules to Follow
	God's Rules Help Page 122	To demonstrate how to follow God's rules	☐ Crayons or markers ☐ Copies of Activity Master 28, p. 124A ☐ Pencils	✝ **Scripture:** Matthew 19:18–19
3 Celebrate	**Thanking Prayer** Page 123	To praise and thank Jesus for his help in making good choices	☐ Music CD ☐ Bible or Lectionary	🌸 **Let Us Pray:** Thanking Prayer 🔥 **Hymn:** Love One Another

Activities	Enrichment

Let's Begin

Act out the situation.

(OPTIONAL) **Activity Master 27: Making Good Choices, p. 119E**

• **Reaching All Learners:** Tactile and Visual Learners

Activity

Circle the right choice.

(OPTIONAL) **What would you do?** Multiple Intelligence: Interpersonal

• **Justice and Peace:** Choosing to Help

❷ Discuss God's rules.

(OPTIONAL) **Following Rules** Multiple Intelligence: Bodily/Kinesthetic

Activity

Draw yourself making a good choice.

(OPTIONAL) **Activity Master 28: Make a Thank You Note, p. 124A**

(OPTIONAL) **Safety Rules** Multiple Intelligence: Visual/Spatial

• **Liturgy Link:** Attendance at Mass

• **Lectionary Link:** Break Open the Word

Pacing the Chapter

Parish
Meets once a week

In parish religious education classes, plan for approximately 60 minutes of class time.

Invite 10 minutes
Explore 40 minutes
Celebrate 10 minutes

The abundance of activity and enrichment options will allow flexibility in planning for longer sessions if needed.

School
Meets 5 days per week

In school religious education classes, plan for lesson 5 days per week for about 30 minutes. The lesson can be easily adapted for a 4-day week as well.

Day 1: Invite   **Day 4:** Explore
Day 2: Explore   **Day 5:** Celebrate
Day 3: Explore

The abundance of activity and enrichment options will allow flexibility in planning for longer sessions if needed.

CALL to FAITH e connect

• Online planning tools include chapter background and planner, activity master, customizable test, and more.
• Enhancement activities for each step of the catechetical process, including alternative prayer experiences and blessings.
• Games, activities, interactive review, alternative assessment, and more for children.

www.calltofaitheconnect.com

Home Connection

Chapter 14 Family Faith, p. 124
Take-home activities, chapter content review, saint features and prayer

 For more family activities
www.harcourtreligion.com

Name _____ Date _____

Making Good Choices

Directions: Your teacher will read some choices to you. Circle the box with the better choice.

Which clothes would you wear in cold weather?

Which food would make a healthy lunch?

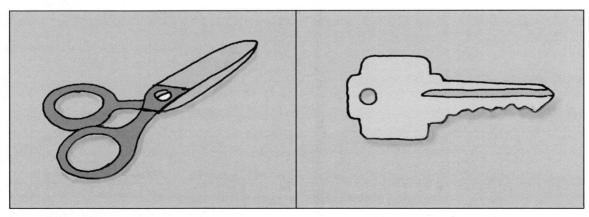

Which tool would help you open a door?

Good Choices

The law of the Lord is perfect.

Psalm 19:8

Read to Me

Let's Begin

Tanya's Choice

Tanya is in a big hurry.

She wants to play with her friend George.

Tanya must cross the street.

She can play with George sooner if she crosses in the middle of the block.

What should Tanya do?

● **What other rules help keep you safe?**

Possible response: No running inside.

119

Objective: To consider how rules keep everyone safe

 Let Us Pray

Sing the psalm verse to a simple tune. Have children sing it after you.

Let's Begin

Tanya's Choice

- Select two children to play the parts of Tanya and George.
- Have them act out the situation as you read it aloud.
- Refer to the illustration to clarify the situation.
- Discuss the choice that Tanya must make.
- Discuss how knowing a rule would help Tanya make the safest choice.
- Review safety rules with the group.
- Ask the text question and elicit responses from children.

OPTIONAL ACTIVITY

Activity Master 27: Making Good Choices: Distribute copies of the activity found on page 119E.

- Tell children they will be making choices.
- Ask them to circle the good choices.

▲ Activity Master 27

★ REACHING ALL LEARNERS

Tactile and Visual Learners Some children may benefit from other demonstrations of the situation involving Tanya and George.

- Draw a street and sidewalks on a sheet of poster board. Use toy cars and action figures to show the situation.
- In addition to showing the danger Tanya could be in, show the correct way for her to cross the street safely.

Objective: To realize that people help us make good choices

Help with Choices

Remind children that they make choices every day, just as Tanya did.

Ask children who it is that helps them make choices. Possible responses: Jesus, parents, teachers

- Read aloud the text.

- Ask children what kinds of choices they made that morning. Possible responses: what to eat, what to wear

Activity

- Hand out pencils.
- Read aloud the following situations. After you read, pause for children to circle the right choice.
- For the first set of pictures, say: "Sally's mother told her to share her toys with her friend. She wants to play by herself. What should she do?"
- For the second set of pictures, say: "Dylan's father told him to play on the path. He would rather play anywhere he wants to. What should he do?"

Help with Choices

You make choices every day.
Parents help you make choices.
Teachers help you make choices.
God the Holy Spirit helps you, too.

Activity

 Circle the picture with the choice the child should make.

120

✝ JUSTICE AND PEACE

Choosing to Help An important part of Christian morality is the obligation of the wealthy to happily choose to assist the poor.

- Every person is entitled to life's necessities.
- Those who have an excess of wealth are urged to help those who do not have enough.

Catholic Social Teaching: Option for the Poor

OPTIONAL ACTIVITY

What Would You Do? Make a "choice jar."

- Write situations similar to those above on small slips of paper, and put them in a jar.
- As time permits, ask a child to draw one from the jar and discuss with the group what to do.

Multiple Intelligence: Interpersonal

God's Rules

Jesus reminded his followers about God's rules.

Matthew 19:18–19

Jesus Teaches

Don't hurt anyone.
Take care of your body.
Don't take other people's things.
Tell the truth.
Obey your father and mother.
Love others as you love yourself.

Based on Matthew 19:18–19

? What are some ways you can follow God's rules?

121

Objective: To learn what Jesus tells everyone about God's rules

God's Rules

Recall with the group that rules help us make good choices.

• Tell children that God gave us rules for living. Jesus taught about those rules.

Jesus Teaches

• Proclaim the Gospel reading.

• Discuss the text question.

• Call attention to the illustration, pointing out that God's rules are for people of all ages.

✝ SCRIPTURE BACKGROUND

Rules to Follow These rules are taken from Jesus' advice to the rich young man in *Matthew 19:16-22*.

• Jesus enumerates many of the commandments and adds the commandment to love one another.

• Shortly after this, the rich young man went away discouraged.

• In the same passage, Jesus gave heart to his followers by pointing out that they would have a special place in heaven.

OPTIONAL ACTIVITY

Following Rules Play Red Light, Green Light.

• Tell children to march around the room.

• When you say "Red light," they must freeze in position.

• Tell them they must stay in that position until you say "Green light."

Multiple Intelligence: Bodily/Kinesthetic

Good Choices 121

Objective: To demonstrate how to follow God's rules

God's Rules Help

Recall that Jesus reminded his followers about God's rules.

- Explain that God gave these rules to his people long before Jesus was born.
- Read aloud the text.
- Talk about how classroom rules help children show love and care.

Activity

- Remind children of the different choices they have read about in the chapter.
- Ask them to pick one choice they may have to make today.
- Read aloud the activity directions.
- Hand out crayons or markers, and have children draw in the activity space.

Explore

God's Rules Help

God's rules help you make good choices.

God's rules help you love yourself and others.

God's rules are called the Ten Commandments.

Activity

Draw yourself making a good choice.

122

OPTIONAL ACTIVITY

Activity Master 28: Make a Thank-You Note Distribute copies of the activity found on page 124A.

- Help children write and decorate their notes.
- Send the notes to each child's "special person".

▲ Activity Master 28

OPTIONAL ACTIVITY

Safety Rules This is an excellent time to review rules for pedestrian safety with the group.

- Invite a police officer or crossing guard to meet with children and discuss pedestrian safety.
- If there is a crosswalk or traffic light near your school, help children practice crossing the street safely.

Multiple Intelligence: Visual/Spatial

Thanking Prayer

Leader: Jesus, you show us how to help others.

All: **You show us how to help others.**

Leader: You teach us about God's rules.

All: **You teach us about God's rules.**

Leader: Thank you for your help!

All: **Thank you for your help! Amen.**

Sing together.

Love one another,
Love one another,
as I have loved you.

Care for each other,
Care for each other,
as I care for you.

Love One Another

123

Objective: To praise and thank Jesus for his help in making good choices

 **Let Us Pray**

Tell children they will thank Jesus for his help.

Thanking Prayer

Prepare

Consider moving the prayer service to your parish church, in an area near religious art representing Jesus.

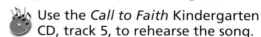 Use the *Call to Faith* Kindergarten CD, track 5, to rehearse the song.

Gather

Invite children into the prayer space.

• Tell children that they will repeat several short prayers after you.

Pray

• Pray aloud the prayers, and prompt children's responses.

• Encourage children to sing the song.

 LITURGY LINK

Attendance at Mass Point out to children that God's commandments tell us to keep the Lord's Day holy.

• We do this by going to Mass once a week, on Saturday evening or Sunday. We go to give thanks and praise to God. We hear Scripture and celebrate Jesus' gift of himself.

 LECTIONARY LINK

Break Open the Word Read last week's Sunday Gospel. Talk about how this reading helps us follow Jesus. For children's questions related to the weekly Gospel reading, visit our Web site.

GO ONLINE **Visit www.harcourtreligion.com for weekly scripture readings and seasonal resources.**

Wrap-Up

Family Faith

Remind children to discuss the Family Faith page at home. Encourage them to talk with family members about what they have learned about making good choices.

Family Project

- Encourage children to complete the activity with family members.

People of Faith

Remind children that Moses led God's people long before Jesus was born.

- God gave Moses the Commandments on two stone tablets.
- Moses was on a mountain when he received the Commandments.
- Encourage children to pray the prayer at home with their families.

  Visit **www.harcourtreligion.com** for weekly scripture readings and seasonal resources.

Catholics Believe

Dear Family,
In Chapter 14, the children learned that parents, teachers, and God help them make good choices. The children also learned about the Ten Commandments.

SCRIPTURE

Read Matthew 19:18–19 together with your child.

www.harcourtreligion.com For weekly scripture readings and seasonal resources

Family Project

Making Good Choices
Make an artistic reminder of the steps to making good choices. On a sheet of paper, draw a stoplight. In the top light, write STOP; in the middle light, write THINK; in the bottom light, write CHOOSE. Have your child color each part of the light with the proper color. Reinforce the ideas of stopping before making choices, thinking about rules that will help make the choices, and choosing wisely.

STOP

THINK

CHOOSE

People of Faith

God gave the Ten Commandments to Moses. The Ten Commandments help people know how to show love to God and other people.

Moses, 12th Century B.C. ▶

Family Prayer

God our Father, thank you for the rules you gave to Moses. Help us follow your rules and show love for others. Amen.

124 **CCC** *See Catechism of the Catholic Church 2472, 2070 for further reading on chapter content.*

? HOW DID I DO?

My week was

☐ *one of the best ever!* ☐ *pretty good.* ☐ *in need of improvement.*

In what discussions and activities were children most interested?

_____

What activity did I most enjoy teaching?

_____

In what area do I need to improve?

_____

Name _____ Date _____

Make a Thank You Note

Directions: Think of someone who helps you make good choices. Write his or her name on the first line. Write your name on the last line. Decorate the note, and send it to the person who helps you.

Dear _____,

You help me make good choices. Thank you!

Love,

_____

Faith Focus

- The Church continues Jesus' work of healing in the sacraments of healing. (CCC 1421)

Catechism Connection

The *Catechism* specifies that all forgiveness begins with God. (CCC 2010)

NDC Link

The saving actions of Jesus remind us of our need for conversion, penance, and forgiveness. (See *NDC*, 36B.)

Resources

BOOK
Stay with Us, Lord: Prayer and Reflections for Educators. Caruso, Miahael J., SJ. (editor). NCEA. Provides thoughtful insights that will help sustain a relationship with God.

DVD/VHS
God Wants Me to Forgive Them? (30 min.). Sony. This segment from the Veggie Tales series spotlights forgiveness.

Resources
For interactive lesson planner, chapter resources, and activities
www.harcourtreligion.com

If you forgive others their transgressions, your heavenly Father will forgive you. But if you do not forgive others, neither will your Father forgive your transgressions.

Matthew 6:14–15

Being Forgiven

We are all human; we are all sinners. Fortunately for us, there are many models of sinners in the Bible who have returned to God's good graces, among them Zacchaeus and the prodigal son. We are eligible for the same treatment, if only we ask for it.

The Church welcomes us to Reconciliation, the sacrament of forgiveness. Although your kindergartners are too young to partake of the sacrament fully, they can still be taught about its process on a rudimentary level: think about what you did; express sorrow; make up for your sin; try to do better.

As an adult, you may receive God's forgiveness in this sacrament. But here is the catch: the way to open yourself to receiving God's forgiveness, is to forgive those who have sinned against you. This is not easy.

Forgiving Others

We cannot expect forgiveness if we behave as the unforgiving servant did. We must seek the counsel of the Holy Spirit in finding ways to transform the hurts that we have experienced. Perhaps we can convert these hurts into learning experiences for ourselves. Adopting this attitude may help us become compassionate with those who injured us. At the very least, it may help us forgive them, and in doing so open us to God's forgiveness.

Reflect *How can you become a model of forgiveness to the children in your care?*

Communication Skills

Children acquire language skills by participating in group discussions.

- Facilitate sharing ideas by modeling the skill of communicating. Remind children that it is polite to listen and respond to others. Tell children they should take turns when talking with others.

- Allow children time to interview you or perhaps another classmate. Make sure children take turns listening and speaking. Praise children for being effective communicators.

Problem Solving

- I will occasionally quarrel with my classmates. Respond calmly. Redirect my negative behavior, and encourage me to use my words to solve problems.

- I am a thinker. Role-play "what if" situations with me often. I like to figure things out and this form of talking is a great way for me to process language.

Challenges and Practices

Some challenges in catechesis are adaptive challenges in which changes are required to sustain your spirit. Some adaptive challenges are obvious, while others erode the ability to sustain your spirit.

The best way to respond to adaptive challenges is with specific practices that

- are intentional ways of doing something instead of simply trying to hold on.

- are proactive responses instead of reactive responses.

- require discipline or courage.

Reflect **What is the greatest challenge you face in sustaining your spirit, and how do you deal with it?**

 Prayer

Holy Spirit, I am sometimes hurt by others. Help me view those who hurt me as God's children, too. Help me pray for them and show others how to forgive. Amen.

Weekly Planner

		Objectives	Materials	Prayer & Scripture
1 Invite	**Forgive Others** Page 125	To recognize that some things can be fixed	☐ Copies of Activity Master 29, p. 125E ☐ Pencils ☐ Crayons or markers ☐ Scissors	🌸 **Let Us Pray:** Psalm 25:12
2 Explore	**Help for Hurts** Page 126	To understand the need for forgiveness	☐ Pencils	
	Forgive One Another Page 127	To learn that God wants people to forgive one another	☐ Bag of beans	✝ **Scripture:** Matthew 18:21–22 ✝ **Scripture Background:** Forgiveness
	Special Signs Page 128	To illustrate ways to forgive	☐ Board or chart paper ☐ Pencils ☐ Copies of Activity Master 30, p. 130A ☐ Crayons or markers	✝ **Scripture:** Matthew 18:21–22
3 Celebrate	**Forgiving Prayer** Page 129	To ask God's help in living in love	☐ Music CD ☐ Bible or Lectionary	🌸 **Let Us Pray:** Forgiving Prayer 🎵 **Hymn:** Love One Another

Activities	Enrichment
## Let's Begin Look at the picture and talk about it. (OPTIONAL) **Activity Master 29: Say "I'm Sorry," p. 125E**	• **Reaching All Learners:** Auditory Learners
## Activity Connect the pictures.	• **Quick Tip:** Worrisome Situations • **Chapter Background:** Conflict Resolution
❓ Talk about forgiveness. (OPTIONAL) Bean Counting **Multiple Intelligence:** Mathematical/ Logical	
❓ Discuss signs that show forgiveness. (OPTIONAL) **Activity Master 30: Find the Hidden Message, p. 130A**	• **Cultural Awareness:** Friendship Bracelets
	• **Liturgy Link:** The Sign of Peace • **Lectionary Link:** Break Open the Word

Pacing the Chapter

Parish

Meets once a week

In parish religious education classes, plan for approximately 60 minutes of class time.

Invite	10 minutes
Explore	40 minutes
Celebrate	10 minutes

The abundance of activity and enrichment options will allow flexibility in planning for longer sessions if needed.

School

Meets 5 days per week

In school religious education classes, plan for lesson 5 days per week for about 30 minutes. The lesson can be easily adapted for a 4-day week as well.

Day 1: Invite   **Day 4:** Explore
Day 2: Explore   **Day 5:** Celebrate
Day 3: Explore

The abundance of activity and enrichment options will allow flexibility in planning for longer sessions if needed.

CALL to FAITH e connect

• Online planning tools include chapter background and planner, activity master, customizable test, and more.

• Enhancement activities for each step of the catechetical process, including alternative prayer experiences and blessings.

• Games, activities, interactive review, alternative assessment, and more for children.

www.calltofaitheconnect.com

Home Connection

Chapter 15 Family Faith, p. 130
Take-home activities, chapter content review, saint features and prayer

GO ONLINE **For more family activities**
www.harcourtreligion.com

Name _____ Date _____

Say "I'm Sorry"

Directions: Trace the letters, and color in the sign. Cut it out, and use it to make a friendship better.

I'm

Sorry

©Harcourt Religion

Chapter 15

Forgive Others

God shows them the way to choose.

Based on Psalm 25:12

Read to Me

Let's Begin

Fixing Things

Lisa was worried. "I fell and tore my new dress," she said.

Lisa's mother said, "We can fix it. You can help me. Bring me my sewing box, please."

● **What is Lisa doing in the picture?**

Possible response: helping her mother fix the dress

125

Objective: To recognize that some things can be fixed

Let Us Pray

Brainstorm simple gestures for the psalm verse. Read aloud the pslam verse. Have children say the verse with you as you make the gestures together.

Let's Begin

Fixing Things

- Have children examine the picture on the page.
- Ask children to guess what the story will be about.
- Read aloud the story to check children's predictions.
- Discuss the question.
- Ask children for examples of other things that can be fixed. Possible responses: toys, cars, windows, furniture

---

OPTIONAL ACTIVITY

Activity Master 29: Say "I'm Sorry" Distribute copies of the activity found on page 125E.

- Ask children to trace the letters and color in the sign.
- Tell them to cut it out and use it to make a friendship better.

▲ **Activity Master 29**

★ REACHING ALL LEARNERS

Auditory Learners Have children retell Lisa's story in song. To the tune of "Are You Sleeping," have them sing

Lisa fell and tore her dress.
Oh, too bad! She felt sad!
"Don't worry we can fix it.
We can work together."
Her mom said.
Now Lisa's glad!

Objective: To understand the need for forgiveness

Help for Hurts

Recall the story of Lisa's dress and how her mother fixed it.

- Ask children how they think a hurt friendship can be fixed. Possible responses: with words, with actions

- Read aloud the text.

- Point out that Lisa's mother used an action, sewing, to fix the dress.

- Have children describe actions and words that can fix friendships.

Activity

- Hand out pencils.

- Tell children to look at the top picture in the left column.

- Discuss why this is a hurtful situation.

- Have children find the picture in the right column that solves the problem and draw a line connecting the pictures.

- Complete the activity as a class.

Explore

Help for Hurts

Sometimes friendships are hurt.
You can make a friendship better.
You can use words to help it.
You can do things to help it.

Activity

Connect the pictures to show how to fix a friendship.

126

 CHAPTER BACKGROUND

Conflict Resolution Point out that people may not agree on all things. Explain to children that as Christians we must learn to solve problems peacefully.

- Teach children to use words to express their feelings.

- Model things for children to say in certain situations. For example, "I did something wrong, and I will try harder next time."

Forgive One Another

What should you do if someone is mean to you?

You should forgive that person.

God wants us to forgive others.

Matthew 18:21–22

Forgiveness

Peter asked Jesus how many times he should forgive someone.

"Must I forgive him seven times?" Peter asked.

"No, you must forgive him many more times than that," Jesus said.

Based on Matthew 18:21–22

? **What does Jesus say about forgiveness?**
Jesus said we must forgive many times.

127

Objective: To learn that God wants people to forgive one another

Forgive One Another

Recall that this lesson is about fixing problems in relationships.

- Read aloud the text.
- Ask children what it means to *forgive* someone. Possible responses: It means that you will accept their apology; you will be their friend even after they hurt you.

Forgiveness

- Tell children that you will tell them what Jesus said about forgiving people.
- Proclaim the Gospel reading.
- Discuss the text question.
- Point out the picture. Talk about why Peter looks surprised.

SCRIPTURE BACKGROUND

Forgiveness Jesus' words are adapted here to help children understand forgiveness.

- In the actual Scripture, Jesus' comment on forgiving seven times seventy times reverses the words of Lamech, who wanted to avenge wrongs against himself seventy-sevenfold (*Genesis 4:24*). From this statement, we are to learn that Jesus wants us to forgive limitlessly.

OPTIONAL ACTIVITY

Bean Counting Help children see that Jesus wants us to forgive limitlessly. Supply a bag of beans.

- Have children count out seven beans.
- Have children combine all of their beans and compare them to one group of seven beans.
- Point out that we are to forgive limitlessly.

Multiple Intelligence: Mathematical/Logical

Forgive Others 127

Objective: To illustrate ways to forgive

Special Signs

Remind children that we are to forgive others.

- Write the word *forgive* on the board or on chart paper.
- Review each letter with children and help them to identify the word.
- Ask them to circle the word where it appears on the page.
- Read aloud the text
- Tell children that they will practice signs of forgiveness and friendship.
- Have children look at the illustrations and tell which signs they use for forgiveness.
- Ask children to imitate the signs on the page and to demonstrate other ways of showing forgiveness.

Explore

Special Signs

Special words can help make things better with family or friends.

"I am sorry."

"I forgive you."

Special signs can help you make things better, too.

High-five

Smile

Hug

Kiss

❓ **When do you use these signs?**
Responses will vary.

128

OPTIONAL ACTIVITY

Activity Master 30: Find the Hidden Message Distribute copies of the activity found on page 130A.

- Tell children they will be looking for a hidden message.
- Help children follow directions to find the hidden message.

▲ **Activity Master 30**

CULTURAL AWARENESS

Friendship Bracelets Have children make friendship bracelets, a custom popular in Guatemala.

- The Guatemalan bracelets are made of four strands of brightly colored string that are tied together.
- Supply children with a few strands of yarn that they can tie together at intervals.

Forgiving Prayer

Leader: Dear God, sometimes I hurt others.

All: **Help me live in love.**

Leader: Help me show that I am sorry.

All: **Help me live in love.**

Leader: Sometimes others hurt me.

All: **Help me live in love.**

Leader: Help me show forgiveness.

All: **Help me live in love. Amen.**

Sing together.

Love one another,
Love one another,
as I have loved you.

Care for each other,
Care for each other,
as I care for you.

Love One Another

129

Objective: To ask God's help in living in love

 **Let Us Pray**

Tell children they will pray for help and forgiveness.

Forgiving Prayer

Prepare

Tell children their response will be the same to each of your short prayers.

- Practice the response.
- Have children sing the song as a round, with a second group entering when the first group sings the fourth line of the song.

  Use the *Call to Faith* Kindergarten CD, track 5, to rehearse the song.

Gather

Invite children to gather quietly in the prayer space.

Pray

- After praying each line, prompt children's response.
- Sing the song in rounds as rehearsed.

 LITURGY LINK

The Sign of Peace Point out to children that we share a sign of love at Mass during the Sign of Peace.

- Have children practice shaking hands or any other gesture that is used in your parish.
- Children may also say, "Peace be with you" or simply, "Peace."
- Remind children that it is important to mean what they say.

 LECTIONARY LINK

Break Open the Word Read last week's Sunday Gospel. Talk about how this reading helps us follow Jesus. For children's questions related to the weekly Gospel reading, visit our Web site.

GO ONLINE **Visit www.harcourtreligion.com for weekly scripture readings and seasonal resources.**

Wrap-Up

Family Faith

Remind children to discuss the Family Faith page at home. Encourage them to talk with family members about what they have learned about forgiveness.

Family Project

- Encourage children to discuss forgiveness with a family member.

People of Faith

Remind children that Moses led God's people long ago.

- God gave Moses the Ten Commandments.
- When Moses was getting the Commandments from God, the people sinned. If time permits, read aloud this story from a children's Bible.
- Encourage children to pray the prayer at home with their families.

  Visit **www.harcourtreligion.com** for weekly scripture readings and seasonal resources.

 CHAPTER 15
Family Faith

◎ Catholics Believe

Dear Family,

In Chapter 15, the children learned that friendships can be made better. They heard the Bible story about forgiving others. They also learned words and gestures that show sorrow and forgiveness.

✝ SCRIPTURE

Read together Matthew 18:21–22 with your child.

 www.harcourtreligion.com
For weekly scripture readings and seasonal resources

Family Project

Showing Forgiveness Practice words and ways of repairing hurt relationships. Use hugs, kisses, handshakes, and phrases such as "I forgive you" to show forgiveness. Point out that the Sign of Peace exchanged at Mass shows that we are at peace with one another. Make this part of the Mass more meaningful by adding personal comments of sorrow and forgiveness.

People of Faith

Moses forgave his friends who forgot to love God and others.

Moses, 12th Century B.C. ▶

 Family Prayer

God our Father, help us forgive other people when they hurt us. Help us show sorrow when we hurt others. Amen.

130 **CCC** *See Catechism of the Catholic Church 1421, 2227, 1435 for further reading on chapter content.*

? HOW DID I DO?

The week was

☐ *one of the best ever!*   ☐ *pretty good.*   ☐ *in need of improvement.*

In what discussions and activities were children most interested?

_____

What activity did I most enjoy teaching?

_____

In what area do I need to improve?

_____

Name _____ Date _____

Find the Hidden Message

Directions: Color in the pieces marked with a ♥ in red. Then color in the other pieces with other colors.

©Harcourt Religion

Scripture Story

Jesus and Zacchaeus

(Luke 19:1–10)

Family Note: In class your child has learned that God wants us to make loving choices and to ask forgiveness when we have hurt others. After reading this Scripture Story together, talk about how Zacchaeus changed because of Jesus. The next time you recognize that your child is trying hard to be a better person, praise his or her actions.

Jesus smiled. He said to Zacchaeus, "You are trying to be a better person.

Good for you! You are a special child of God!"

Color in Jesus and Zacchaeus.

8

131

Jesus was traveling with his friends.

They came to a town.

The people in the town were excited about seeing Jesus.

They gathered in a big crowd.

2

Zacchaeus knew what they were saying.

He told Jesus, "I will give away half of what I own.

I will pay back the people who I cheated.

I will give them more than I took from them."

7

132

The people in the town were surprised.

They said, "Why does Jesus want Zacchaeus for a friend? We know that he cheats people."

A man named Zacchaeus lived in the town.

He was very short.

He could not see Jesus because everyone else was so tall.

3

6

133

Zacchaeus had an idea.
He would climb a tree!
Then he could see Jesus
and hear him.

Jesus looked up. He saw
Zacchaeus.
He said, "Zacchaeus,
come down.
I want to eat at your
house today."

4

5

134

Chapter 16

Overview

Faith Focus

■ The sacraments communicate our unity with God. *(CCC 1118)*

Catechism Connection

The *Catechism* explains that the sacraments are meant to make us holy, to strengthen the Body of Christ, and to honor God. *(CCC 1123)*

NDC Link

The *Directory* notes that catechesis helps us move from the signs and symbols of our faith to the mysteries they reveal or make present. (See *NDC*, 33.)

Resources

BOOK
A Crash Course in Teaching Religion. Glavich, Kathleen. Twenty-Third Publications. Provides many concrete tips for new and experienced catechists.

DVD/VHS
Jesus: What He Said and What He Did (18 min.). Oblate Media. Follows Jesus from his Baptism through the Resurrection.

 Resources
For interactive lesson planner, chapter resources, and activities
www.harcourtreligion.com

Holy Signs

CHAPTER BACKGROUND

 Jesus said to him, "Unless you people see signs and wonders, you will not believe."

John 4:48

Seeing and Believing

The sacraments are seven gifts from Jesus, seven signs of God's life within us. In many ways, they bridge the gap between human experience and God. God knows that we are constantly changing. He is aware of our movement toward him to accepting grace. He is aware of our movement away from him when we reject his love. We are not omniscient, however. We need to see signs of God's love, of the changes within ourselves. And that is what the sacraments do for us. They help us believe.

In addition, the sacraments build up the Church. Each time a person receives any sacrament, that person grows in grace. As each Church member becomes closer to God, the Church also becomes closer to God.

Ceremonies and Celebrations

The rituals that comprise the sacraments are set by the Church and are not changed. Inspired by the Holy Spirit, the rituals impart divine grace to those whose hearts are disposed to receive it.

Sacraments are also marked by celebrations. Families and cultures have special ways of celebrating the sacraments and marking the changes they bring to the lives of the faithful. Baptisms, First Communions, and Holy Matrimony, especially, are often enhanced by gatherings of family and friends. The children in your group may be happy to tell you about their families' celebrations of these rituals. Listen to their tales, and be glad of the joy they find in Jesus' gifts.

Reflect   What difference have the sacraments made in your relationship with God?

Sign Language

Help children understand that people are different in many ways and those differences make each person unique and special. Explain that people speak different languages, and some use sign language to communicate.

- Teach the sign of I Love You. Hold up your hand, allow your thumb, pointer and pinkie to extend, fold your middle and ring fingers.

- Invite someone to your class to teach children sign language. Allow children time to ask questions about the language and practice the signs.

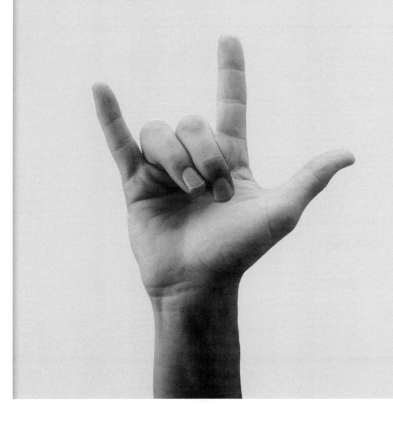

Concrete Things

- I am a concrete learner. I need to touch and explore as much as possible.

- I have a hard time understanding abstract concepts. Relate learning to my world.

Moments of Grace

Catechesis puts you in touch with the longings and dreams of those around you. It is an important spiritual task to listen to and truly hear the inner voices of students and their parents. You may see the unspoken pain in someone's eyes. You may hear important questions that shy souls are afraid to ask.

The practice of collecting moments of grace is a way to stay in touch with the spiritual nature of your work by deliberately paying attention. You can collect moments of grace by noticing when people invite you to come to know them better or let you get a glimpse of their vulnerability. Moments of grace are collected when you realize that the present is sacred and the ordinary is holy.

Reflect   ***What moments of grace have sustained your spirit in the past?***

 Prayer

Jesus Christ, our Lord, thank you for giving us the sacraments. Help us be aware of their power in our lives. Help us use them to become closer to you. Amen.

Weekly Planner

		Objectives	Materials	Prayer & Scripture
1 Invite	**Holy Signs** Page 135	To notice signs that are everywhere	☐ Crucifix ☐ Copies of Activity Master 31, p. 135E ☐ Crayons or markers	🙏 Let Us Pray: Psalm 36:10
2 Explore	**Jesus' Signs** Page 136	To learn that Jesus and the Church use signs	☐ Copies of Activity Master 32, p. 140A ☐ Crayons or markers ☐ Scissors ☐ Glue	
	Blessing Food Page 137	To show how Jesus used signs	☐ Drawing paper ☐ Crayons or markers ☐ Binder	✝ Scripture: Mark 6:34–42 ✝ Scripture Background: Feeding a Multitude
	Signs of God's Love Page 138	To recognize signs of God's love	☐ Bingo markers ☐ Mural paper ☐ Paint	✝ Scripture: Mark 6:34–42
3 Celebrate	**Thanking Prayer** Page 139	To appreciate signs of God's love	☐ Music CD ☐ Bible or Lectionary ☐ Completed Activity Master 31	🙏 Let Us Pray: Thanking Prayer 🎵 **Hymn:** Psalm 126: The Lord Has Done Great Things

Activities	Enrichment

Let's Begin

Talk about signs and what they mean.

OPTIONAL **Activity Master 31: Sign of Love, p. 135E**

OPTIONAL Look for Signs
Multiple Intelligence: Naturalist

❓ Discuss when the Church family uses signs.

OPTIONAL **Activity Master 32: God's-Signs, p. 140A**

• **Reaching All Learners:**
Tactile Learners

❓ Discuss and act out the Gospel story.

OPTIONAL Signs
Multiple Intelligence: Interpersonal

Activity

Play the game about signs.

OPTIONAL Cross-Curricular: Art
Multiple Intelligence: Bodily/Kinesthetic

OPTIONAL Signs in Your Parish Church
Multiple Intelligence: Visual/Spatial

• **Liturgy Link:**
Signs at Mass

• **Lectionary Link:**
Break Open the Word

Pacing the Chapter

Parish

Meets once a week

In parish religious education classes, plan for approximately 60 minutes of class time.

Invite	10 minutes
Explore	40 minutes
Celebrate	10 minutes

The abundance of activity and enrichment options will allow flexibility in planning for longer sessions if needed.

School

Meets 5 days per week

In school religious education classes, plan for lesson 5 days per week for about 30 minutes. The lesson can be easily adapted for a 4-day week as well.

Day 1: Invite   **Day 4:** Explore
Day 2: Explore   **Day 5:** Celebrate
Day 3: Explore

The abundance of activity and enrichment options will allow flexibility in planning for longer sessions if needed.

- Online planning tools include chapter background and planner, activity master, customizable test, and more.
- Enhancement activities for each step of the catechetical process, including alternative prayer experiences and blessings.
- Games, activities, interactive review, alternative assessment, and more for children.

www.calltofaitheconnect.com

Home Connection

Chapter 16 Family Faith, p. 140
Take-home activities, chapter content review, saint features and prayer

 For more family activities
www.harcourtreligion.com

Name _____ Date _____

Sign of Love

Directions: Draw your favorite sign of love.

My Favorite Sign of Love.

Chapter 16 Holy Signs

For with you is the fountain of life.

Psalm 36:10

Read to Me

Let's Begin

Signs Everywhere

We see signs everywhere we go.

Signs give us information.

They give us directions.

Signs can also tell us about love.

● What does this sign mean? What other signs do you know about?

Responses will vary.

135

Objective: To notice signs that are everywhere

 **Let Us Pray**

Invite children to gather in the prayer space and make the Sign of the Cross. In the prayer space, have a crucifix and a Bible opened to the psalm verse.

Read aloud the psalm verse. Have children respond, "Amen."

Let's Begin

Signs Everywhere

- Call attention to the picture.
- Ask children the first text question.
- Read aloud the text.
- Discuss why signs are important. Point out that signs and words give us information about other people and the world.
- Ask the second text question.
- Have children act out some signs they know about.

OPTIONAL ACTIVITY

Activity Master 31: Sign of Love Distribute copies of the activity found on page 135E.

- Tell children they will be drawing.
- Ask them to draw their favorite sign of love and explain it to the class.

Sign of Love

Directions: Draw your favorite sign of love.

My Favorite Sign of Love.

▲ Activity Master 31

OPTIONAL ACTIVITY

Look for Signs Go on a walk to seek signs in the school neighborhood.

- Look for traffic signs, such as lights, stop signs, and crosswalks. Talk about how they keep us safe.
- Look for signs in nature. Clouds may indicate rain to come, or budding flowers may be an early sign of spring.

Multiple Intelligence: Naturalist

Objective: To learn that Jesus and the Church use signs.

Jesus' Signs

Recall that signs teach us about the world.

- Invite children to talk about signs of God's love in the world and in their lives.
- Read aloud the text.
- Point out the illustrations of Jesus and the signs he used.
- Ask children how Jesus used signs to show God's love. Possible response: Jesus used signs like food and words to show God's love.
- Ask the text question.

Explore

Jesus' Signs

The world is full of signs.

Jesus used signs to teach people.

He used signs to show people God's love.

The Church family uses the signs Jesus used.

Water

Light

Food

? **When does the Church family use these signs?** The Church uses these signs at Mass.

136

Activity Master 32: God's Signs Distribute copies of the activity found on page 140A.

- Tell children they will be looking for signs.
- Ask them to find the signs and color them. Then have them cut them out and glue them on the cross.

Name _____ Date _____

God's Signs

Directions: Color the signs of God's love. Cut them out, and glue them on the cross.

▲ Activity Master 32

Tactile Learners The Church uses sacred signs to help us see God's love in our lives. These signs are called sacramentals. Examples of sacramentals include rosaries, holy water, and medals, as well as actions (the Sign of the Cross) and prayers.

- Allow children to hold holy objects. Explain that we treat them with reverence.

Blessing Food

Many people were listening to Jesus. They were hungry.

A boy had brought some bread and fish.

This wasn't enough food for so many! Jesus blessed the boy's food.

Jesus' friends shared the food with everyone. They all had more than enough to eat.

Based on John 6:1–13

❓ What did Jesus do?
Possible response: blessed food, shared food, gave people food to eat

137

Blessing Food

Remind children that Jesus used signs to teach us.

• Tell children that they will hear a story about a sign that Jesus used.

• Proclaim the Gospel reading.

• Refer to the illustration to show the small amount of food and the large crowd.

• Ask children what the blessing and the food showed the people. Possible response: They showed that Jesus had great power; they showed that God loved the people and knew that they needed food.

• Select children to play the parts of Jesus, the boy, Jesus' friends, and the crowd.

• Have children act out the story as you read it aloud again.

• Discuss the text question.

✝ SCRIPTURE BACKGROUND

Feeding a Multitude This story is told in all four Gospels.

• It echoes the theme of the manna that God provided to feed Moses' followers after leaving Egypt.

• It also looks forward to the Last Supper, when Jesus shared a sacred meal with his followers.

OPTIONAL ACTIVITY

Signs Make a book of favorite signs.

• Have children draw traffic signs and other signs that they encounter every day.

• Collect the drawings, laminate them, if possible, and place them in a binder or other cover.

• Have children take turns taking the book home and sharing it with family members.

Multiple Intelligence: Interpersonal

Objective: To recognize signs of God's love

Signs of God's Love

Recall the Gospel reading.

• Read aloud the text .

• Ask children why blessings and food are signs of God's love. Possible responses: Blessings are special prayers that remind us of God; food makes people happy.

Activity

• **Tell** children they will be playing a game about signs.

• Distribute markers that would be suitable for a bingo game.

• Read aloud the directions.

• Read aloud these clues; vary the order in which they are read.
a place to pray (church)
the Holy Spirit (dove)
God's stories (Bible)
where Baby Jesus slept (manger)
Jesus calling his friends (Jesus motioning to apostles)
love (heart)
how Jesus died (cross)
God's creation (world)

Signs of God's Love

Jesus blessed the bread and fish.

The blessing and the food were signs of God's love.

Activity

Your teacher will give you a clue.

Find the sign that fits the clue.

Cover the sign with a marker.

138

Cross-Curricular: Art The purpose of this exercise is to remind children that they should follow God's signs.

• Have children paint with their feet on a long sheet of paper.

• Use the foot prints to make a bulletin board with the title "We Walk with God."

Multiple Intelligence: Bodily/Kinesthetic

Signs in Your Parish Church Challenge children to find signs in your church building.

• Prior to taking children into the building, visit it yourself to discover signs that the children would recognize. These could be in religious art, for example.

• Take children into the church building. Help them discover and interpret the signs.

Multiple Intelligence: Visual/Spatial

Thanking Prayer

Leader: God our Father, you have given us many signs of your love. We have our beautiful world. We have our friends and families. These are wonderful signs. But the best sign of your love is your Son, Jesus. Thank you for all of your love.

All: Amen.

 **Sing together.**

The Lord has done great
   things for us;
We are filled with joy,
We are filled with joy.

Psalm 126:
The Lord Has Done
Great Things

Objective: To appreciate signs of God's love

 Let Us Pray

Tell children they will thank God and sing with joy.

Thanking Prayer

Prepare

Have children bring the signs of love they created earlier.

Use the *Call to Faith* Kindergarten CD, track 6, to rehearse the song.

Gather

Ask children to carry their signs of God's love into the prayer space.

- Have children stand in a circle around the prayer table.

Pray

- Have children look at their sign of love as you pray aloud.
- Sing the song.
- Have children return to their places.

139

 LITURGY LINK

Signs at Mass   Have children look for signs that show God's love at Mass. Point out the following:

- As the Mass begins, altar servers carry in candles, a sign of light and warmth.
- The deacon carries the Book of the Gospels, a sign of God's Word in the Bible.
- The priest blesses the people with the Sign of the Cross, a sign of God's care.
- Have children look for other signs and report on them during the next class.

 LECTIONARY LINK

Break Open the Word   Read last week's Sunday Gospel. Talk about how this reading helps us follow Jesus. For children's questions related to the weekly Gospel reading, visit our Web site.

 Visit www.harcourtreligion.com for weekly scripture readings and seasonal resources.

Wrap-Up

Family Faith

Remind children to discuss the Family Faith page at home. Encourage them to talk with family members about what they have learned about signs.

Family Project

- Encourage children to do the activity with family members.

People of Faith

Tell children about Saint John the Baptist.

- John the Baptist's parents were Zachary and Elizabeth. Elizabeth was the cousin that Mary visited after the Annunciation. Elizabeth was expecting John the Baptist when Mary visited.

- Encourage children to pray the prayer at home with their families.

  Visit **www.harcourtreligion.com** for weekly scripture readings and seasonal resources.

Catholics Believe

Dear Family,

In Chapter 16, the children learned that special signs tell about God's love for us. Jesus used signs when he taught people. They also reviewed some of the signs of God's love that they have learned about this year.

✝ SCRIPTURE

Read Mark 6:34–42 together with your child.

 www.harcourtreligion.com For weekly scripture readings and seasonal resources

Family Project

Signs of Love Send a sign of love to a friend or family member who is far away. Take your child to a local post office, and allow him or her to purchase a postcard. Help your child write a message of love on the card and address it. With your child, mail the card. Talk about how the message will brighten the day of the receiver. Relate this happiness to the happiness we receive from God's messages of love to us in the Bible.

People of Faith

John the Baptist was Jesus' cousin. God sent John as a sign of love to his parents and to all the people that he met.

Saint John ▶ the Baptist, 1 B.C.–32 A.D.

Family Prayer

God our Father, thank you for your signs of love to us. Help us see and appreciate them. Amen.

140 CCC *See Catechism of the Catholic Church 459, 1749, 1131 for further reading on chapter content.*

? HOW DID I DO?

This week was

☐ *one of the best ever!*   ☐ *pretty good.*   ☐ *in need of improvement.*

In what discussions and activities were children most interested?

_____

What activity did I most enjoy teaching?

_____

In what area do I need to improve?

_____

Name _____ Date _____

God's Signs

Directions: Color the signs of God's love. Cut them out, and glue them on the cross.

Overview

Faith Focus

- Baptism is the gateway to the sacraments and to Christian life. *(CCC 1213)*

Catechism Connection

The *Catechism* tells us that Baptism makes us new creatures, members of the Church, adopted children of God, and dwelling places of the Holy Spirit. *(CCC 1265)*

NDC Link

The *Directory* reminds us that Baptism is the foundation of and the gateway into the Christian life. (See *NDC*, 36A1.)

Resources

BOOK
Grace for the Moment, Volume II. Lucado, Max. Liturgical Press. Provides a Scripture-based thought for each day of the year.

DVD/VHS
The New Birthday Club (15 min.). Oblate Media. Explains that Baptism is a rebirth and explores its ritual and symbols.

Resources
For interactive lesson planner, chapter resources, and activities
www.harcourtreligion.com

Peter [said] to them, "Repent and be baptized, every one of you, in the name of Jesus Christ for the forgiveness of your sins; and you will receive the gift of the holy Spirit."

Acts 2:38

Saving Waters

Since the creation of the world, water has been recognized as a symbol of spiritual regeneration. In the Old Testament, it is one of the first elements named in creation, plays a part in the flood, and symbolizes freedom as the People of God cross the Red Sea.

Water's role in our salvation becomes even more clear in the New Testament when it becomes allied with baptism. The central event inaugurating Jesus' public life was his baptism at the hands of John the Baptist. Jesus promised living water to the woman at the well. Before his Ascension, Jesus charged his Apostles with traveling to share the news of salvation and to baptize anyone who confessed belief in him.

The Gateway Sacrament

Baptism brings us into membership in the Church and makes us eligible to celebrate all other sacraments. The richness of the ritual tells us of its importance to salvation. Its rites include the Sign of the Cross, reading of the Word of God, promises and exorcisms, and anointing with oil of catechumens. The essential element of the sacrament, which must be present for a valid Baptism, is the immersion into water or the pouring of water onto the candidate as the words of the sacrament are spoken.

As with all sacraments, Baptism signifies a new beginning. The white garment of the ritual identifies the new member with the risen Christ. The baptismal candle symbolizes Christ's enlightenment. Thus, the newly baptized person begins a beautiful journey toward salvation.

Reflect ***How have you fulfilled the promise of your Baptism?***

Baby Pictures

Children love to hear stories and see pictures of themselves now and from their past. They are aware of growing up and often like to hear stories of what they can do now that they couldn't do as babies.

- Ask family members to send in pictures of their children. Allow children time to share their pictures with the group. Have children tell a story about what was taking place in the picture.

- Share with children your own baby picture, and share a story from your own childhood.

Prayer

- I am beginning to read and write. Have simple prayers posted around the room for me to read and copy.

- I like to create motions to go with simple prayers. This helps me remember the words.

Remember Who You Are

You can be overwhelmed by the religious, educational, and emotional expectations of others. Unless you adapt to the challenge of superhuman expectations, you may become fatigued and ineffective.

You may not be able to change others' superhuman expectations of you, but you can practice remembering who you are. This means intentionally reclaiming what you do best and what you care most about.

Remembering who you are encompasses including tasks in your life that come naturally, so that you preserve those sources of fulfillment.

Reflect **Which of your natural talents or interests do you need to remember and reclaim?**

Prayer

Holy Spirit, who made the holy waters of the first creation, help the children and me appreciate the rich symbolism of water, which in Baptism shows the promise of new life in you. Amen.

Weekly Planner

	Objectives	Materials	Prayer & Scripture
1 Invite **Baptism** Page 141	To recognize that water is all around	☐ Board or chart paper ☐ Copies of Activity Master 33, p. 141E ☐ Pencils ☐ Waterproof container ☐ Soap and sponges ☐ Other objects	🙏 **Let Us Pray:** Psalm 23:2
2 Explore **Life from Water** Page 142	To understand that all living things need water	☐ Crayons or markers	
A Sign of Love Page 143	To show how Jesus' followers used water as a sign		✝ **Scripture:** Acts 8:35–40 ✝ **Scripture Background:** The Conversion of the Ethiopian
A Special Celebration Page 144	To learn that Baptism makes a person a member of the Church	☐ Baptism pictures or video ☐ Copies of Activity Master 34, p. 146A ☐ Pencils ☐ Crayons or markers ☐ Scissors	✝ **Scripture:** Acts 8:35–40
3 Celebrate **Prayer of Praise** Page 145	To thank God for water and Baptism	☐ Music CD ☐ Bible or Lectionary	🙏 **Let Us Pray:** Prayer of Praise 🎵 **Hymn:** Psalm 126: The Lord Has Done Great Things

Activities	Enrichment
## Let's Begin Solve the riddle. (OPTIONAL) **Activity Master 33: How We Use Water, p. 141E** (OPTIONAL) Fun with water **Multiple Intelligence: Naturalist**	
❓ Talk about how water is used. ## Activity Find the things that use water. (OPTIONAL) Water Safety **Multiple Intelligence: Naturalist**	• **Reaching All Learners:** Children with Visual Difficulties
❓ Discuss Baptism and why it makes people happy.	• **Chapter Background:** Baptism
❓ Discuss your Baptism. (OPTIONAL) **Activity Master 34: Make a Baptism Banner, p. 146A**	• **Quick Tip:** A Church Tour
	• **Liturgy Link:** Baptism in the Liturgy • **Lectionary Link:** Break Open the Word

Pacing the Chapter

Parish
Meets once a week

In parish religious education classes, plan for approximately 60 minutes of class time.

Invite	10 minutes
Explore	40 minutes
Celebrate	10 minutes

The abundance of activity and enrichment options will allow flexibility in planning for longer sessions if needed.

School
Meets 5 days per week

In school religious education classes, plan for lesson 5 days per week for about 30 minutes. The lesson can be easily adapted for a 4-day week as well.

Day 1: Invite   **Day 4:** Explore
Day 2: Explore   **Day 5:** Celebrate
Day 3: Explore

The abundance of activity and enrichment options will allow flexibility in planning for longer sessions if needed.

CALL to FAITH
e connect

• Online planning tools include chapter background and planner, activity master, customizable test, and more.

• Enhancement activities for each step of the catechetical process, including alternative prayer experiences and blessings.

• Games, activities, interactive review, alternative assessment, and more for children.

www.calltofaitheconnect.com

Home Connection
Chapter 17 Family Faith, p. 146
Take-home activities, chapter content review, saint features and prayer

For more family activities
www.harcourtreligion.com

Name _____ Date _____

How We Use Water

Directions: Connect the pictures that belong together to show how water is used.

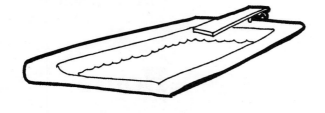

Baptism

 To safe waters you lead me.

Psalm 23:2

Read to Me

Let's Begin

A Riddle

What is in the rain but not in a chain?

What is in a creek but not in a cheek?

What is in a tear but not in a cheer?

● **Where else can you find water?**

Possible responses: in the ocean, creeks, puddles, rivers

141

Objective: To recognize that water is all around

 Let Us Pray

Invite children to make up gestures for the psalm. Read aloud the psalm verse. Have children do the gestures as they repeat the psalm after you.

Let's Begin

A Riddle

• Tell children that today's lesson begins with a riddle.

• Read aloud the riddle.

• Have children look at the picture for clues about solving the riddle.

• Work with children to help them discover the answer.

• Write *water* on the board or on chart paper.

• Discuss the question.

OPTIONAL ACTIVITY

Activity Master 33: How We Use Water Distribute copies of the activity found on page 141E.

• Tell children they will be connecting pictures.

• Help children follow the directions to complete the activity.

▲ **Activity Master 33**

OPTIONAL ACTIVITY

Fun with Water Have children perform some sink or float experiments with water. Use a large waterproof container.

• Have children predict whether items such as soap, sponges, etc. will float. Record predictions.

• Test predictions by tossing the items into the water. Check the actual results against the predictions.

Multiple Intelligence: Naturalist

Objective: To understand that all living things need water

Life from Water

Recall with children that water is important for our lives.

• Point out that water is in every living thing.

• Read aloud the text.

• Discuss the text question.

Activity

• Hand out crayons or markers to children.

• Tell children that four things that use water are hidden in the puzzle.

• Ask children to find the four things and color them.

• When children have finished, have them identify each thing and tell how the fish, the turtle, the child, and the cat use water.

Explore

Life from Water

Every thing needs water to live.
You drink water.
People wash and cook with water.
Some animals live in water.

❓ **How else do you use water?**
Possible responses: for playing, for fountains, for gardening

Activity

Find and color all the things that use water.

142

⭐ **REACHING ALL LEARNERS**

Children with Visual Difficulties Some children may not easily find the items that are hidden in the puzzle. Possible ways of assisting them include:

• Pairing such children with a partner who can help with the task.

• Outlining the items so that they are easier for the child to recognize.

• Marking the items with an *X*.

OPTIONAL ACTIVITY

Water Safety Remind children that even though water is a great gift from God, we must use it wisely.

• Take swimming lessons and have an adult with you when you swim.

• Don't touch a pot or pan of hot water.

• Don't run on a slippery floor.

• Always wear a life jacket in a boat.

Multiple Intelligence: Naturalist

A Sign of Love

Jesus' followers used water as a sign of God's life and love.

They used water to baptize new Church members.

A New Member

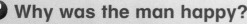

Philip told a young man about Jesus.

The young man said, "I want to follow Jesus. Please baptize me."

The young man went into the water and was baptized. He was very happy.

Based on Acts 8:35–40

? Why was the man happy?
Possible responses: He knew he belonged to the Church; he became a follower and friend of Jesus.

143

Objective: To show how Jesus' followers used water as a sign

A Sign of Love

Remind children that water is used in many ways in our lives.

• Read aloud the text.

• Tell children that everyone who belongs to the Church was baptized at some time.

A New Member

• Ask children to listen as you tell a Bible story about a baptism.

• Proclaim the scripture story.

• Have children look at the illustration and discuss it.

• Choose children to act out the roles of the young man and Philip. Have them act out the story as you read it aloud again.

• Discuss the text question.

SCRIPTURE BACKGROUND

The Conversion of the Ethiopian This story takes place as Philip is traveling to share the Gospel.

• The young man who converts so happily is an official of the Ethiopian court; he works for the queen.

• Philip meets him as he is pondering a passage from Isaiah, and the young man asks Philip to explain it to him.

• The passage shows the spread of the early Church beyond the Holy Land.

CHAPTER BACKGROUND

Baptism This first Sacrament of Initiation brings a new member into the Church. Baptism involves pouring water over the head of the new member and saying the words, "*Name,* I baptize you in the name of the Father, and of the Son, and of the Holy Spirit." The new member may either be dipped or plunged into water.

Objective: To learn that Baptism makes a person a member of the Church

A Special Celebration

Recall with children that water is used at Baptism.

- Ask children if any have attended a Baptism. If so, encourage them to tell what they remember.
- Read aloud the text to children.
- Tell children that the priest says the name of the person and "I baptize you in the name of the Father, and of the Son, and of the Holy Spirit."
- Ask children which prayer this sounds like. the Sign of the Cross
- Have children interpret the illustration.
- Discuss the text question.
- Consider playing videotapes or showing pictures of children's Baptisms if any are available.

A Special Celebration

Baptism is a special Church celebration.

At Baptism, a person becomes a member of the Church.

Like Philip, the priest uses water to baptize.

The priest also says special words.

Then the person belongs to the Church family.

❓ What do you know about your Baptism?
Responses will vary.

144

Activity Master 34: Make a Baptism Banner Distribute copies of the activity found on page 146A.

- Tell children they will be making a banner.
- Help children follow directions for writing, decorating, and cutting the banner.

▲ **Activity Master 34**

QUICK TIP

A Church Tour

- Plan a time to take children to the baptismal font in your church.
- If necessary, get permission in advance.
- Arrange for a parish priest to meet the class in the church and explain the Sacrament of Baptism.

Prayer of Praise

Leader: Water is in all living things.

All: **We praise you for water.**

Leader: Water helps plants grow.

All: **We praise you for water.**

Leader: Water takes away our thirst.

All: **We praise you for water.**

Leader: Water welcomed us into your Church.

All: **We praise you for water. Amen.**

Sing together.

The Lord has done great
things for us;
We are filled with joy,
We are filled with joy.

Psalm 126: The Lord
Has Done Great Things

145

Objective: To thank God for water and Baptism

 **Let Us Pray**

Tell children they will praise God for water.

Prayer of Praise

Prepare

Arrange to have this prayer service in your church building, near the Baptismal font.

- Teach children the response.
- Review the Sign of the Cross with children.

 Use the *Call to Faith* Kindergarten CD, track 6, to rehearse the song.

Gather

Take children to the church building. Be certain that they bless themselves with holy water as they enter. Help them make the Sign of the Cross.

- Gather children around the Baptismal font.

Pray

- Read aloud the leader's part, and have children pray the response.
- Conclude with the song.

LITURGY LINK

Baptism in the Liturgy   Baptisms are ideally celebrated in the presence of the entire parish community.

- Find out when a Baptism will be part of a weekend Mass. Encourage children to attend and pay attention to the words and actions that welcome a Church member.
- Often adults are baptized at the Easter Vigil. Invite a newly baptized adult to tell the group about his or her experience.

LECTIONARY LINK

Break Open the Word   Read last week's Sunday Gospel. Talk about how this reading helps us follow Jesus. For children's questions related to the weekly Gospel reading, visit our Web site.

 GO ONLINE **Visit www.harcourtreligion.com for weekly scripture readings and seasonal resources.**

Wrap-Up

Family Faith

Remind children to discuss the Family Faith page at home. Encourage them to talk with family members about what they have learned about water and Baptism.

Family Project

- Encourage children to do this activity with family members.

People of Faith

Remind children that Saint John the Baptist was Jesus' cousin.

- Tell children that Saint John's job was to come before Jesus and tell other people that Jesus would lead them to God.

- Encourage children to pray the prayer at home with their families.

 Visit **www.harcourtreligion.com** for weekly scripture readings and seasonal resources.

Family Faith

Catholics Believe

Dear Family,

In Chapter 17, the children learned that water is a sign of God's life and love. The Church uses water to baptize new members. The children also learned that they became members of the Church family at Baptism.

SCRIPTURE

Read Acts 8:35–40 together with your child.

www.harcourtreligion.com For weekly scripture readings and seasonal resources

Family Project

Share a Baptism Story Tell your child about his or her Baptism. Tell how you selected his or her godparents and how felt as your child was being baptized. If have pictures or a videotape of the ever share them with your child. The next tim you visit your parish church, remind you child to bless himself or herself with hol water. Point out that these blessings re our Baptism.

People of Faith

John told people how to love God. He baptized many people in the Jordan River.

Saint John the Baptist, I B.C.–32 A.D.

Family Prayer

Dear God, thank you for the sacrament of Baptism. Help us be good members of your Church family. Amen.

146 *See Catechism of the Catholic Church I, 1218, 1228 for further reading on chapter content.*

HOW DID I DO?

This week was

☐ *one of the best ever!* ☐ *pretty good.* ☐ *in need of improvement.*

In what discussions and activities were children most interested?

_____

What activity did I most enjoy teaching?

_____

In what area do I need to improve?

_____

Name _____ Date _____

Make a Baptism Banner

Directions: Write the name of someone who was recently baptized on the line. Decorate the banner, cut it out, and send it to the person.

Chapter 18

Overview

Faith Focus

■ The Eucharist unites Christ and all members of the Church in praising and thanking God the Father. *(CCC 1407)*

Catechism Connection

The *Catechism* emphasizes that Jesus is present with us in the Blessed Sacrament in a form that shows his love for us and in which we adore him. *(CCC 1380)*

NDC Link

The *Directory* notes that preparation for participation in the Eucharist is a primary means of catechesis. (See *NDC*, 17C.)

Resources

BOOK
*God Speaks to Us in Feeding Stories.** Getty-Sullivan, Mary Ann. Liturgical Press. "Jesus' Supper." Retells the story of the Last Supper.

DVD/VHS
This Sacred Meal (21 min.). Twenty-Third Publications. A catechumen learns about the Eucharist.

*Available at www.harcourtreligion.com

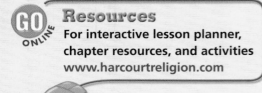

Resources
For interactive lesson planner, chapter resources, and activities
www.harcourtreligion.com

Eucharist

CHAPTER BACKGROUND

 Jesus said to them, "I am the bread of life; whoever comes to me will never hunger, and whoever believes in me will never thirst."

John 6:35

In Memory of Jesus

At the Last Supper on the first Holy Thursday, an amazing thing happened. Jesus gave us a wonderful way of remembering him: the Eucharist. The mystery of how the bread and wine become the Body and Blood of Christ is beyond mere human understanding, but we have been told by our Savior that this is so, and so we believe.

However, the sacrament is more than a memorial. The very meaning of *Eucharist* is thanksgiving, and it is our great offering of gratefulness to the God who has been so good to us. As part of the Mass, it also gives praise to him. It tells of his great glory. And, finally, it is a sign of Emmanuel, "God with us," now and forever. It is the physical presence of Jesus in our midst.

Sharing the Sacrifice

We gather for Sunday Eucharist as the Body of Christ. We share ourselves when we participate in the Mass as we bring our bodies, our joys, our problems, our work—indeed, our lives—with us to the altar. Our personal offerings are added to those of other Church members and Jesus to make one offering to God the Father.

During the Eucharistic prayer, at the Mass, we also remember the faithful departed who have not yet entered heaven as a way of joining our prayers to theirs and benefiting them. What this means is that all of the Church—members in heaven and on earth—share in the communion of sacrifice. We are united in our praise and thanksgiving.

*Reflect **How do you show your belief in the presence of Christ in the Eucharist?***

Repetition = Success

Interacting with the same text in a variety of ways promotes learning.

- Hearing a verse aloud and then singing that same verse is always helpful.

- Joining that verse with movement helps to build a better sense of comprehension.

Patience

- I like to talk more than listen. Teach me to listen to my friends.

- I don't like to wait. Give me something to do. While waiting in line at the water fountain, teach me a waiting song, 12345,678910 that's enough, it's time for another friend.

Accepting Mediocrity

Acceptance of mediocrity is the quietest and most harmful of all the challenges you face. Accepting mediocrity makes you ineffective and may eventually lead to apathy.

Whether mediocrity is found in colleagues who have lowered expectations, materials that are inadequate, or environments that are in disrepair, its lullaby is the same: "It's good enough."

Testimony is the courageous practice of making a public statement—to one person or many, with words or with actions—that "It's not good enough for me." Even if you don't know how to improve a situation, truthfully testifying that something is not good enough strengthens the fire of your spirit.

Reflect **To what area of mediocrity might you now need to apply the practice of Testimony?**

 Prayer

Jesus, Son of God, thank you for your gift of yourself in the Eucharist. Help me share with the children an appreciation for all the gifts you give us. Amen.

Weekly Planner

	Objectives	Materials	Prayer & Scripture
1 Invite **Eucharist** Page 147	To consider the importance of bread	☐ Board or chart paper ☐ Copies of Activity Master 35, p. 147E ☐ Crayons or markers ☐ Scissors ☐ *A Peek Into My Church*	🙏 Let Us Pray: Psalm 23:5
2 Explore **A Sign of Life** Page 148	To learn about the Last Supper		✝ Scripture: Mark 14:22–24 ✝ Scripture Background: The Last Supper
The Mass Page 149	To discover what happens at Mass	☐ Board or chart paper	✝ Scripture: Mark 14:22–24
Really Jesus Page 150	To learn that Jesus' Body and Blood are shared at Mass	☐ Crayons or markers ☐ Copies of Activity Master 36, p. 152A	✝ Scripture: Mark 14:22–24
3 Celebrate **Pray With God's Word** Page 151	To listen to God's word from the Bible	☐ Music CD ☐ Bible or Lectionary	🙏 Let Us Pray: Pray with God's Word 🎵 Hymn: Psalm 126: The Lord Has Done Great Things

Activities	Enrichment
Let's Begin Talk about different kinds of bread. (OPTIONAL) **Activity Master 35: Make A Bread Mobile, p. 147E** (OPTIONAL) Children's Literature **Multiple Intelligence:** Verbal/Linguistic	
❓ Discuss when the Church says the words of Jesus.	• **Reaching All Learners:** Visual Learners

Activity
Describe what is taking place in the pictures.
	• **Cultural Awareness:**
	  Sample Bread
	
	• **Chapter Background:**
	  The Mass

Activity Draw yourself in the picture. (OPTIONAL) **Activity Master 36: Color the Picture, p. 152A**	• **Justice and Peace:** Working

	• **Liturgy Link:**
	  The Consecration
	
	• **Lectionary Link:**
	  Break Open the Word

Pacing the Chapter

Parish
Meets once a week

 In parish religious education classes, plan for approximately 60 minutes of class time.

Invite	10 minutes
Explore	40 minutes
Celebrate	10 minutes

The abundance of activity and enrichment options will allow flexibility in planning for longer sessions if needed.

School
Meets 5 days per week

 In school religious education classes, plan for lesson 5 days per week for about 30 minutes. The lesson can be easily adapted for a 4-day week as well.

Day 1: Invite   **Day 4:** Explore
Day 2: Explore **Day 5:** Celebrate
Day 3: Explore

The abundance of activity and enrichment options will allow flexibility in planning for longer sessions if needed.

- Online planning tools include chapter background and planner, activity master, customizable test, and more.
- Enhancement activities for each step of the catechetical process, including alternative prayer experiences and blessings.
- Games, activities, interactive review, alternative assessment, and more for children.

www.calltofaitheconnect.com

Home Connection

Chapter 18 Family Faith, p. 152
Take-home activities, chapter content review, saint features and prayer

 For more family activities
www.harcourtreligion.com

Name _____ Date _____

Make a Bread Mobile

Directions: Color the different kinds of bread. Then cut them out and make a mobile with them.

©Harcourt Religion

Eucharist

You set a table before me.

Psalm 23:5

Read to Me — Let's Begin

Bread

Brown toast for breakfast,
bagels for lunch,
shortbread for snack.

Flat pitas for wrapping,
bent croissants for dipping,
square matzo for munching.

Bread is shared
in near and far places.
It gives us full stomachs
and happy faces.

● Why do you eat
bread? Possible responses:
because it tastes good, to get energy

147

1 Invite

Objective: To consider the importance of bread

Let Us Pray

Read aloud the psalm verse. Have children act out sitting at a banquet as they repeat the psalm verse after you.

Let's Begin

Bread

Direct children's attention to the photograph.

- Have children name their favorite kind of bread. List their responses on the board or on chart paper.
- Alert children to listen for their favorite bread as you read aloud the text.
- Discuss the text question.

OPTIONAL ACTIVITY

Activity Master 35: Make a Bread Mobile Distribute copies of the activity found on page 147E.

- Tell children they will be making a mobile.
- Ask them to color the different types of bread and cut them out.
- Help them assemble the mobile.

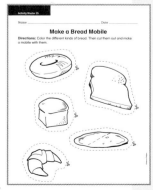

▲ Activity Master 35

OPTIONAL ACTIVITY

Children's Literature Read *A Peek Into My Church* by Wendy Goody and Veronica Kelly (WhipperSnapper, 1998). This book is an entertaining and informative introduction to the Catholic religion.

Multiple Intelligence: Verbal/Linguistic

Objective: To learn about the Last Supper

A Sign of Life

Remind children that bread is eaten by people all over the world.

- Tell them that Jesus taught his followers to share food with others.
- Read aloud the text.

The Last Supper

- Have children look at the illustration and predict what the story will be about.
- Proclaim the Gospel reading.
- Ask children what Jesus shared with his friends. bread, wine, a special meal, his Body, his Blood
- Discuss the text question.
- Ask children to pay special attention at Communion time when they attend Mass next week.

Explore

A Sign of Life

Jesus ate bread, too.
He shared bread with his friends.

Mark 14:22–24

The Last Supper

Jesus and his friends were sharing a special supper.
Bread and wine were on the table.
Jesus blessed the bread and gave it to his friends.
He said, "This is my body."
Then Jesus gave thanks over the wine and shared it.
He said, "This is my blood."

Based on Mark 14:22–24

When does the Church say these words of Jesus?
at Mass

148

Visual Learners Have children make a class collage or bulletin board on the theme of sharing bread.

- Provide magazines that contain photographs and drawings of people sharing food.
- Have children select and cut out their favorite illustrations.
- Combine the illustrations in a collage or on a bulletin board.
- Label your work: "We All Share Bread."

SCRIPTURE BACKGROUND

The Last Supper In this passage, the Gospel writer connects the Old Testament sacrifice with the sacrifice Jesus will soon make on the cross.

- Through their participation in the supper, the disciples are asked to share in Jesus' death as well as in the heavenly banquet that awaits Jesus' followers.

The Mass

The Church remembers the Last Supper at each Mass.

At Mass you hear readings from the Bible.

Everyone gathered gives thanks and praise to God.

The priest says and does what Jesus did at the Last Supper.

Look at the Mass pictures. Describe what is taking place in each.

149

The Mass

Objective: To discover what happens at Mass

The Mass

Recall with children that Jesus offered the gift of himself at the Last Supper.

• Ask children what they know about the Mass.

• Write their responses on the board or on chart paper.

• Tell children the Mass is a special Church celebration.

• Read aloud the text.

• Point out that the priest blesses bread like Jesus did.

Activity

• Assist children in correctly identifying the Mass parts.

CULTURAL AWARENESS

Sample Bread   Have children sample breads from around the world.

• Gather different types of bread, such as Greek pita bread, Mexican tortillas, Italian garlic bread, Irish soda bread.

• After determining that students do not have food allergies, allow children to taste different breads, identifying the bread as it is distributed.

CHAPTER BACKGROUND

The Mass   The Mass has two main parts: the Liturgy of the Word and the Liturgy of the Eucharist.

• The assembly listens to God's proclaimed word and reflects on its meaning in their lives.

• The assembly shares in the Body and Blood of Christ which unites them more closely to Christ and one another.

Eucharist   149

Objective: To learn that Jesus' Body and Blood are shared at Mass

Really Jesus

Remind children what takes place at Mass.

- Read aloud the text.
- Explain that Jesus is truly and really present in the Eucharist.
- Invite children to describe what happens at Mass in their parish.

Activity

- Point out the illustration of the Mass.
- Explain that each time we go to Mass, we celebrate God's love and Jesus' gift of himself in Body and Blood.
- Hand out crayons or markers, and have children draw themselves in the picture.

Really Jesus

The blessed Bread and Wine at Mass are called the Holy Eucharist.

The blessed Bread and Wine are really Jesus' Body and Blood.

Jesus told his friends that he is the Bread of Life.

Sharing the Eucharist brings Church members closer to Jesus.

Draw a picture of yourself in Church.

OPTIONAL ACTIVITY

Activity Master 36: Color the Picture Distribute copies of the activity found on page 152A.

- Tell children they will be looking for symbols.
- Help children follow the directions for the activity.

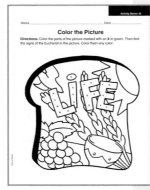

▲ Activity Master 36

✚ **JUSTICE AND PEACE**

Working During the Eucharistic Prayer, we reflect on how wheat and grapes grown through human efforts are made into the Body and Blood of Christ. Similarly, our labors at any task contribute "to the realization of God's plan on earth." (*On Human Work,* Donders, #25)

Catholic Social Teaching: Dignity of Work

Pray with God's Word

Leader: Let us listen to God's word from the Bible.

Read Mark 14:22–24.

The word of the Lord.

All: Thanks be to God.

Sing together.

The Lord has done great things for us;
We are filled with joy,
We are filled with joy.

Psalm 126: The Lord Has Done Great Things

151

Objective: To listen to God's word from the Bible

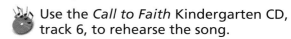
Let Us Pray

Tell children they will pray.

Pray with God's Word

Prepare

Place the Bible on the prayer table.

- Tell children they will hear a reading from the Bible.
- Practice children's response to the reading.
- Use the *Call to Faith* Kindergarten CD, track 6, to rehearse the song.

Gather

Have children process into the prayer space.

- Direct children to bow before the Bible and then sit in front of the prayer table.

Pray

- Proclaim the Gospel reading.
- Prompt children's response.
- Conclude with the song.

LITURGY LINK

The Consecration After this lesson, children will be more aware of the consecration in the Eucharistic Prayer.

- If possible, have children visit the parish church and see the sacred vessels used for Holy Communion.
- Have a priest, deacon, or sacristan show them to the children and explain their use.

LECTIONARY LINK

Break Open the Word Read last week's Sunday Gospel. Talk about how this reading helps us follow Jesus. For children's questions related to the weekly Gospel reading, visit our Web site.

GO ONLINE Visit www.harcourtreligion.com for weekly scripture readings and seasonal resources.

Wrap-Up

Family Faith

Remind children to discuss the Family Faith page at home. Encourage them to talk with family members about what they have learned about the Eucharist.

Family Project

• Encourage children to participate in this activity with family members.

People of Faith

Remind children that Saint John the Baptist was Jesus' cousin.

• John said that Jesus was greater than he was. When Jesus asked John to baptize him, John said that he was not worthy, and that Jesus should baptize him. Jesus insisted, and John performed Jesus' baptism. (*Mark 3:13-16*)

• Encourage children to pray the prayer at home with their families.

  Visit **www.harcourtreligion.com** for weekly scripture readings and seasonal resources.

Family Faith

◎ Catholics Believe

Dear Family,

In Chapter 18, the children learned that at the Last Supper, Jesus celebrated the first Eucharist. He changed bread and wine into his Body and Blood. At Mass, Jesus is again with us in the Holy Eucharist.

✝ SCRIPTURE

Read Mark 14:22–24 together with your child.

 www.harcourtreligion.com For weekly scripture readings and seasonal resources

Family Project

Baking Bread Find a simple recipe for bread, assemble the ingredients, and have your child help you measure, mix, and knead the dough. As the bread bakes, talk about how people all over the world eat some form of bread. Before eating your bread, bless it and thank God for this gift.

People of Faith

Saint John the Baptist told people about Jesus before he baptized them.

Saint John the Baptist, I B.C.–32 A.D. ▶

🙌 Family Prayer

Saint John the Baptist, you shared stories about Jesus and lead others to God. Pray for us that we may be like you. Amen.

152 CCC *See Catechism of the Catholic Church 1333, 1337, 1341 for further reading on chapter content.*

? HOW DID I DO?

This week was

☐ *one of the best ever!*   ☐ *pretty good.*   ☐ *in need of improvement.*

In what discussions and activities were children most interested?

_____

What activity did I most enjoy teaching?

_____

In what area do I need to improve?

_____

Name _____ Date _____

Color the Picture

Directions: Color the parts of the picture marked with an **X** in green. Then find the signs of the Eucharist in the picture. Color them any color.

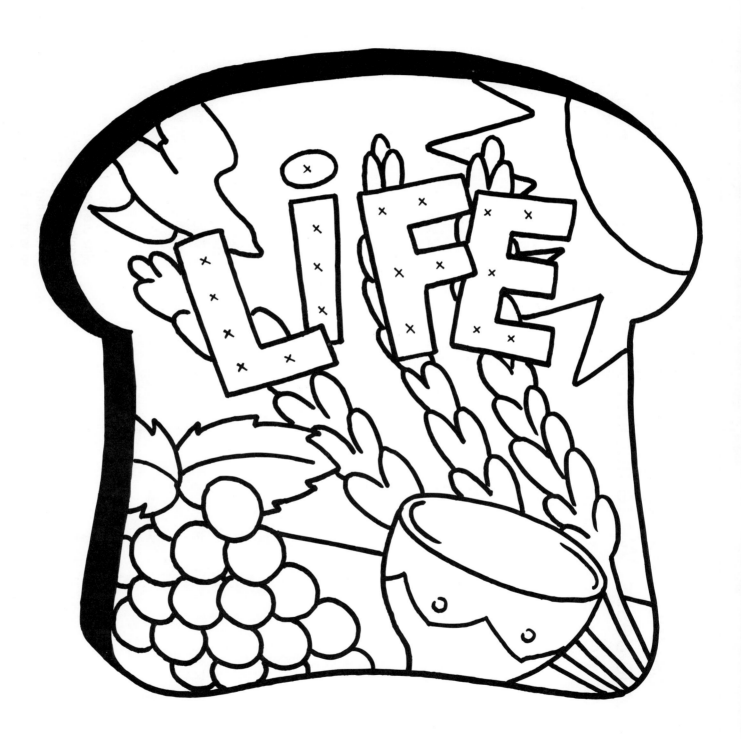

At Mass, the bread and wine become Jesus. We remember him as he asked us to.

153

Read to Me Scripture Story
The Last Supper

(Mark 14:22–26)

Family Note: In class your child has learned that bread and wine are signs of God's love. After reading this Scripture Story together, ask your child to tell you what Jesus said about his body and blood. The next time you attend Mass with your child, point out that Jesus is really present in the bread (host) and the wine of the Eucharist.

8

Jesus and his friends had a
very special dinner.
We call it the Last Supper.

2

Jesus said, "This is my Blood.
When you drink, remember me."

7

154

Then Jesus gave thanks over the wine.

This was the last meal Jesus would eat with his friends.

They had bread and wine.

3

6

155

Jesus blessed the bread and shared it.

Jesus said, "This is my Body."

4

5

156

Overview

Faith Focus

- There is life beyond death. (CCC 1020)

Catechism Connection

The *Catechism* affirms that all people yearn for heaven, which is a state of complete and everlasting joy. (CCC 1024)

NDC Link

Learning and following the message of the Beatitudes puts us on a path leading to God's eternal home and a recognition of our true vocation. (See *NDC*, 45I.)

Resources

BOOK
To Everything There Is a Season. Daly, Jude (illustrator). Eerdmans Books for Young Readers. Illustrates the famous passage from Ecclesiastes with scenes from Africa.

DVD/VHS
Final Blessing (52 min.). USCCB. Examines the spiritual aspect of the lives of the terminally ill.

Resources
For interactive lesson planner, chapter resources, and activities
www.harcourtreligion.com

 [R]ejoice because your names are written in heaven.

Luke 10:20

The Life Beyond

On earth, happiness is always temporary. We think that new clothes, more friends, or a larger home will make us happy, and sometimes this is true. But they do not bring true happiness.

This is not the case in heaven. If we are in God's grace at the moment of death and need no purification, we will enter heaven immediately. There, we will experience happiness beyond our earthly understanding. We will see God!

If we need purification, we will receive it in purgatory. If we die in the state of serious sin, we cannot hope to see God, and we will suffer eternal damnation. He and the Church do not wish these punishments on human souls. He and the Church wish for and work for the salvation of everyone. It is human choices that result in a soul being sent to purgatory or hell.

Working for Good

The image of hell should not be what motivates us to do good works. We cannot gain heaven out of avoidance. Rather, our actions should be based on love of God and his creations. We should use our freedom to act to further the kingdom of God, to remain in grace and friendship with God because this is the right and loving thing to do.

After we have been made part of the glory of heaven, we will still be working for God's will. We will intercede for those who need help to join us in God's presence, in everlasting happiness.

Reflect *How do you work to be in God's grace and friendship?*

Tracking Words

Emerging readers sometimes have difficulty keeping their place as they read. It is often useful to have them use their pointer finger to track the words they are reading.

- While reading a chart, use a pointer to track left-to-right, top-to-bottom orientation.

- Make pointers with paint stirrers. Have children use colored masking tape or markers to decorate their pointers. Encourage children to use their pointer to help them keep their place while reading.

Play

- I love to play. Let me discover things on my own. Set up my environment for successful exploration.

- I like to talk. Allow me to explain my discoveries to you.

Coming to the Balcony

Pursuing catechetical excellence is increasingly complex. The challenges erode your willingness to shift, evaluate, and grow. As a result, you may find yourself doubting your effectiveness.

In *Leadership Without Easy Answers,* Ronald Heifetz proposes the practice of Coming to the Balcony: occasionally rising above the dance floor to get a better view of the dynamics, interactions, and pace making up the complexity of your catechetical dance. When Coming to the Balcony, seek the Wisdom of the Ratio, which can be found not by choosing one approach over the other but by determining when you are doing too much or not enough of different approaches.

Reflect ***How can you practice Coming to the Balcony?***

 Prayer

Loving God, help us all see that we have no lasting happiness here on earth. We are on a journey—on our way to everlasting joy and a perfect home with you in heaven. Amen.

Weekly Planner

		Objectives	Materials	Prayer & Scripture
1 Invite	**Being with God** Page 157	To reflect on happy places	☐ Crucifix ☐ Copies of Activity Master 37, p. 157E ☐ Crayons or markers ☐ Ball of yarn	🌷 **Let Us Pray:** Psalm 11:4
2 Explore	**A Perfect Place** Page 158	To learn about heaven		
	What Is Heaven Like? Page 159	To discover how special heaven is	☐ Copies of Activity Master 38, p. 162A ☐ Crayons or markers	✞ **Scripture:** 1 Corinthians 2:9 ✞ **Scripture Background:** Paul's Description of Heaven
	In God's Home Page 160	To learn that heaven is where people will see Jesus	☐ Crayons or markers ☐ Empty toilet tissue rolls ☐ Paint ☐ Construction paper ☐ Tape ☐ Clothesline	✞ **Scripture:** John 14:1–31 ✞ **Scripture Background:** Many Rooms
3 Celebrate	**Prayer of Praise** Page 161	To celebrate the idea of heaven	☐ Music CD ☐ Bible or Lectionary	🌷 **Let Us Pray:** Prayer of Praise 🎵 **Hymn:** We Are Walking in the Light

Activities	Enrichment

Let's Begin

Talk about happy places.

OPTIONAL **Activity Master 37: Find the Hidden Word, p. 157E**

OPTIONAL Acts of Kindness
Multiple Intelligence: Interpersonal

• **Chapter Background:**
Theology of Heaven

• **Reaching All Learners:**
Heaven

❓ Discuss what heaven is like.

OPTIONAL **Activity Master 38: Follow the Path, p. 162A**

Activity

Draw yourself in God's house.

OPTIONAL Angels
Multiple Intelligence: Visual/Spatial

• **Liturgy Link:**
Alleluia!

• **Lectionary Link:**
Break Open the Word

Pacing the Chapter

Parish
Meets once a week

In parish religious education classes, plan for approximately 60 minutes of class time.

Invite	10 minutes
Explore	40 minutes
Celebrate	10 minutes

The abundance of activity and enrichment options will allow flexibility in planning for longer sessions if needed.

School
Meets 5 days per week

In school religious education classes, plan for lesson 5 days per week for about 30 minutes. The lesson can be easily adapted for a 4-day week as well.

Day 1: Invite   **Day 4:** Explore
Day 2: Explore   **Day 5:** Celebrate
Day 3: Explore

The abundance of activity and enrichment options will allow flexibility in planning for longer sessions if needed.

• Online planning tools include chapter background and planner, activity master, customizable test, and more.

• Enhancement activities for each step of the catechetical process, including alternative prayer experiences and blessings.

• Games, activities, interactive review, alternative assessment, and more for children.

www.calltofaitheconnect.com

Home Connection

Chapter 19 Family Faith, p. 162
Take-home activities, chapter content review, saint features and prayer

 For more family activities
www.harcourtreligion.com

Name _____ Date _____

Find the Hidden Word

Directions: Color in the space with a ? in them to find the hidden word. Then color in the rest of the spaces.

©Harcourt Religion

Being with God

 The Lord's throne is in heaven.

Psalm 11:4

Let's Begin

God's House

God's house is a happy place
Where you will not see a sad face.
A place so shiny and so bright
Because it's filled with holy light.
No need to be sad or to cry
Because God's love is so nearby.

● What sort of place does this poem describe?
a happy place

157

Objective: To reflect on happy places

 Let Us Pray

Invite children to gather in the prayer space and make the Sign of the Cross. In the prayer space, have a crucifix and a Bible opened to the psalm verse.

Arrange children in a circle. Read aloud the psalm verse. Have children repeat the psalm verse after you and say "Amen."

Let's Begin

God's House

- Tell children that you will read a poem about a happy place.
- Read aloud the poem.
- Ask children to describe other happy places. Possible responses: their house, a playground, an amusement park
- Discuss differences between happy and sad places.
- Discuss the text question.

OPTIONAL ACTIVITY

Activity Master 37: Find the Hidden Word Distribute copies of the activity found on page 157E.

- Tell children they will be looking for a hidden word.
- Ask them to color in the spaces with a question mark in them to find the hidden word.

▲ Activity Master 37

OPTIONAL ACTIVITY

Acts of Kindness This may be done as an indoor or outdoor activity.

- Have children stand in a circle.
- Have them toss a ball of yarn from person to person.
- Instruct children to say something nice about the person to whom they are throwing the ball.

Multiple Intelligence: Interpersonal

Objective: To learn about heaven

A Perfect Place

Recall with children the happy place poem.

- Invite children to close their eyes and think of a wonderful place.
- Have children open their eyes and tell about what they imagined. Praise their imagination.
- Read aloud the text.
- Point out that heaven will be better than anything we can imagine.
- Be sensitive to those children who may have loved ones who have passed away.
- Call attention to the illustrations. Point out what will NOT be in heaven. Have children suggest other things that will not be in heaven.
  Possible responses: dying, natural disasters, fights

Explore

A Perfect Place

Heaven is where God is.

God wants all of his children to be with him in heaven.

Everything is perfect in heaven.

Everyone is happy in heaven.

In heaven no one gets sick.

In heaven no one is sad.

In heaven no one gets hurt.

158

CHAPTER BACKGROUND

Theology of Heaven Be certain that children understand that heaven is not a geographical or physical place.

- It is not on earth, nor is it in the clouds.
- Heaven is best described as a "state of being" in which we will be together with God.

★ REACHING ALL LEARNERS

Heaven The topic of heaven provides several opportunities for children to express themselves.

- Have bodily/kinesthetic learners act out what they believe heaven will be like.
- Invite children to make a class mural of heaven. Have children make small sketches of their ideas and then add these ideas to a large sheet of butcher paper.

What Is Heaven Like?

God has wonderful things planned for the people who love him.
Heaven is better than anything that anyone has ever seen or heard.

Based on I Corinthians 2:9

❓ What do you think will be the best thing about heaven? Possible responses: having everyone you care about together, seeing God

159

Objective: To discover how special heaven is

What Is Heaven Like?

Tell children that heaven is being with God forever.

• Read aloud the text to children.

• Ask why God would want to plan a wonderful place for people who love him. Possible responses: because he loves them, because he thinks it would make them happy

• Direct children's attention to the illustration. Point out that this is one artist's idea of heaven, and that no one knows for certain what it looks like.

• Discuss the text question.

Activity Master 38: Follow the Path Distribute copies of the activity found on page 162A.

• Tell children they will be looking for a path to Jesus.

• Ask them to draw the path that they should take to get to Jesus.

▲ Activity Master 38

✝ SCRIPTURE BACKGROUND

Paul's Description of Heaven This verse is part of a passage about God's plan for our redemption.

• This particular verse echoes *Isaiah 64:3,* which tells of the wonderful things God does for his followers.

• Paul focuses on love as the necessary quality for enjoying salvation.

Explore

Objective: To learn that heaven is where people will see Jesus

In God's Home

Recall that heaven is where we will see Jesus.

- Proclaim the Gospel reading.

- Explain that Jesus used ideas that we would easily understand. That is why he said that heaven was like a big house. Be certain that children understand that heaven is not a physical place, but that there is room for everyone there.

Activity

- Direct children's attention to the illustration.

- Point out that people of all ages and nationalities will enjoy heaven together.

- Tell children that this is a picture of Jesus' idea.

- Hand out crayons or markers, and have children draw themselves in God's house.

In God's Home

Jesus told us about heaven, too.

Jesus said, "Heaven is like a huge house.

God's house has many rooms.

I will make a place for you there."

Based on John 14:1–31

Activity

 Draw yourself in God's house.

160

✝ SCRIPTURE BACKGROUND

Many Rooms The lesson on this page is based on the Last Discourse of Jesus during the Last Supper.

- In *John 14:1-31,* Jesus assures the Apostles that their faith in God will be rewarded with a place in heaven.

- Jesus also informs his followers that he will return and guide them to the Father.

OPTIONAL ACTIVITY

Angels Have children make angels.

- Paint or cover toilet tissue rolls with paper.

- Make wings and heads out of heavy paper, and tape them to the tissue rolls.

- "Fly" the angels from clothesline strung across the room.

Multiple Intelligence: Visual/Spatial

Prayer of Praise

Leader: God our Father, we love you.

All: Alleluia!

Leader: Thank you for making heaven.

All: Alleluia!

Leader: We want to be with you and Jesus there someday.

All: Alleluia! Amen.

Sing together.

We are walking in the light,
in the light,
in the light.
We are walking in the light,
in the light of God.

We Are Walking in the Light

161

Objective: To celebrate the idea of heaven

 Let Us Pray

Tell children they will pray a prayer of praise.

Prayer of Praise

Prepare

Explain that *Alleluia* is a happy word used in prayers and songs. Teach children to say "Alleluia!" with joyous expression.

• Tell children this will be their prayer response. Encourage them to raise their arms high when they say the word.

 Use the *Call to Faith* Kindergarten CD, track 7, to rehearse the song.

Gather

Invite children into the prayer space.

Pray

Begin the prayer, and prompt children's response.

• Have children march around the room as they sing the song.

 LITURGY LINK

Alleluia! This acclamation is the Hebrew term meaning "Praise the Lord!"

• It is part of our Jewish heritage and appears often in prayers such as the Psalms.

• Because of the penitential nature of Lent, "Alleluia" is not included in the Mass from Ash Wednesday until the Easter Vigil.

 LECTIONARY LINK

Break Open the Word Read last week's Sunday Gospel. Talk about how this reading helps us follow Jesus. For questions related to the weekly Gospel reading, visit our Web site.

 GO ONLINE Visit www.harcourtreligion.com for weekly scripture readings and seasonal resources.

Wrap-Up

Family Faith

Remind children to discuss the Family Faith page at home. Encourage them to talk with family members about what they have learned about heaven.

Family Project

• Encourage children to complete the activity with family members.

People of Faith

Tell children about Saint Thérèse of Lisieux.

• Thérèse was from a big family. She was the youngest of nine children. She called herself "the little flower."

• Encourage children to pray the prayer at home with their families.

Visit **www.harcourtreligion.com** for weekly scripture readings and seasonal resources.

Family Faith

Catholics Believe

Dear Family,

In Chapter 19, the children discussed heaven in simple terms. They learned that heaven is a perfect place. Jesus is preparing a home for us there.

SCRIPTURE

Read I Corinthians 2:9 together with your child.

GO ONLINE www.harcourtreligion.com
For weekly scripture readings and seasonal resources

Family Project

Draw Together With your child, draw a picture of what you think heaven looks like. Draw Jesus, God the Father, the Holy Spirit, patron saints, relatives, and others who you think are in heaven. Everyone should look happy. Talk about how we love and serve God on earth so that we can join God in heaven someday.

People of Faith

When Thérèse was very young, she wanted to serve God. She gave money to the poor because she worried about them. When she was fifteen years old, she chose to become a nun.

Saint Thérèse ▶ of Lisieux, 1873–1897

Family Prayer

Loving God, help us learn about you and serve you well. Help us love others as you have loved us. Amen.

162 **CCC** *See Catechism of the Catholic Church 30, 1844, 223 for further reading on chapter content.*

HOW DID I DO?

This week was

☐ *one of the best ever!* ☐ *pretty good.* ☐ *in need of improvement.*

In what discussions and activities were children most interested?

_____

What activity did I most enjoy teaching?

_____

In what area do I need to improve?

_____

Name _____ Date _____

Follow the Path

Directions: Draw the path that the child should take to get to Jesus.

©Harcourt Religion

Overview

Faith Focus

- Our relationship with the saints is strengthened when we ask them to pray for us. *(CCC 958)*

Catechism Connection

The *Catechism* explains that saints intercede for us with Christ. *(CCC 956)*

NDC Link

The *Directory* emphasizes that each person is called to do whatever he or she can to carry out the mission of Jesus. *(See NDC, 1.)*

Resources

BOOK
Butler's Saint for the Day. Burns, Paul. Liturgical Press. Presents a saint for each day of the year, emphasizing twentieth-century figures.

DVD/VHS
Big Al Live: Gospel Values for Children, Vol 3. * Harcourt Religion Publishers. "Have You Ever Seen a Giant?" (4:49 min.). Points out that actions make us important.

*Available at www.harcourtreligion.com

Resources
For interactive lesson planner, chapter resources, and activities
www.harcourtreligion.com

 Therefore, my beloved brothers, be firm, steadfast, always fully devoted to the work of the Lord, knowing that in the Lord your labor is not in vain.

1 Corinthians 15:58

Heading for Heaven

The Church on earth is an imitation of what heaven will be like. Granted, it is a pale imitation seen through a dark glass. But this small model teaches us that each of us has gifts that we can use to contribute to the common good. Indeed, we are obliged to use our gifts to help others, for it is the Holy Spirit who gives them to us. We are stewards of our physical and spiritual gifts.

When we use gifts for the common good, we are acting in a way that pleases God and unites us more closely to him. This strengthens us personally and strengthens the Church as a whole.

The Saints

The saints understand the difficulties of life on earth. Having been through temptation and having chosen the better way, the saints have experience with exactly the same trials that we have before us. They were once pilgrims on the same road. They can be valuable allies.

What this means is that the saints are a wonderful bridge between God and us. With their view of the Almighty, they can plead our case to God, or they can work to assist us with problems and decisions. This is why we ask them to pray for us, why we adopt patron saints, and why we honor their memory with churches and shrines.

Reflect   In what ways do you honor the saints?

TIPS FOR TEACHING KINDERGARTNERS

Show and Tell

Communicating is a child's way of acquiring language skills. Provide opportunities to freely and openly share ideas.

- Designate a special time during the day for sharing time. Allow children time to share what they learned at the end of the day. Ask children to offer specific examples.

- Show and Tell is a great way to allow students the opportunity to express themselves freely. Have children bring in an item from home to share with the group. Allow children to ask those presenting questions about their item.

KINDERGARTNERS SAY

Attention Span

- I want independence. Provide times for child-selected activities.

- I will stay involved and maintain my focus when playing and learning with things I choose.

- I like to do things over and over again. Repetition is my way of making sense of things.

SUSTAINING YOUR SPIRIT

Confession

Psychologists tell us that we unconsciously create enemies to avoid responsibility for a problem, to bond closer with the colleagues on our side, or to better define who we are. In catechetics, we can make such an imagined enemy out of parents, the pastor, or a certain group of students.

The struggle to sustain your spirit is difficult enough without carrying such a burden. The courageous practice of Confession enables you to let go of the illusion of an enemy and freely carry on the noble work of catechetics. Your virtuous act of Confession can help you refrain from contributing to the enemy illusion.

Reflect **What enemy comes to your mind as you consider the practice of Confession?**

 Prayer

Saints in Heaven, I appreciate the example you have given me. Pray for me to show these young saints their potential to serve God and to meet you in heaven someday. Amen.

Weekly Planner

		Objectives	Materials	Prayer & Scripture
1 Invite	**Be Like God** Page 163	To understand that people can serve God by doing little things	☐ Copies of Activity Master 39, p. 163E ☐ Pencils	🌸 **Let Us Pray:** Psalm 36:11
2 Explore	**Holy People** Page 164	To understand that saints served God and others while on earth	☐ Pencils ☐ Crayons or markers	
	Saints Page 165	To learn how to be like the saints	☐ Copies of Activity Master 40, p. 168A ☐ Pencils ☐ Crayons or markers	✝ **Scripture:** Ephesians 5:1–2, 7–10 ✝ **Scripture Background:** Being Like God
	As You Grow Page 166	To show how to grow in God's love	☐ Crayons or markers ☐ *Waiting for Wings*	✝ **Scripture:** Ephesians 5:1–2, 7–10
3 Celebrate	**Prayer for Help** Page 167	To celebrate little ways of helping others	☐ Music CD ☐ Bible or Lectionary ☐ Battery operated candles	🌸 **Let Us Pray:** Prayer for Help 🔔 **Hymn:** We Are Walking in the Light

Activities	Enrichment

Let's Begin

Talk about little things you can do.

OPTIONAL **Activity Master 39: Make a List, p. 163E**

• **Reaching All Learners:**
Naturalistic Learners

Activity

Name a saint.

OPTIONAL **Helping Professionals**
Multiple Intelligence: Interpersonal

• **Justice and Peace:**
Sainthood

❓ Discuss what pleases God.

OPTIONAL **Activity Master 40: Make a Saints Banner, p. 168A**

Activity

Connect the pictures.

OPTIONAL **Children's Literature**
Multiple Intelligence: Verbal/Linguistic

• **Quick Tip:**
Serving God

• **Liturgy Link:**
Feast Days

• **Lectionary Link:**
Break Open the Word

Pacing the Chapter

Parish
Meets once a week

In parish religious education classes, plan for approximately 60 minutes of class time.

Invite	10 minutes
Explore	40 minutes
Celebrate	10 minutes

The abundance of activity and enrichment options will allow flexibility in planning for longer sessions if needed.

School
Meets 5 days per week

In school religious education classes, plan for lesson 5 days per week for about 30 minutes. The lesson can be easily adapted for a 4-day week as well.

Day 1: Invite **Day 4:** Explore
Day 2: Explore **Day 5:** Celebrate
Day 3: Explore

The abundance of activity and enrichment options will allow flexibility in planning for longer sessions if needed.

• Online planning tools include chapter background and planner, activity master, customizable test, and more.

• Enhancement activities for each step of the catechetical process, including alternative prayer experiences and blessings.

• Games, activities, interactive review, alternative assessment, and more for children.

www.calltofaitheconnect.com

Home Connection

Chapter 20 Family Faith, p. 168
Take-home activities, chapter content review, saint features and prayer

 For more family activities
www.harcourtreligion.com

Name _____ Date _____

Make a List

Directions: List three things you can do to make God happy.

1. _____

2. _____

3. _____

©Harcourt Religion

Chapter 20 Be Like God

Invite

 Continue your kindness toward your friends.

Psalm 36:11

Let's Begin

Little Things

"What makes God happy?" Jerry asked.

"God is happy with little things," his mother said.

"What kind of little things?" His mother thought.

"Be nice to other people.

Cheer up people who are sad.

Help at home and school.

Making other people happy makes God happy."

 What is a little thing you can do at home or school?

Possible responses: helping with dishes, playing nicely with a sibling

163

Objective: To understand that people can serve God by doing little things

Let Us Pray

Pair each child with another child from the group. Have children make friendly gestures as you read aloud the psalm verse.

Let's Begin

Little Things

- Remind children that God is a special friend to them.

- Read aloud the text to children.

- Pause after each of the mother's suggestions. Ask children for specific ideas for being nice, cheering up sad people, helping others, and making other people happy.

- Discuss the text question.

OPTIONAL ACTIVITY

Activity Master 39: Make a List Distribute copies of the activity found on page 163E.

- Tell children they will be making a list.

- Have them list three things they can do to make God happy.

Activity Master 39

Name _____ Date _____

Make a List

Directions: List three things you can do to make God happy.

1. _____
2. _____
3. _____

▲ **Activity Master 39**

★ REACHING ALL LEARNERS

Naturalistic Learners Make the theme of growth and development more concrete.

- Grow plants from seeds. Monitor the growth by recording measurements and observations.

- Display animal pictures in the classroom. Discuss how the animals increase not only in size, but in ability to take care of themselves as they grow.

Objective: To understand that saints served God and others while on earth

Holy People

Tell children that saints are special followers of Jesus who have died and are in heaven with God.

- Read aloud the text to children.
- Tell children that each of them has a special friend in heaven. That friend is their patron saint.
- Explain that a person's patron saint shares a name or a special interest with that person.
- Point out that children can ask their patron saints to help them lead good lives.

Activity

- Hand out pencils.
- Help children write their favorite saint's name on the line.
- Hand out crayons or markers.
- Allow children time to color in the frame.
- Have children share their favorite saint's name with the group.

Holy People

God wants everyone to be good and happy.
Saints are friends of God and holy followers of Jesus.
Each day they helped people.
Each day they prayed.
Now they are in heaven.

Activity

Write the name of your favorite saint on the line below.

Saint

_____

pray for us.

164

OPTIONAL ACTIVITY

Helping Professionals Invite members of helping professions to talk with children about their life's work.

- Have parents who are medical personnel, safety workers, or other professions come to class.
- Invite parents to tell what they do, how they feel about their work, and how they became interested in joining this profession.

Multiple Intelligence: Interpersonal

Saints

Saint Paul told us how to be like the saints.

Ephesians 5:1–2, 7–10

Live in the Light

Be like God, and live with love.

Stay in God's light because it will make you good.

God's light will make you truthful.

Find out what pleases God, and then do it.

Based on Ephesians 5:1–2, 7–10

❓ How can you find out what pleases God?
Possible responses: Read the Bible; follow Jesus' teachings.

165

Objective: To learn how to be like the saints

Saints

Remind children that saints are holy people.

- Tell children that many people can tell them how to become saints.
- Point out that the Bible is full of ideas for becoming a holy person.
- Tell children that you will read Saint Paul's ideas for becoming a saint.

Live in the Light

- Proclaim the Scripture.
- Ask children to repeat in their own words the advice Saint Paul gave us. Possible responses: Live with love; find out what God wants you to do; do what God wants you to do.
- Talk about what light means in this passage. Explain that light helps us see what is good.
- Discuss the text question.

OPTIONAL ACTIVITY

Activity Master 40: Make a Saints Banner Distribute copies of the activity found on page 168A.

- Tell children they will be making a banner.
- Have them fill in a saint's name and color the banner.
- Ask them to use it as a reminder to pray to that saint.

▲ Activity Master 40

✝ SCRIPTURE BACKGROUND

Being Like God This passage from Saint Paul outlines Christian behavior.

- It tells us to be imitators of Christ in love of our neighbors.
- It also contrasts Christians with those who live in darkness; the images of growth and change in the light of the Lord invite us to learn and develop our own good characteristics.

Objective: To show how to grow in God's love

As You Grow

Remind children that they will have a long time to learn about God and to serve others on earth.

- Point out that the lessons they are learning will help them live good lives.
- Read aloud the text to children.
- Ask children why God loves what they do now. Possible responses: because they are helping others, because they are following Jesus' teachings

Activity

- Read aloud the directions to children.
- Point out the picture of the child who is sharing lunch. Ask children which adult is doing something similar. the one who is feeding people
- Have children connect those two pictures.
- Continue with the rest of the activity in a similar fashion.

As You Grow

God loves the small things you do for him now.
You will not always be small.
You will grow up someday.
God will love what you do then, too.

Activity

 Connect each picture of a child with the picture of an adult who is helping people in a similar way.

166

Children's Literature Read *Waiting for Wings* by Lois Ehlert (Harcourt, 2001). In this picture book, four ordinary caterpillars blossom into beautiful butterflies in a story that explores the life cycles of one of the world's most fascinating creatures.

Waiting for Wings Lois Ehlert

Multiple Intelligence: Verbal/Linguistic

QUICK TIP

Serving God Explain that Jesus asks us to help others.

- Arrange for your class to participate in a clothing drive or food drive.
- Another service option would be to ask your local humane society if you could collect pet food for an animal food drive.

Prayer for Help

Leader: Thank you, God, for little things.

All: **Thank you, God, for little things.**

Leader: Help us help others in little ways.

All: **Help us help others in little ways.**

Leader: Help us stay in your light.

All: **Help us stay in your light. Amen.**

Sing together.

We are walking in the light,
in the light,
in the light.
We are walking in the light,
in the light of God.

We Are Walking in the Light

3 Celebrate

Objective: To celebrate little ways of helping others

 **Let Us Pray**

Tell children they will ask God's help to help others.

Prayer for Help

Prepare

Prepare the prayer space for the celebration.

 Use the *Call to Faith* Kindergarten CD, track 7, to rehearse the song.

Gather

Invite children into the prayer space.

- Hand out candles, and quiet the group.
- Tell children to repeat what you say.

Pray

- Pray the leader's part, and prompt children's response.
- Have children process to their places as they sing the song. Let them carry the candles as they move.

 LITURGY LINK

Feast Days Explain to children that almost every day in the year is associated with a particular saint or group of saints. On that Saint's day, also called a feast day, certain parts of the Mass honor the saint's memory. Some families celebrate patron saints' feasts by calling them "name days."

- Obtain a liturgical calendar and find feast days for children in the class.
- Have children write the date on a family calendar and plan a special celebration.

 LECTIONARY LINK

Break Open the Word Read last week's Sunday Gospel. Talk about how this reading helps us follow Jesus. For children's questions related to the weekly Gospel reading, visit our Web site.

 Visit www.harcourtreligion.com for weekly scripture readings and seasonal resources.

Be Like God   167

Wrap-Up

Family Faith

Remind children to discuss the Family Faith page at home. Encourage them to talk with family members about what they have learned about saints.

Family Project

- Encourage children to complete the activity with family members.

People of Faith

Remind children that Saint Thérèse of Lisieux called herself "the little flower."

- Even though Saint Thérèse was often sick, she still prayed and tried to serve God every day.
- Encourage children to pray the prayer at home with their families.

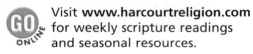

Visit **www.harcourtreligion.com** for weekly scripture readings and seasonal resources.

Catholics Believe

Dear Family,
In Chapter 20, the children learned that God is pleased with little acts of kindness. They learned that saints are holy people in heaven. Children learned that as they grow, they will do many things for God.

SCRIPTURE

Read Ephesians 5:1–2, 7–10 together with your child.

GO ONLINE **www.harcourtreligion.com** For weekly scripture readings and seasonal resources

Family Project

Make a Chart This week, emphasize the small jobs that your child does to help in your household. To help your child keep up with chores without being reminded, make a simple job chart. Have your child use stickers or make check marks to show that a job is completed. Review the chart regularly, and praise your child's contributions to family work. Point out that even little jobs, done well, please God and help the family.

My Jobs	
Sunday	
Monday	☆
Tuesday	
Wednesday	✓
Thursday	
Friday	
Saturday	

People of Faith

Thérèse wrote about serving God in little ways. Even when she was sick, she trusted God and loved him very much.

Saint Thérèse of Lisieux, 1873–1897 ▶

Family Prayer

Saint Thérèse, help us be like you. Help us do little things for God. Amen.

168 **CCC** *See Catechism of the Catholic Church 833, 958, 955 for further reading on chapter content.*

? HOW DID I DO?

This week was

☐ *one of the best ever!* ☐ *pretty good.* ☐ *in need of improvement.*

In what discussions and activities were children most interested?

_____

What activity did I most enjoy teaching?

_____

In what area do I need to improve?

_____

Name _____ Date _____

Make a Saints Banner

Directions: Fill in a saint's name. Then decorate the banner. Put it in a place where it will remind you to pray to the saint.

Saint

_____

_____

_____ ,

pray for us!

Overview

Faith Focus

■ We can bless God because he has blessed us. *(CCC 2645)*

Catechism Connection

The *Catechism* stresses the need to give thanks and praise to God for everything that happens to us. *(CCC 2648)*

NDC Link

In order to lead individual and communities to deeper faith, catechesis should encourage and provide an atmosphere of prayer and worship. (See *NDC*, 34.)

Resources

BOOK
Guided Meditations for Children.* Reehorst, Jane, BVM. Harcourt Religion Publishers. "The Annunciation." This meditation calls to mind Mary's role as Jesus' mother.

DVD/VHS
Prayer of Praise (10 min.). Saint Anthony Messenger Press. Shows children how to praise God with their prayers.

*Available at www.harcourtreligion.com

Resources
For interactive lesson planner, chapter resources, and activities
www.harcourtreligion.com

In all circumstances give thanks, for this is the will of God for you in Christ Jesus.

1 Thessalonians 5:18

Thanks

Before classes end for the year, plan one last celebration with the children. Let them help you give thanks for the year and praise God for his goodness.

Giving thanks to God is different from praising him. A prayer of thanks is associated with a gift, just as a note of thanks is sent for a specific favor. Because everything we receive is a gift, we can pray prayers of thanks for our talents, physical goods, elements of creation, and the people in our lives.

Praise

Praise, however, is a type of prayer that glorifies God for being God. It does not center on creation or anything in our lives; it reflects the joy and wonder of understanding God in the small way that we are able. It is noting and reveling in the splendor of the Father, Son, and Holy Spirit.

As your year closes, thank God for the children and for the time that you have spent learning with them. And exalt God for who and what he is.

Reflect **How can you show thanks and praise to God?**

Mark Milestones

Some parishes and schools have graduation ceremonies for their kindergarten class. The last class is a great time to acknowledge all that children have done in class.

- Invite family members to come to a closing ceremony.

- Have children take turns describing the year and naming one special thing they have learned.

Words of Praise

- It feels good to be loved. Catch me doing the right thing, and acknowledge my choice.

- I need to hear encouraging words. I will perform in positive ways when I know what is expected.

The Promise to Become

Your commitment to catechesis has enabled others to address their promise to become the kind of person God has called them to be. You have given them opportunities to gain knowledge, develop attitudes, and identify behaviors. These things can help them respond spiritually to the Call to Faith.

Reflect **Circle any of the following to revisit and cultivate as you continue to follow your vocational commitments.**

Engagement with Others	Coming to the Balcony
Habits of Mind	Confession
Keeping Company	Moments of Grace
Motivations	Vocational Seasons
Remember Who You Are	Blessed Assurance

 **Prayer**

God of wisdom, thank you for a wonderful year with children who have taught me so much about you and your love. I praise you for your goodness. Amen.

Weekly Planner

		Objectives	Materials	Prayer & Scripture
1 Invite	**Praise God** Page 169	To reflect on what has been learned during the year	☐ Board or chart paper ☐ Copies of Activity Master 41, p. 169E ☐ Pencils ☐ Crayons or markers ☐ Drawing paper	🙏 **Let Us Pray:** Psalm 145:2
2 Explore	**Thanks and Praise** Page 170	To learn that God can be praised anytime	☐ Crayons or markers ☐ Copies of Activity Master 42, p. 174A ☐ Pencils ☐ Large drinking straws ☐ Scissors ☐ Tape	
	Ways to Praise Page 171	To show ways to praise God	☐ Craft books	✝ **Scripture:** Psalm 150:1, 3–5 ✝ **Scripture Background:** Psalm 150
	Praising and Loving Page 172	To remember to praise God for his goodness	☐ Empty toilet tissue rolls ☐ Crayons or markers ☐ Glue gun ☐ Hole punch ☐ Yarn	✝ **Scripture:** Psalm 150:1, 3–5
3 Celebrate	**Prayer of Praise** Page 173	To praise God the Father, the Son, and the Holy Spirit	☐ Music CD ☐ Bible or Lectionary	🙏 **Let Us Pray:** Prayer of Praise 🎵 **Hymn:** We Are Walking in the Light

Activities	Enrichment
### Let's Begin	
Discuss what you have learned about God.	
OPTIONAL **Activity Master 41: Make a Picture, p. 169E**	
OPTIONAL Notes of Thanks **Multiple Intelligence:** Interpersonal	
### Activity	
Draw yourself praising God.	• **Cultural Awareness:** Teach a Spiritual
OPTIONAL **Activity Master 42: Make a Baton, p. 174A**	
❓ Discuss how you praise God.	
OPTIONAL Making Music **Multiple Intelligence:** Musical	
OPTIONAL Seeing and Praising **Multiple Intelligence:** Visual/Spatial	• **Reaching All Learners:** We Serve God
	• **Liturgy Link:** Dismissal
	• **Lectionary Link:** Break Open the Word

Pacing the Chapter

Parish
Meets once a week

In parish religious education classes, plan for approximately 60 minutes of class time.

Invite 10 minutes
Explore 40 minutes
Celebrate 10 minutes

The abundance of activity and enrichment options will allow flexibility in planning for longer sessions if needed.

School
Meets 5 days per week

In school religious education classes, plan for lesson 5 days per week for about 30 minutes. The lesson can be easily adapted for a 4-day week as well.

Day 1: Invite   **Day 4:** Explore
Day 2: Explore   **Day 5:** Celebrate
Day 3: Explore

The abundance of activity and enrichment options will allow flexibility in planning for longer sessions if needed.

CALL to FAITH e·connect

- Online planning tools include chapter background and planner, activity master, customizable test, and more.
- Enhancement activities for each step of the catechetical process, including alternative prayer experiences and blessings.
- Games, activities, interactive review, alternative assessment, and more for children.

www.calltofaitheconnect.com

Home Connection

Chapter 21 Family Faith, p. 174
Take-home activities, chapter content review, saint features and prayer

For more family activities
www.harcourtreligion.com

Name _____ Date _____

Make a Picture

Directions: Complete the sentence. Then draw a picture of yourself celebrating.

I learned a lot
about ̶G̶o̶d̶.̶

Chapter 21 Praise God

I will praise your name forever.

Psalm 145:2

Read to Me

Let's Begin

Celebrate, Celebrate

The year is ending.

You have learned so much this year!

You have learned a lot about God.

● Tell one thing you learned about God.

Responses will vary.

169

Objective: To reflect on what has been learned during the year

Let Us Pray

Ask children to suggest ways of praying the psalm verse. Use one of their suggestions. Read aloud the psalm verse.

Let's Begin

Celebrate, Celebrate

• Ask children to tell you what *celebrate* means. Possible responses: to have a party, to do happy actions

• Read aloud the text.

• Discuss what children learned about God.

• Record their responses on the board or on chart paper.

OPTIONAL ACTIVITY

Activity Master 41: Make a Picture   Distribute copies of the activity found on page 169E.

• Tell children they will be making a picture.

• Ask them to complete the sentence. Then have them draw a picture of themselves celebrating.

Activity Master 41

Make a Picture

Directions: Complete the sentence. Then draw a picture of yourself celebrating.

I learned a lot about God

▲ **Activity Master 41**

OPTIONAL ACTIVITY

Notes of Thanks   Send thank-you notes to people who helped you during the school year.

• Have children recall special people, such as your pastor, school administrators, parent volunteers, and others.

• Have children draw or write about special things that those people did. Have children write "Thank You," and send the note to the person.

Multiple Intelligence: Interpersonal

Objective: To learn that God can be praised anytime.

Thanks and Praise

Ask children why they should praise God. Possible responses: because he is good to us, because we love him

Recall with children what they have learned about God's gifts to them.

• Read aloud the text.

• List things that they have learned about God this year. Possible responses: God is the Father, Son, and Holy Spirit; God loves us; Jesus taught us about God the Father; the Holy Spirit helps us today.

Activity

• Ask children how they praise God. Possible responses: by praying, by singing

• Hand out crayons or markers.

• Tell children to draw themselves praising God in the morning and in the evening.

• Have children share their drawings when they are finished.

Explore

Thanks and Praise

Thank God for what you learned.

You can thank God by praising him.

You can praise God in the morning.

You can praise God in the evening.

Activity

Draw yourself praising God in the morning and in the evening.

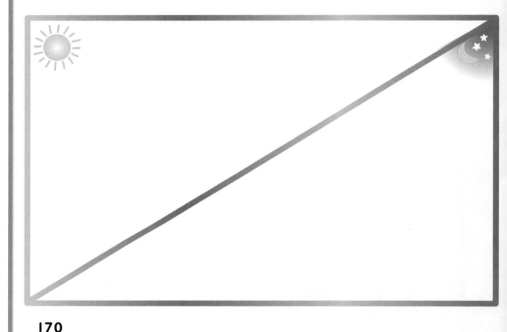

170

Activity Master 42: Make a Baton Distribute copies of the activity found on page 174A.

• Tell children they will be making a baton.

• Help them follow the directions to complete the activity.

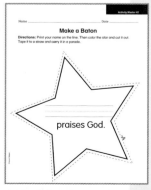

Name _____ Date _____

Make a Baton

Directions: Print your name on the line. Then color the star and cut it out. Tape it to a straw and carry it in a parade.

praises God.

▲ **Activity Master 42**

CULTURAL AWARENESS

Teach a Spiritual Help children become more aware of traditional African-American music.

• Explain that the rhythms of African-American music traveled with slaves from Africa. The songs are highly repetitive because they were passed on orally, not in writing.

• Teach children a spiritual. An appropriate one for this unit's theme is "Chatter with the Angels."

Explore

Psalm 150:1, 3–5

Ways to Praise

Praise God in heaven.
Praise him with blasts of the horn,
Praise him with harp and lyre,
Praise him with tambourines and dancing.
Praise him with flutes and strings.
Praise him with cymbals.

Based on Psalm 150:1, 3–5

❓ How can you praise God?
Possible responses: with words, with actions

171

Objective: To show ways to praise God

Ways to Praise

Remind children that God wants us to praise him.

• Tell children that the Psalms are prayers that were written long ago. Jesus prayed the Psalms when he was young like them. The Psalms are found in the Bible.

• Proclaim the Scripture.

• Explain any unfamiliar terms to children. Use reference books, if necessary.

• Ask children to act out the psalm as you read it aloud again.

• Discuss the text question.

SCRIPTURE BACKGROUND

Psalm 150 This psalm is the last entry in the Book of Psalms and thus serves as its conclusion.

• Fittingly, the psalm praises God and asks all in heaven and on earth to join in celebrating God's goodness and his actions.

• The psalm tells how temple musicians should praise God, listing traditional Biblical instruments.

OPTIONAL ACTIVITY

Making Music Look through craft books to find ways of making instruments that are named in the psalm.

• Assemble materials and have children make a variety of instruments. Have them pretend to play their creations.

• Read aloud the psalm. Invite children to demonstrate their instruments at the appropriate moment.

Multiple Intelligence: Musical

Explore

Objective: To remember to praise God for his goodness

Praising and Loving

Remind children that we praise God because he is good to us.

• Point out that God showed his goodness to us by giving us the world.

• Have children look at the photograph. Ask what gifts from God the children might see through their binoculars. Possible responses: animals, plants, other people

• Ask what gift from God cannot be seen. Possible response: love

• Read aloud the text to children.

• Ask why loving the world is another way to praise God. Possible response: If you love a person, you want to take care of the gifts you receive from the person.

Praising and Loving

God will always love you.

God gave you the world because he loves you.

God wants you to love the world.

Loving others and the world is a way to praise God.

172

 REACHING ALL LEARNERS

We Serve God   Have children tell ways that they have served God or ways they can do so in the future.

• Display all the answers on a bulletin board for all the school to see.

• Choose a service project to do together as a class.

OPTIONAL ACTIVITY

Seeing and Praising   Have children make binoculars.

• Have children decorate two empty toilet tissue rolls.

• Have an adult use a glue gun to glue each child's pair of rolls together and punch holes for a yarn neck strap.

• Have them use the binoculars to observe the world.

Multiple Intelligence: Visual/Spatial

Prayer of Praise

Leader: We praise you God the Father.

All: **We praise you God the Father.**

Leader: We praise you God the Son.

All: **We praise you God the Son.**

Leader: We praise you God the Holy Spirit.

All: **We praise you God the Holy Spirit.**

Sing together.

We are walking in the light,
in the light,
in the light.
We are walking in the light,
in the light of God.

We Are Walking in the Light

173

3 Celebrate

Objective: To praise God the Father, the Son, and the Holy Spirit

 Let Us Pray

Tell children that they will praise God.

Prayer of Praise

Prepare

Tell children you will be praying an echo prayer. They will repeat your words.

Use the *Call to Faith* Kindergarten CD, track 7, to rehearse the song.

Gather

Invite children into the prayer space.

Pray

• Begin with the Sign of the Cross.

• After you pray aloud each sentence, prompt children to echo your words.

• Conclude with the song.

 LITURGY LINK

Dismissal Explain to children that the priest or deacon sends us forth every time we leave Mass. He tells us to "Go in peace to love and serve the Lord." We answer "Thanks be to God." His words tell us that we are to do God's work every day of the week.

• Practice the dialogue with children until they know it.

• Encourage children to attend Mass throughout the summer.

 LECTIONARY LINK

Break Open the Word Read last week's Sunday Gospel. Talk about how this reading helps us follow Jesus. For children's questions related to the weekly Gospel reading, visit our Web site.

 Visit www.harcourtreligion.com for weekly scripture readings and seasonal resources.

Wrap-Up

Family Faith

Remind children to discuss the Family Faith page at home. Encourage them to talk with family members about what they have learned throughout the year.

Family Project

• Encourage children to complete the activity with a family member.

People of Faith

Remind children that Saint Thérèse of Lisieux did little things to serve God.

• Tell children that the leader of Saint Thérèse's group asked her to write a book that would help other people find God.

• Encourage children to pray the prayer at home with their families.

 Visit **www.harcourtreligion.com** for weekly scripture readings and seasonal resources.

 **CHAPTER 21**
Family Faith

Catholics Believe

Dear Family,
In Chapter 21, the children celebrated the end of the year. They reviewed key ideas from the year. They talked about praising God with music and prayer.

✝ SCRIPTURE

Read Psalm 150:1, 3–5 together with your child.

GO ONLINE www.harcourtreligion.com
For weekly scripture readings and seasonal resources

Family Project

Remember to Pray Make a door hanger that will help your child remember to pray throughout the summer. Cut a sheet of paper or poster board about 4" x 11". Cut a hole so that it can slip over a doorknob, or use yarn to make a loop for hanging. Write "Remember to pray!" on the hanger. Have your child decorate the remaining space and hang it on his or her bedroom door or other frequently used door.

People of Faith

Thérèse taught other sisters about God. She also wrote a book. People still read her book to learn how to serve God and other people.

Saint Thérèse ▶ of Lisieux, 1873–1897

Family Prayer

Almighty God, we love you. We praise you for what you have done for us. Thank you for our world. Amen.

174 **CCC** *See Catechism of the Catholic Church 54, 2639, 2097 for further reading on chapter content.*

? HOW DID I DO?

This week was

☐ *one of the best ever!* ☐ *pretty good.* ☐ *in need of improvement.*

In what discussions and activities were children most interested?

_____

What activity did I most enjoy teaching?

_____

In what area do I need to improve?

_____

Name _____ Date _____

Make a Baton

Directions: Print your name on the line. Then color the star and cut it out. Tape it to a straw and carry it in a parade.

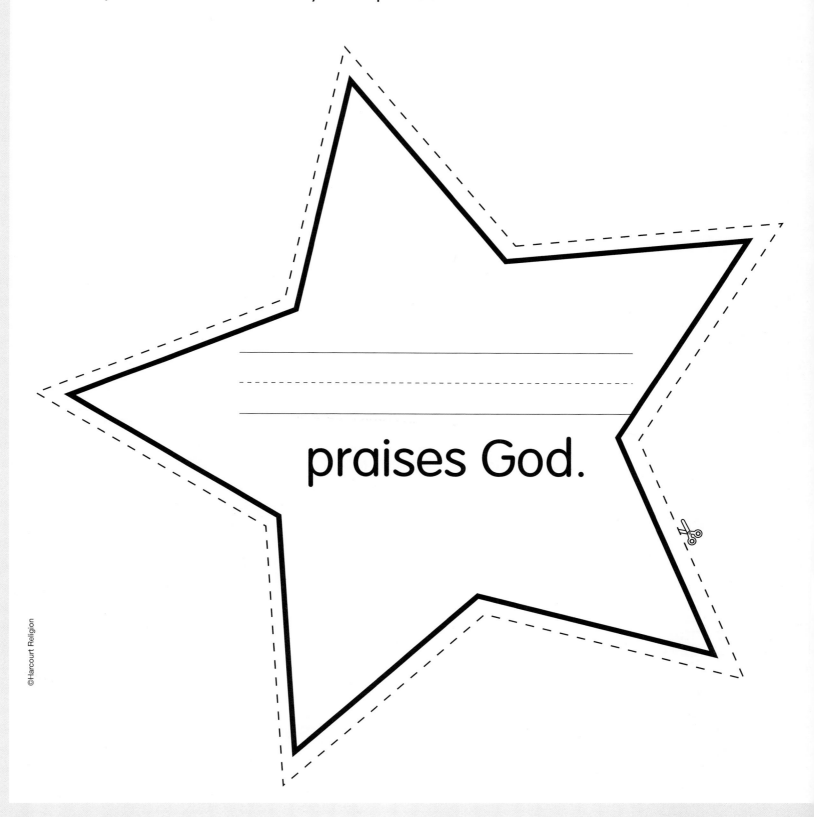

praises God.

©Harcourt Religion

Scripture Story

Easter

(Mark 15:1–16:6; John 20:1–16)

Jesus told Mary, "Tell my friends that I have new life from God the Father.

I will visit them soon!"

We celebrate Jesus' new life on Easter.

Family Note: In class your child has learned that Jesus died to save us. After reading this Scripture Story together, talk about how Jesus rose from the dead, met with his friends, and later returned to heaven to be with the Father. Then pray the Lord's Prayer together.

8

175

Many people did not like what
Jesus was teaching.
They took him to their leaders.
The leaders said that Jesus
should die.

2

Then Mary looked up.
Jesus was right in front of her!
Mary was very happy!

7

176

Mary Magdalene was one of the women at the tomb.

She was crying outside the tomb.

Someone asked her why she was sad.

She said, "I don't know where Jesus is."

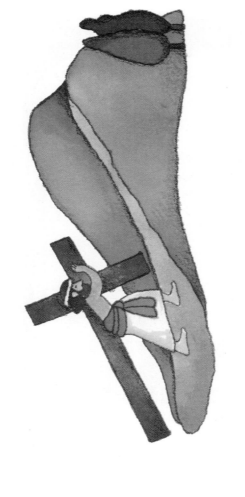

6

Jesus died on the cross.

He prayed for us while he was on the cross.

3

Jesus' friends took his body.

They put it into a tomb that was cut into a rock.

They closed the tomb with a big rock.

All of Jesus' friends were very sad.

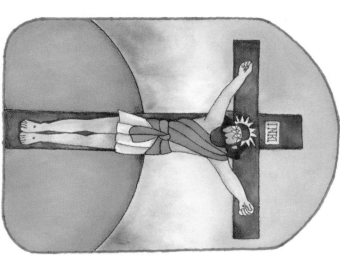

4

The next Sunday, some women went back to Jesus' tomb.

The rock was rolled back.

An angel was inside the tomb.

The angel said, "Jesus was raised from the dead! He is not here!"

5

178

Catholic Prayers

The Church Year

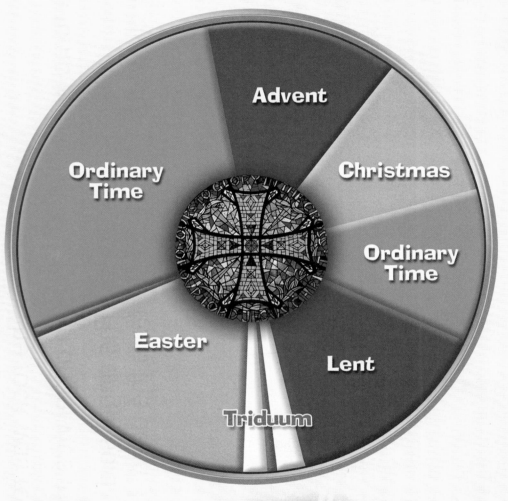

Advent

Christmas

Ordinary Time

Lent

Triduum

Easter

Ordinary Time

179

CALL to FAITH

Prayers

The Sign of the Cross

In the name of the Father,
and of the Son,
and of the Holy Spirit.
Amen.

In the name of the Father,

and of the Son,

and of the Holy Spirit.

Amen.

180

Glory to the Father

Glory to the Father,
and to the Son,
and to the Holy Spirit:
as it was in the beginning,
is now,
and will be forever. Amen.

The Lord's Prayer

Our Father, who art in heaven,
hallowed be thy name;
thy kingdom come;
thy will be done on earth as it is in
heaven.
Give us this day our daily bread;
and forgive us our trespasses
as we forgive those who trespass
   against us;
and lead us not into temptation,
but deliver us from evil.
Amen.

182

183

Hail Mary

Hail Mary, full of grace,
the Lord is with you!
Blessed are you among women,
and blessed is the fruit of your
   womb, Jesus.
Holy Mary, Mother of God,
pray for us sinners,
now and at the hour of our death.
Amen.

184

185

Blessing Before Meals

Bless us, O Lord,
and these your gifts,
which we are about to receive
from your goodness.
Through Christ our Lord. Amen.

Thanksgiving After Meals

We give you thanks for all your gifts,
  almighty God,
living and reigning now and forever.
Amen.

187

CALL to FAITH

Words of Faith

Words of Faith

A is for an angel,
a messenger of God.

B is for Bible,
the Church's holy book.

188

C is for Church,
our family of faith.

D is for day;
we thank God each day
for all creation.

189

© Harcourt Religion

E is for Eucharist,
the Church's holy meal.

F is for forgiveness,
a sign of God's love.

190

G is for God,
who made us and loves us.

H is for the Holy Spirit,
who helps Jesus' friends
and followers.

191

I is for imitate,
to act more like Jesus.

J is for Jesus,
the Son of God, who
shares his life with us.

192

K is for the three kings,
who visited the baby Jesus.

L is for love,
God's love and our
love for others.

193

M is for Mary,
the Mother of Jesus.

N is for Noah,
who took care of
God's creatures.

194

O is for obey,
to listen to God
and our parents.

P is for prayer,
talking and listening
to God.

195

Q is for questions
we ask about God's world.

R is for the rainbow
Noah saw in the sky
after the flood.

196

S is for saints,
God's friends who show us
how to follow Jesus.

T is for the Trinity:
God the Father, God the Son,
and God the Holy Spirit.

197

U is for up and down
and all around; God is
with us everywhere.

V is for visit,
when the angel visited Mary
to tell her about Jesus.

198

W is for our world,
where all people are
God's children.

X looks like a cross,
the sign of Jesus.

199

Y is for "yes";
your family said "yes" to God
for you when you were baptized.

Z is for zebras
and all the other creatures
God made with love.

Illustration Credits
Hector Borlasca 8-9, 115, 158; Nan Brooks 12-13, 43-46, 65-68, 87-90, 175-178; Olivia Cole 72, 82, 142, 164; Carolyn Croll 7, 18-19, 26, 60, 70, 78, 109-112, 121, 136, 137; Shelly Dieterichs 94, 166; Julie Durrell 76, 150; Patrick Girouard 83, 106; Amanda Harvey 39, 120; Jenny Kostecki 29, 35, 57; Anthony Lewis 131-135; Moira Maclean 114; Susan Nethery 33; Diane Paterson 10-11; Mick Reid 98, 127, 143, 153-156; Bill Smith Studio 2-7, 100; Matt Straub 27, 28, 30, 36, 40, 42, 48, 52, 56, 58, 61, 77, 84, 91, 93, 96, 105, 122, 124, 138, 140, 162, 168, 170, 174, 188-200; Peggy Tagel 63; John Wallace 32, 126; Bari Weissman 160; Lois Woolley 30, 36, 42, 52, 58, 64, 74, 80, 86, 96, 102, 108, 118, 124, 130, 140, 146, 152, 159, 162, 168, 174.

Photo Credits
Page iv, Mel Yates/Getty Images; 1, Rubberball Productions; 6, SW Productions/Getty Images; 7, Yang Liu/Corbis; 8, Royalty-Free/Corbis; 14, Myrleen Ferguson Cate/Photo Edit; 16, ASAP Ltd./Index Stock Imagery; 20, Father Gene Plaisted, OSC; 22, zefa/Masterfile; 24, Melissa Bocock; 25, M Llorden/Getty Images; 29, zefa/Masterfile; 31, Production/ Index Stock Imagery; 34 (bl), Ariel Skelley/Corbis; 34 (tr), Bill Schild/Corbis; 34 (tl), Kim Robbie/Corbis; 34 (br), Steve Casimiro/Getty Images; 35 (bg), Jan Tove Johansson/Getty Images; 35 (r), Darwin Wiggett/Corbis; 36, Arte & Immagini srl/Corbis: 37, Ian Woollams/Getty Images; 38, Double Exposure/Getty Images; 41, 47 Ariel Skelley/Corbis; 49, Jim Cummins/Getty Images; 50 (b), Jim Boorman/Age Fotostock; 50 (c), (t), Jose Luis Pelaez, Inc./Corbis; 51, Ariel Skelley/ Corbis; 53, Jon Feingersh /Masterfile; 54 (b), (t), Larry Williams/Corbis; 55 (t), ROB & SAS/Corbis; 55 (b), Stockbyte/ PictureQuest; 55 (c), SW Production/Index Stock Imagery; 57, Myrleen Ferguson Cate/Photo Edit; 59, zefa/ Masterfil; 61 (tl), Craig Hammell/Corbis; 61(b), Emilio Ereza/AgeFotostock; 61 (tr), Rudi Von Briel/Photo Edit; 62, Royalty-Free/Corbis; 64, David Young-Wolff/Photo Edit; 69, Myrleen Ferguson Cate/Photo Edit; 71, Bill Wittman; 73, L. Powell/Superstock; 74, Stuart Pearce/AgeFotostock; 75, Larry Williams/Corbis; 79, Dennis MacDonald/Photo Edit; 80 (b), Archivo Iconografico, S.A./ Corbis; 80 (t), Tony Freeman/ Photo Edit; 81, Banana Stock/ AgeFotostock; 85, Royalty-Free/ Corbis; 86, Myrleen Ferguson Cate/Photo Edit; 91, Don Hebert/Getty Images; 92, Mitch Wojnarowicz/The Image Works; 95, Laura DeSantis/Getty Images; 97, zefa/Masterfile; 99 (r), Jim Cummins/Getty Images; 99 (l), JLP/Jose L. Pelaez/Corbis; 99 (c), SW Production/Index Stock Imagery; 101, Simon Cook/Bridgeman Library; 102 (b), Archivo Iconografico, S.A./Corbis; 102, Michael S. Yamashita/Corbis; 103, S.I. Shoot-Charon/Index Stock Imagery; 104, Steve Gorton/DK Images; 107, Ariel Skelley/ Corbis; 108, Myrleen Ferguson Cate/Photo Edit; 113, Dave Nagel/Getty Images; 116 (t), Bob Thomas/Getty Images; 116 (b), Stockbyte/ Stockbyte/ PictureQuest; 117, Randy Miller/Masterfile; 118, Lawrence Lawry/Getty Images; 119, IFA Bilderteam/eStock Photo/ PictureQuest; 123, Lake County Museum/Corbis; 124, Steve Skjold/Photo Edit; 125, Claudia Kunin/Getty Images; 129, Charles Gupton/Corbis; 130, Myrleen Ferguson Cate/Photo Edit; 135, Elyse Lewin/Getty Images; 139. Royalty-Free/ Corbis; 141, Michael Keller/ Corbis; 144, Jose Carillo/Photo Edit; 145, Raoul Minsart/ Masterfile; 146, Michael Newman/Photo Edit; 147, Arthur Tilley/i2i Images/ PictureQuest; 148, PoodlesRock/ Corbis; 149 (l), Bill Wittman; 149 (r), Father Gene Plaisted, OSC; 149 (c), 151, Myrleen Ferguson Cate/Photo Edit; 152, Masterfile Royalty Free; 157, Roy Morsch/ AgeFotostock; 161, Masterfile Royalty-Free Division; 163, George Shelley/Masterfile; 165, Dorit Lombroso/Index Stock Imagery; 167, David Sacks/ Getty Images; 168, Seraphic Icons/Bridge Building Images; 169, Eric O'Connell/Getty Images; 171, Pat Doyle/Corbis; 172, Melissa Bocock; 173, LWA-Sharie Kennedy/ Corbis; 179 (b), LWA-Sharie Kennedy/Corbis; 179 (t), Father Gene Plaisted, OSC; 180, Thinkstock/Getty Images; 183, Royalty-Free/Corbis; 185, 186, Myrleen Ferguson Cate/Photo Edit. For permission to reprint copyrighted material, grateful acknowledgment is made to the following sources:

Confraternity of Christian Doctrine, Washington, D.C.: Scriptures from the *New Americn Bible.* Text copyright © 1991, 1986, 1970 by the Confraternity of Christian Doctrine. All rights reserved. No part of the *New American Bible* may be used or reproduced in any form, without permission in writing from the copyright owner.

Hope Publishing Company, Carol Stream, IL 60188: Lyrics from "We Are the Church" by Richard K. Avery and Donald S. Marsh. Lyrics © 1972 by Hope Publishing Company.

International Commission on English in the Liturgy: English translation of the Psalm Response from "Psalm 126: The Lord Has Done Great Things" in *Lectionary for Mass.* Translation © 1969, 1981, 1999 by International Committee on English in the Liturgy, Inc.

International Consultation on English Texts: English translation of Glory to the Father and Hail Mary by the International Consultation on English Texts (ICET).

OCP Publications, 5536 NE Hassalo, Portland, OR 97213: Lyrics from "Praise to You, O Christ, Our Savior" by Bernadette Farrell. Lyrics copyright © 1986 by Bernadette Farrell.

Illustration Credits

8A Hector Borlasca; 10A Diane Paterson; 12A Nan Brooks; 18A Carolyn Croll; 20A the Crosiers/Father; 25A Nan Brooks; 31A John Wallace; 47A Matt Straub; 59A Carol Croll; 70 Roger Payne; 75A Julie Durrell; 81A Patrick Girouard; 81B(l) Melissa K. Bocock; 92 Lois Woolley; 97A Mike Reid; 113B Mora Maclean: 119A Carolyn Croll; 125A Mike Reid; 141A Mike Reid; 143 Shannon Stirnweiss; 147A Julie Durrell; 149 Carolyn Croll; 157A Lois Woolley; 159 The Mazer Corporation; 160 The Mazer Corporation

Photo Credits

ix Getty Images/590003; xviii Getty Images/OS47072; xxiii Getty Images/590002; 3 Getty Images/24206; 4 The Mazer Corporation; 11 Jack Holtel/Photographik Company; 12 SW Productions/Getty Images; 14A Photo Edit; 14 Getty Images/OS50049; 15 Jack Holtel/Photographik Company; 16A IndexStock; 16 Getty Images/60262; 22A Masterfile; 23 Getty Images OS19023; 25B(r) Getty Images/24021; 31B(l) Getty Images/24168; 31B(r) Getty Images/SS16013; 32 Getty Images/41176; 37A Getty Images; 37B(r) Getty Images/SS16015; 39 Getty Images /OS54082; 47B(l) Getty Images/24093; 53A Corbis; 53B(r) Getty Images/SS16020; 53 Getty Images/333090; 59B(r) Getty Images/OS47097; 69A W.P. Wittman Limited; 69B(r) Getty Images/SS30313; 75B(r) Getty Images/041021C; 77 Jack Holtel/Photographik Company; 81 Getty Images/8293; 91A Mitch Wojnarowicz/The Image; 91B(l) Getty Images/010009B; 91B(r) Getty Images/26190; 91B(l) Getty Images/80153; 91B(r) Getty Images/SS16011; 98 Getty Images/11589; 99 The Mazer Corporation; 103A DK Images; 103B(r) Getty Images/OS44061; 106 Jack Holtel/Photograhik Company; 113B(tl) Getty Images/80155; 113B(bl) Getty Images/63014; 113B(r) Getty Images/107023; 115 Getty Images/3316021; 116 Jack Holtel/Photographik Company; 119B(l) Getty Images/24120; 119B(r) Getty Images/OS47057; 123 Jack Holtel/Photographik Company; 125B(r) Getty Images/16012; 126 Getty Images/OS54082; 127 Getty Images/54137; 135B(r) Getty Images/SS16022; 136 The Mazer Corporation; 137 Bread: Getty Images/30051 Fish: Harcourt Index/Corbis; 147B(l) Getty Images/24031; 147B(r) Getty Images/41049; 147B(l) Getty Images/80154; 163A Dovit Lombroso/Index Stock Imagery; 163B(l) Getty Images/04031B; 163B(r) Getty Images/41027; 166 Getty Images/59126; 169A Pat Doyle/Corbis

Notes

Notes

_____

_____

_____

_____

_____

_____

_____

_____

_____

_____

_____

_____

_____

_____

_____

_____

Notes

Notes

Notes

Notes